ENKO

ENKOP AI

(MY COUNTRY)

MY LIFE WITH THE MAASAI

CATHERINE ODDIE

SIMON & SCHUSTER
AUSTRALIA

ENKOP AI
First published in Australasia in 1994 by
Simon & Schuster Australia
20 Barcoo Street, East Roseville NSW 2069

Reprinted 1994

A Paramount Communications Company
Sydney New York London Tokyo Singapore

National Library of Australia
Cataloguing in Publication data

Oddie, Catherine.
Enkop ai.

ISBN 0 7318 0420 1.

1. Oddie, Catherine : Marriage. 2. Ole Rerente, Robert
Oloimooja — Marriage. 3. Masai (African people) —
Biography. 4. Interracial marriage — Kenya. I. Title.

306.846

Designed by Jack Jagtenberg
Typeset in Australia by Asset Typesetting Pty Ltd
Printed in Singapore by Kim Hup Lee Printing Co. Pte Ltd

CONTENTS

DEDICATION

For Mesianto
May *Enkai* help me to guide you, and you me.

'If we want things to stay as they are, things will have to change. D'you understand?'

Guiseppe di Lampedusa *The Leopard*

TECHNICAL DETAILS

This book was written away from mains power using an Apple Powerbook 140 generously supplied by Apple Australia. Power from the sun was harnessed using an M16 (16 watt) solar panel courtesy of Showa Solar Energy Far East Pty Ltd and a 75 AH Carbide Exide solar battery purchased in Nairobi. The whole rig was connected up with a car cigarette lighter socket from the Rainbow Power Company and a 12 volt car adaptor designed especially for Macintosh Powerbooks by Fosh Australia Pty Ltd.

AUTHOR'S NOTE

This book in no way sets out to be a comprehensive portrait of the culture of the Maasai of Kenya and Tanzania. The Maasai customs and traditions I describe are only what I have seen in one small corner of Kenya with the Nkidongi subclan of the Ilaiser clan of the Loita Maasai. I apologise to any Maasai readers for what may seem to be my limited knowledge and understanding of their rich culture. All opinions and, of course, any mistakes are entirely mine.

ROBERT'S FAMILY TREE

(commencing from his paternal grandfather)

Senteu ole Mbatiany m **Intereshet** *(fourth wife of approximately 15)*
|
Redeti (f)
Nalaron (f)
Seine (f)
Mengoru Lekuta Rerente Ololoreshe/Papa (third-born)
married Siabe/Kinyikita/Mumai* *(first wife)*

1. Morintat/ Nolarianga (f)	2. Nakariso/ Nolmunai (f)	3. Olkilia	Sianoi/Nolkiseeyia (f)
m	m	m	m
Ole Nairowa	Lenaiposha Numbaso	Mertu/Meiyoki/ Yeiyio Kiti	Ole Keser
*Arambow	*Saingo (f)	*Sembeta	*Musiere
*Nakato (f)	*Saiyui (f)	*Narotiai (f)	*Nanakoi (f)
*Shilato (f)	*Nankaiya (f)	*Enkaiyoni b 1992	
*Tipapa			
*Senue			

married Nenkokwain ene Sunge/Noltetian/Mama *(second wife)*

Ol Morijoi	Ntanin/Nolmeshuki (f)	Sinante (f)	Daniel Njoie
m	m	m	m
Nailole/Helen	Lomali ole Koiye	Ole Sepere	Esele/Narygunkishon
*Entito b 1992		*Olkamasie	*Sintiman
		*Ngoto Inkerra (f)	(m Ole Keriase)
		(m Sendura Ole Murrianga)	*Leseamon
			*Sitaiyo (f)
			*Gunisai (f)
			*Mesianto/Ndoondo (f)
			*Melubo

Langisa	James Ilampala Nkaroya	Nasango/Noongishu (f)	Robert Oloimooja
m	m	m	m
1. Toris/Nadupoi	1. Lesiato/Nosotua	Ole Numbaso	1. Catherine/Nasha
*Sanare	*Lendoiyan	*Namoshe	*Mesianto (Ndoondo)
*Enkaiyoni b 1992	*Nashunyi	*Ranan	
		*Ekaiyoni b 1992	
2. Nolmedotie	2. Nasango ene Numbaso		2.Nakoiyaan/ Enoolomala

married Nolterito/Yeiyio/Kokoo *(third wife)*

|

Daughter-in-law   Samuken/Nolmemeri/Memi

*David Pariken

*Singua/Niroshi (f)

(m Ole Njapeet)

*Peter Saitoti Loldudula

*Toonga/Naisua (f)

(m Ole Kiyiook)

*Nataiya (f)

*James Momposhe

*Hannah and Napalell (twins f)

*Matanga (f)

Enkaiyoni b 1993

married Kwosenga/Paashe *(fourth wife)*

|

Ngaiyo Shangwa

m

1. Nolkipenperia/Mary

*Lekenya

*Merise (f)

Entito

2. Nelengon/Joyce

Robert's father and his four wives are listed in bold type in this family tree. Their children are listed in normal roman type, while *their* children — the grandchildren of Robert's father — are marked with an asterisk. The spouses of grandchildren are indicated in brackets below the name of their partner. To avoid added confusion, I have not listed the great grandchildren of Robert's father.

Women usually have three names; the name their parents give them as children (*enkarna apa* — the name for long ago), the name their husband's age group gives them on the wedding night (*enkarna ol porror*), and a pet name that the children give them. In addition they may have a school name.

Maasai men also accumulate several names over the course of their life. However, the name given to them by their parents remains throughout. They are also known politely as the son of their father (or sometimes another man that they may tend cattle for). They will have stock names used by friends and family, pet names used by children, and a school name. Men also receive an additional name at the *Olkiteng lorrbaa* ceremony in middle age.

Young and as yet unmarried children are referred to as *Enkaiyan* or *Entito,* and I have indicated them with italics.

I have used all names wherever they are known to me.

KENYA

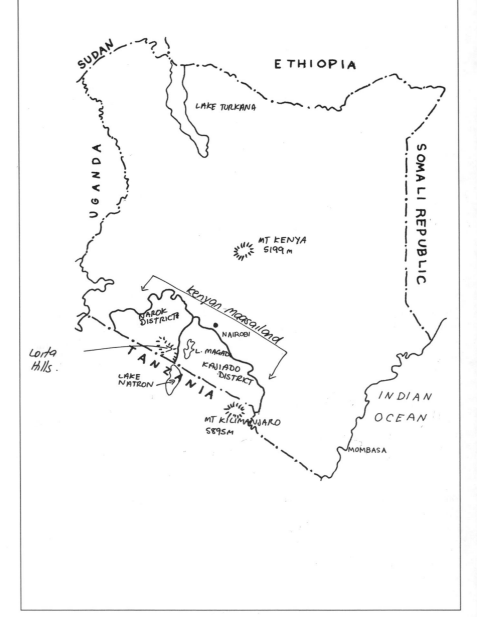

Olapa oibor inkera

Children are the bright moon

MAASAI PROVERB

THE WARMTH FROM THE FIRE COMFORTED NOLTETIAN AS SHE LAY propped on her elbows on the hard cowhide bed. She had been in labour for six hours now. Already in her forties, this pregnancy had been unexpected and she hoped this would be the last time she had to go through all this. She had borne her husband more children than all his other three wives put together. *Enkai* had indeed blessed her and this tiny life pushing its way into the world would make number eight. Her first son, Ol Morijoi, had been given to her when she was a young bride. He was a junior elder now, but had not yet married because he was blind. It was hard to find a wife for a blind man. The first-born girl had been married five years ago and had gone to live far away with her husband's family, and the second-born girl two years later. Her next son, Njoie, was a senior warrior and ready to take a wife himself. The next two children were both boys, Langisa now aged ten and Nkaroiya who was only four. Both were sleeping in the children's house in another part of the *enkang*. The youngest child, a girl, was only twenty-four months old and lay asleep on the bed on the opposite side of the room. She had been named Nasango during her *Enkarna Enkerai* (naming ceremony) held more than a year and a half ago now.

Assisting with the birth in the smoky hut was Noltetian's sister, who had walked far to help with the birth, and Mumai, her co-wife. Mumai had four children and was an experienced midwife as well as being Noltetian's dear friend. She was the first, and therefore senior wife in the village, but she was not the favourite. That position was reserved for Kokoo, the third wife. Noltetian herself was the second wife. Also in the house were all of the women from the *enkang*, there to lend their support and celebrate the birth.

The pregnancy had been tiresome, especially towards the end when her back ached terribly. Mumai and Kokoo had taken on most of the heavier duties like carrying firewood, but Noltetian was still expected to walk almost a kilometre to the river and carry thirty litres of water on her back each day and, of course, help with some of the milking. She craved the taste of fresh milk, but was not permitted to drink it lest the baby grow too fat and make the birth difficult. It was imperative for both mother and foetus to remain slim and, like all Maasai women, Noltetian was very careful with what she ate throughout the pregnancy. A small amount of curdled milk is permitted since the baby does not receive this milk 'direct' from the mother's stomach. To compensate for the lack of milk, Noltetian indulged her cravings for meat. Her husband, a senior elder, was a generous man and very happy to be adding another child to his family. He slaughtered several goats so that Noltetian had plenty of meat and also a supply of nourishing soup made with the offal and selected plants from the forest. Pregnant women are also expected to eat certain herbs and roots to purify the blood and keep the stomach healthy. Noltetian knew the various uses of all the plants that grew in the forest, and had used them appropriately throughout her pregnancy.

In the *olale* (calf pen) next to her bed, she was vaguely aware of the young calves stirring. Dawn was not far away. Noltetian did not cry out as her pain worsened. Not because she was particularly brave, but because she had learnt how to endure sharp pain quietly. Also she was vain enough to derive some measure of satisfaction from her stoic silence. Even as a young girl more than twenty-five years ago she had refused to cry out when she had been circumcised inside her mother's house. Her grandmother had begged her to scream so that the warriors would not be affronted by her courage, but she had already taken her mind far away from the pain and did not hear what her grandmother said.

Mumai had been observing the progress of the birth from her position next to the fire. Now she moved closer to Noltetian as the baby's head appeared. The greasy black body slithered out quickly into Mumai's hands. *'Enkaiyoni,'* she crooned, *'Ashe Enkai.'* Thank you God, a boy. The tiny body was placed on his mother's stomach while the placenta was delivered. Mumai prepared to cut the umbilical cord. She looked intently at the baby as she pronounced the words that greet every Maasai child: 'You are now responsible for your life as I am responsible for mine.' Later the placenta was taken outside and thrown in the centre of the cattle enclosure, thus connecting the life of the new baby with the herd. The connection symbolised the link between children and cattle, *Enkai's* gift to his people, the twin riches of the Maasai.

As the sun rose over the Great Rift Valley one day in August 1964 a Maasai boy was born into the Nkidongi subclan to Mengoru Lekuta Rerente and Noltetian ene Sunge. He was his father's last-born child, his mother's special blessing from God, a member of the sacred Iloibonok family and my future husband.

MAASAILAND
(Narok District)

NAROK DISTRICT

1. morijo
2. Narotian
3. Empurputia
4. Entasekera Centre
5. olmesutye
6. Ilkerin
7. olongarua

4

CHAPTER ONE
ENKITERUNOTO
(Beginning)
A u g u s t   1 9 8 9

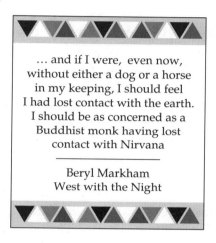

... and if I were, even now,
without either a dog or a horse
in my keeping, I should feel
I had lost contact with the earth.
I should be as concerned as a
Buddhist monk having lost
contact with Nirvana

Beryl Markham
West with the Night

I HAD ALWAYS WANTED TO GO TO AFRICA, AS I THOUGHT OF IT THEN. LIKE most westerners, I considered Africa to be one big country instead of a continent with an incredible mixture of colours, cultures and languages. Almost five years after my first visit to Kenya, I am a little less ignorant, though I only claim to know one tiny corner of the country where I have made my home.

My mother puts my fascination with Africa down to watching too many episodes of the cartoon, 'Kimba the White Lion' during my formative years. I think it was a combination of 'Kimba', 'Wild Kingdom' and *Born Free*. One of my earliest memories is of being given a box of thick felt textas, which I used to draw pictures of lions until the inks ran out. Years later the Sidney Pollack film *Out of Africa*, which immortalised the neurotic Baroness von Blixen and colonial Kenya, rekindled my desire to go there. The film had the same effect on thousands of westerners who subsequently flocked to Kenya like the pink flamingos they had come to photograph.

My main interest was in the wildlife. I longed to see the great herds and their predators before they disappeared forever, as they had in other places on this earth.

Animals have been a big part of my life for as long as I can remember. Every phase of my life has been connected with the cats and dogs that we owned, and even those that we didn't. When I was a small girl, our next door neighbour's dog was a splendid golden labrador named Pepper. He would take himself for walks down to the shops. If we bumped into him down there, he would catch a lift back up the hill in our car. Not far from our house in suburban Epping was a tiny paddock with a palomino horse, and I invented an elaborate fantasy that the horse was mine. I started pretending that I was really a cat when I was in kindergarten. I grew out of that before primary school, where I spent recess and lunch time running around the oval pretending I was a horse.

Tasha was our first cat. I remember my mother saying that when my father was really ill with the cancer that would eventually kill him, he would sometimes ask for Tasha to be brought to his bed. Somehow the cat made him feel better. The company of animals has always made me feel better too. In fact without the companionship of a dog, cat, horse or other animal in my life, I would feel lost. So, I have to admit straight out, that I am slightly unbalanced when it comes to animals. I love being with them, drawing them, watching wildlife documentaries, and reading fiction and non-fiction about animals and the people that worked with them. When I was a small girl, I never played with dolls. I only played with stuffed animals. When I got a bit older, my animal friends were real, not stuffed, and by and large I preferred them to the human ones. Small wonder I dreamed of travelling to Africa.

I was born in Sydney, where I grew up. There were two of us, me and my brother Mark, who is eighteen months younger than me. Both my parents were very intelligent people, politically aware and avid readers. They instilled in my brother and me an appreciation of literature and music, as well as a commitment to humanitarian values and politics. The strongest message I was given by my parents was that I could do anything I set my mind to.

I was seven when my father died. The pain is still too raw to say much about that. I blocked a lot of it out and have always been too scared to plumb the depths of my seven-year-old self. I feel the loss of my father every day of my life.

From that time on, we, that is, the three of us and the cats, moved around a lot. I guess after my father's death we were unsettled for a long time. As a result I attended four different primary schools, and the chopping and changing strengthened my independence that was already pretty well developed. My mother had to go back into the work force, which she hadn't done for a long time. For the next twenty-five years she held down a variety of mind-numbing jobs as an unskilled worker with Philips, Hoover, the ABC canteen, and some draconian factory.

When I was nine years old, my mother started going to the opera. I remember she'd get dressed up, usually in something long and tie-dyed, and smell of Arpège. She always brought Mark and I back a surprise, like an after dinner mint, and I would read the glossy opera programme. This was my first taste of the theatre. My second was more of a transfusion. I was taken to see *Jesus Christ Superstar* and sat transfixed from start to finish. The music, mechanics, lighting and performances electrified me. It made an indelible impression, and I am indebted to that production of *JCS* for giving me such a wonderful introduction to the world of theatre which remained a magic place to me for many years afterwards.

I don't remember too much about my brother Mark in my school years. We sort of lost mental contact until we each sorted ourselves out in our early twenties. I do however remember Ester, a golden labrador my mother gave me when I was eleven — she was my first dog. We went to obedience training every Sunday afternoon at Brush Farm, a big park in West Ryde where we lived for two years along with my aunt Judy and her family. At obedience training I met Virginia Warren, aged twelve, who was there with her cocker spaniel, Lacey. For four years, spanning Grade 6 to Form 3, Virginia and I were best friends. We shared a love of dogs, theatre and Skyhooks.

Virginia's house was always full. She had at least four siblings and because her parents bred cocker spaniels and standard poodles as a hobby, sometimes twice that number of dogs. I remember the Warrens as a warm and casual household. The sort of place where a sleeping dog might be roused from a good chair to make way for a human guest. I travelled all over New South Wales with Virginia and her family. We stayed in caravan parks and entered the dogs, Ester included, in the country shows. Mrs Warren, an academic, taught both of us elocution and drama and we toured the suburbs performing monologues, duologues, speeches and poems in eisteddfods. We enjoyed moderate success with our performance of Alice and Caterpillar, even Bernard King gave us a good score on the seminal Australian talent show 'Pot of Gold'. I was the caterpillar.

Though we continued to move house another four times in my teen years, I did manage to stick in the one high school, Cheltenham Girls, where my father had taught economics and geography. I was the only girl in my group of friends whose family voted Labor. I loved English, history and art, hated maths with a passion and generally managed to skip sport and scripture.

When I was fifteen, I joined my next big family, the Australian Theatre for Young People. Most of the young people who participated in the workshops and youth theatre productions were a bit eccentric, precocious and came from single parent families, so I fitted in very well. My world revolved around rehearsals, productions, workshops and the new group of friends I had discovered, a handful of whom I still count among my dearest friends to this day.

After high school, I was accepted into the Western Australian Academy of Performing Arts. Our home for the last few years had been dominated by one or another of my mother's drunken boyfriends. Home made me feel isolated, angry and depressed, and I was more than happy to move to Perth where I pursued a diploma in Theatre and Arts Administration. In Perth I had the opportunity to buy a standard poodle puppy, Raa. I had always loved standard poodles (the big ones, not the little yappy things) since my days with Virginia Warren. Because they grow to the size of a small pony, I figured a poodle would be the next best thing to a horse — a life-long desire of mine.

Upon graduation, I landed a plum job as administrator of a youth arts centre in Melbourne. At first I was very lonely in Melbourne. Because I didn't have my own place to stay, Raa had remained in Sydney with my ex-boyfriend. I was determined not to blow my first job, and so put all my efforts into work. There were a couple of my colleagues who were fortunately not put off by the gruff all-work-and-no-play barricade I constructed around myself. One in particular, the company publicist Carolyn Logan, was very persistent in asking me out to see the pub band she managed, Zurich Zoo. I never made it to the band but nevertheless we gradually became firm friends. When I left youth arts and started working in commercial theatre, Carolyn followed and branched out into the music industry. In 1988, she moved into the beautiful 1950s style flat I rented in the Melbourne suburb of Prahran with me and Raa, who had by now moved back into my life.

I had three major relationships in my teens and early twenties. My first boyfriend was gay, the above-mentioned second boyfriend was definitely straight but eighteen years older than me, and the third one was an actor who probably swung both ways, though I can't say for sure. Not exactly an upward growth curve you might say. Still, I learnt a lot and had had a chance to 'play house', so that was out of my system. By the time I was twenty-five, I found myself happily ensconced in Melbourne with a great new job, good friends, my dog, a cat and at long last a horse of my own. There was so much going on in my life that I felt more than happy being single. I did promise myself though that my next relationship was going to be with someone truly exceptional. Above all, someone who knew more than I did. I thought a marine biologist or a mammal researcher might be nice, a man who could introduce me to another aspect of the natural world.

There were in fact men in my life at this time; they were five outrageous platform-soled rockers who made up the Melody Lords, a glam rock band specialising in a scathing parody of the 1970s. I worked as one half of their management team looking after publicity and tour management. The Melody Lords were my third big family, and I managed to blend them together with Carolyn, other friends, Raa and my Anglo-Arab mare, Siska. Most of my free time revolved around Siska and my riding lessons, which I adored. To me, learning to ride was like learning to speak a new language. Even when I was on tour with a theatre show in Sydney and Adelaide, I managed to find time to have lessons. Earlier in 1989, I had broken my left arm in a fall, which had shaken my confidence and slowed me down a bit. However, this was a time when my work, home and social spheres were at a peak. I expected life to be wonderful, and it was. I even viewed the period spent with my arm in a cast as time to learn more about myself. By mid-1989 an opportunity to turn a dream into reality presented itself.

For years I had collected a file of clippings about travelling in Africa, knowing that one day I would make it there. East Africa seemed to be the Mecca for game viewing, so even though other countries beckoned with wilderness and wildlife, my interest stayed focused on Kenya and Tanzania. My opportunity to travel there arrived unexpectedly when I heard about a group of women who planned to horsetrek across Kenya's Maasai Mara Game Reserve. The trip, organised by Linda Tellington-Jones, brought together my interests in wildlife and horse-riding. Linda leads a group she calls the Animal Ambassadors on a horse-riding trip each year. She is an American woman I greatly admired for her non-violent training and healing work with animals. She bases this on her training in the Feldenkrais technique. Her organisation, TEAM (Tellington-Jones Equine Awareness Method), conducts workshops all over the world. I had attended one the year before, near Melbourne. When my riding teacher passed on the information about Linda's riding safari, I decided instantly that I would be on that trip. The chance to learn Linda's techniques first hand was almost as great an attraction as the trip itself. I called Linda in New Mexico that same night and reserved the final place.

I also wanted to see the Ngorongoro Crater and the Serengeti Plains in Tanzania, and I shopped around for a budget safari. The airfares from Australia to Kenya were expensive (and still are), so I wanted to pack in as much as I could on this trip. When I booked a Tanzanian camping safari, I remember telling my travel agent that I only wanted to see wildlife — not any tribespeople. I had read about the Maasai, East Africa's most famous tribe, but I had no desire to meet them. Culture? What culture? I was going strictly for the zebras.

The Melody Lords were breaking over Christmas and January, so it was a perfect time for me to go overseas. The only problem was money. I didn't have any, so I arranged to borrow $6000 from my bank and organised a credit card with another one. I was only planning to go on a holiday and so I had no qualms about my ability to pay the money quickly. My other responsibilities were my horse

Siska and dog Raa. Siska was easy, for she agisted with my riding teacher just outside of Melbourne and was well cared for. I would have to take Raa to my mother's home on the New South Wales Central Coast. Carolyn would take care of our flat for six weeks. My financial, work and domestic details in place, I had just over four months until my trip.

A few weeks later I woke with a raging fever. My glands were swollen and I felt as though I had been hit by a Mack truck. A blood test confirmed glandular fever. I was physically tired from constant work with the Melody Lords. Plus I was emotionally exhausted after a traumatic episode where Raa had nearly died from intestinal bloat. All the deep sadness I had experienced in the last few days while he recovered from major surgery had left my already stressed system exhausted and vulnerable. I was knocked for six and seriously ill for the first time in my life. After Raa came home from the vet's, the two of us must have been a sight as we lay on the pillows doing our best 'Camilles'. Raa was sore from surgery and I was too weak to move. Carolyn did all the right things with chicken soup and warm baths. But as my condition deteriorated, she started making noises about taking me to hospital. That's when I called in the cavalry and phoned my mother.

She flew down from Sydney the next day, picked up all my dirty tissues from the bedroom floor, and nursed Raa and me back to the point where we set ourselves up in the lounge room watching videos of 'The Young Ones'. I laughed myself better. I was advised to have total rest for two months. Mum hired a car and drove Raa and me back to the New South Wales Central Coast. I insisted on taking the beautiful flowers sent by my friends in a bucket of water. We stopped the night in Gundagai on the way through and smuggled Raa into the motel unit. He was over the worst and enjoyed the whole journey.

I rested completely at my mother's home on the beach. During the first weeks I was too weak to even read and would just lie in bed thinking. This was the first time I had stopped working since I started out at nineteen in the entertainment industry. I couldn't understand the thought processes I was going through until I realised one day that I was in fact just living. Not planning or worrying or stressing out or making lists of all the things I had to achieve that day, but simply living each moment as it came. Quite a revelation to someone who had once upon a time sworn an oath to herself that nothing would ever stand in the way of her career.

Life never fails to present you with challenges appropriate to the time. Although I was not conscious of it, this period of convalescence was crucial as it provided an opportunity to quietly re-evaluate my life. Ideas that had been floating around in my mind came into focus. I emerged from my enforced cocoon of introspection a changed person. The daily bump and grind of show business seemed shallow. As a glam rock parody act, the Melody Lords had a built-in 'use by' date. They were a happy hiccup in my career that would probably burn out and leave me back where I started in commercial theatre.

With that in mind, I realised that I no longer found entertainment very satisfying. I had embarked upon a course that I no longer wished to complete. I started to dream about getting out of the entertainment industry and moving to the country with my horse. Maybe start a new career as an administrator for the local pony club.

After I recovered and returned to work, everyone assumed that I could not possibly be continuing with my planned trip to Kenya in December. They were wrong.

To the horror of my mother and friends, I continued with my travel plans. They were all convinced that I would suffer a relapse on safari and die dramatically in the bush, or at the very least have a bummer of a holiday. To rebuild my strength, I started walking regularly and even attended aerobics classes (I am not into exercise). For the next two months I curtailed all social activities, worked sensible hours and was in bed each night by 8.30.

Such sacrifice was easy, for I had sensed from the start that it was very important that I get to Africa. In addition to photographing zebras and charging about on horseback, I had a vague sense that 'something' was waiting for me there. I thought perhaps it had to do with my dreams of a career with horses and Linda Tellington-Jones, and in a way it did — though not at all as I imagined. With this in the back of my mind, I set off for Kenya to keep my date with destiny.

SAFARI (Journey)

D e c e m b e r   1 9 8 9

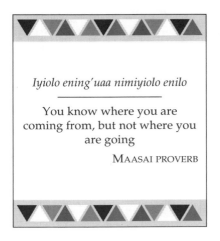

Iyiolo ening'uaa nimiyiolo enilo

You know where you are
coming from, but not where you
are going

MAASAI PROVERB

IN THE LAST WEEKS BEFORE MY DEPARTURE, ALL MY ENERGY WAS FOCUSED on getting on the plane, and getting to Africa. I was excited about the horse-riding and, even more, about seeing the wildlife. Soon the time came. I went up to the New South Wales Central Coast to say goodbye to Mum and then my brother Mark took me to the airport and I was off.

If they gave out gold stars for the most overprepared tourist, then I would have won. I had read every book I could on travelling in general and about East Africa especially. I knew to drink plenty of water on the plane, spray my face regularly with Evian, keep a spare change of undies in my hand luggage and do leg exercises to keep my blood circulating. I was thoroughly versed on how to eat in Africa and survive: don't drink the water; no ice in drinks; no salads; no unboiled milk; no seafood; eat only freshly cooked, well-done meat and fruits that you can peel yourself. I took to heart the suggestion that dubious cutlery could be cleaned with a splash of scalding hot tea and, if you must eat with your fingers, then don't eat the part of the food that you have been holding.

My first sight of Africa was from 3220 metres up as we flew over Madagascar. The island looked wrinkled and old. A sandy river snaked its way through the green-brown jungle. Soon we were nearing the end of a sixteen-hour flight and the attendants had begun to smile again. On the tarmac in Harare a red neon sign declared WELCOME TO ZIMBABWE. This is usually the first port of call for Australians flying to Africa. My connecting flight to Kenya left the next morning, so I had to spend one night in Harare. By the time I got through customs, hired a taxi and checked into my room it was 4 am Australian time, though only 8.30 pm local time. In line with my paranoia I decided against a toasted sandwich from room service — the safety factor was not good — and instead just ordered a coke, no ice. I added iodine to the jug of water in my room and risked brushing my teeth. I lay in bed with my overactive imagination and listened to footsteps creep up and down the hallway.

I woke at 4.30 am to the sounds of birds calling. They sounded so different. The sky was a beautiful dove grey. I stood at my window enthralled as the dawn ever so slowly tinged it a deep apricot. A thin sliver of moon still hung low in the sky. I missed my dog, Raa. I heard a rustle outside my room: was it the owner of the footsteps come to murder me? No, only the Zimbabwe *Herald* being shoved under my door. The headline proclaimed '69 killed in bus horror'. The lurid report came complete with grisly pictures. I ate a packet of fruit pastilles and finished reading the paper. It was going to be a hot day. I felt glad to be in Africa and decided that I had better relax.

I watched through my window as smartly groomed children and office workers made their way to school and work. After having a bath and dressing, I negotiated my way through breakfast. Chilled grapefruit, black tea and toast with bright red sickly sweet jam. I didn't touch the milk and left the corner of toast I held. There was only time for a short walk before heading off to the airport again, so I hurried out for my first taste of African sunshine. Harare is a very clean city with the feel of a big country town. The streets are wide and the footpaths unpaved. The jacarandas were in bloom and I walked on a carpet of mauve petals. There were cream and pink frangipanis and orange flame trees too.

Soon it was back to the airport again. The Air Zimbabwe flight to Nairobi took only two and a half hours, and arrived around 4 pm local time. The taxi I hired from the airport was a twenty-seven-year-old Volvo that broke down twice before we reached the centre of Nairobi. My first impression was of a city much more polluted and populated than Harare, with people walking everywhere. My destination was the Ambassadeur Hotel in the city centre. Convenient location, I had thought. Four years down the track, I have developed the ability to sleep comfortably anywhere and have lost my dependence upon western-style accommodation. However, in November 1989, I must admit that the Ambassadeur was not the best choice for a wide-eyed tourist travelling on her own. It was noisy, rundown and in the centre of one of the busiest sections of downtown Nairobi. That first day I suffered severe culture shock. Everyone was black. I know that sounds stupid, but that is how it struck me. I was in the minority for the first time in my life. As a learning experience, I recommend this to everyone. However, my response at the time was to hide in my hotel room for the next two days.

Upon the advice of a British couple I met, I changed my accommodation to the Milimani Hotel outside the city centre. The quiet atmosphere and green outlook had an immediate effect upon me. I began to relax. I learnt how to chill out, go with the flow and act like I belonged — even if I didn't really feel it.

After two days of this, I was due to meet up with the American group led by Linda Tellington-Jones at the Norfolk Hotel. Suddenly I was no longer alone. With a whole four days under my belt, I knew more about Nairobi than my companions. There were sixteen of us, all women. Fourteen Americans, one English woman and me.

We spent the rest of the day visiting Daphne Sheldrick and the orphaned elephant calves at her home inside the Nairobi National Park. Daphne has, after many years of heartbreaking disappointment, discovered how to raise orphaned infant elephants aged under twelve months. The calves we met were all victims of the ivory poachers. After shooting the adults, the poachers then go in with chainsaws to hack out the ivory. The tuskless (and therefore worthless) calves witness the massacre and mutilation of their mothers, sisters, subadult brothers, cousins, aunts and grand-mothers. By the time Daphne gets them, they are in a deep state of shock and can grieve for more than twelve months. Daphne, her family and staff manage to get them through that period and rekindle their will to live by becoming a substitute family for the orphans. Elephant babies are not unlike human babies in that they need not only food and protection but lots of love. After growing up with Daphne, they are then moved down to the Tsavo National Park and gently re-introduced to the wild. They roam in their own herd led by Eleanor, orphaned herself and now the self-appointed matriarch of the orphans.

It was wonderful to meet the elephant calves, Olmeg, Dika, Edo and Taru, plus the young rhino and resident warthogs. However, it was meeting the inspiring Daphne Sheldrick herself that was the high point of the visit for me. Her home overlooked a grassy plain dotted with acacia trees and wildlife. It seemed like heaven on earth.

Next we stopped by the Langata Giraffe Centre for a meeting with the rare Rothschild giraffe. This sanctuary and education centre does much to promote awareness of conservation to Kenyan school children and it is great fun for giraffe fans of all ages. The raised viewing platform really does allow you an eye-to-eye encounter with one of Africa's most exotic and glamorous species.

The next day we started out on safari in four-wheel-drive vehicles. Just outside the capital, the sealed road turns into a mess of potholes; the metropolitan skyline fades and the world belongs to rural Africa. We drove through the fertile Kikuyu farmlands where tea and coffee are grown. The green of the crops contrasted with the rich blood-red of the soil. All of a sudden the vast expanse of the Great Rift Valley made a dramatic appearance. Nowhere in Africa is the Rift more clearly defined than in Kenya, where it is also known as the 'Gregorian Rift' after the geologist Gregory who first described it. The towering walls can reach as high as 1200 metres and the floor is studded with volcanoes. These include Olorgesailie, Suswa, Longonot, Menengai and Londiani. Like most place names close to the Great Rift Valley, these are Maasai words.

The view across the valley floor was breathtaking. As we descended and headed towards Tanzania, I began to see the first signs of an animal kingdom unrivalled anywhere in the world. Gazelles, wildebeests and zebras grazed. Secretary birds and beautiful crowned cranes stalked by on long legs. Giraffes bent their elegant necks to nibble the low acacia bushes that grow here. It is one thing to see a giraffe on television or in a zoo, and another thing entirely to see one standing stock still beside the road in the middle of nowhere. I'll never forget my first one. He was golden and brown, beautiful beyond words and blinking at me with a set of lashes that a starlet would kill for.

After passing through the bustling Maasai trading town of Narok, we forked south-west and headed up into the Loita Hills that lie close to the Tanzanian border. As we drove along a rough dirt track, past herds of cattle returning to their Maasai homesteads, and past more game, I knew that all the clichés about Africa were true. It was indeed magical.

We arrived at our camp at Narotian at dusk. The horses had arrived earlier and now grazed on a 'picket line' on the top of a small rise. Our tents had been set up in a wooded glade of acacia trees next to a small stream. A lone star shone in the soft grey sky. Birds and monkeys sang out in a final rush of evening activity. It was the most perfect place I had ever seen. Of course I had no idea this area would become my home. We were introduced to a Maasai elder, Daniel ole Mengoru. As the dusk deepened, he shook each of us by the hand and solemnly greeted us, 'Supa'. I had learnt my first Maasai word.

It was immediately apparent that we were in a very special place. I learnt later that the Loita Hills are the home of the Nkidongi dynasty — the most conservative and traditional section of the Kenyan Maasai. The Nkidongi are the spiritual leaders of the entire Maasai. This, plus their geographic isolation, has helped protect their culture from western influences, making the Loita Hills the last stronghold of the old Maasai ways in Kenya. We had arrived in the very heart of Maasailand.

The next morning we were assigned horses. Linda encouraged us to take over the grooming and saddling, usually a task handled by the grooms, or *syces* as they are known in Kenya. We were all keen to do this. The horses immediately responded to the gentle massage techniques taught by Linda. Her pioneering work was based on the Feldenkrais technique, except she had learnt to apply it to animals. The horses had been trucked into the Loita Hills in

17

huge 4WD lorries. The ascent is very steep and rough. It is amazing that drivers manage to get up there at all. The horses must have had a very hard time of it in the back of the lorries.

Linda pointed out to me the symptoms of shock that the horses were all experiencing, most notably the shaking limbs, staring into space and listlessness. I felt reluctant to put a saddle on my horse after all that she had been through the previous day but I was also tremendously excited at the thought of riding out into an unknown land.

The rule was that we led our horses for a short distance and gave them a drink. This was to ensure that the saddle and girth settled into a comfortable position before we actually mounted. Despite this precaution and despite the addition of sheepskin blankets and corrective saddle padding, many of the horses had nasty sores on their withers and backs before the twelve-day ride was over.

We mounted and set off. I rode a bouncy little mare whose name I no longer remember. We slowly rode up into the hills that surrounded the Narotian Valley. In the trees above us colobus monkeys croaked to their friends and the sounds of highland birds filled the air. By the time we stopped for lunch, I was feeling nauseous. I put it down to a touch of altitude sickness. The Loita Hills start at about 1800 metres which is high for someone who is used to living at sea level.

Linda and her friend Copper, a Texan redhead who had a special fondness for all things Australian, settled me in the shade and applied their Feldenkrais-based healing technique to my feet and head. They paid particular attention to my earlobes, pulling and rubbing them firmly. I later learnt that by massaging the earlobes you can prevent shock and nausea.

When it came time to mount up again, I decided I needed a quieter horse to ride back to camp on. This is when I was introduced to Kisima, a gentle giant of a horse who was an absolute challenge to mount. He was seventeen hands high at the shoulder, and I just make 152 centimetres. Once up in the saddle, he carefully carried me home to camp. For a big horse, he had a surprisingly small and cautious step. We finally worked out that this was being caused by an ill-fitting saddle and we were able to alleviate the pressure by building up the saddle with special foam pads the Americans had brought over with them. The *syces* were shown how to use the corrective padding too. Kisima was a true gentleman who seemed to sense that I was feeling fragile and never gave me reason to doubt him as we negotiated the stony path back down to the camp.

That night we dined out under the stars. The table was laid with coloured cloth and candles. Soup was followed by a roast with vegetables and a hot pudding for dessert. It was all served onto our plates with meticulous care by Jasper and John, two Kenyans who worked for the safari operator, Tony Church. As much as I enjoyed the food and the romantic setting, I didn't feel comfortable being waited on by Africans. The whole scene was much too colonial for my taste. I would much rather have been sitting at the staff fire, sharing a simpler meal and talking to the Kenyans, than have them wait on me.

The next day I was too feverish to ride, and it indeed seemed as if all the warnings had been right. I didn't have altitude sickness; it seemed the glandular fever was back. I went by vehicle with Linda to the next camp and watched amazed as the staff set up an entire tented safari camp in under two hours. I was propped up on a camp bed under a magnificent yellow fever tree. Linda was massaging acupressure points in my feet when, in my feverish state, I noticed a Maasai warrior stalk past wearing a red toga, a spear, and a pair of Nikes at the end of his long legs. He stopped and looked down at us intently for a few moments before asking in English if I was sick. Linda explained what she was doing and after a few moments he strode off. That was how, under a clear African sky while hallucinating from fever, I first met Robert Oloimooja ole Rerente.

Over the next few days, the local warriors or *moran* would often wander into our camp. They were very good-natured about posing for photos. One of our group, Nancy, had a Polaroid Instamatic camera which delighted the *moran* no end. They took turns in operating the Polaroid. I felt too shy to join in the photographic fun and was content to admire them from a distance. In comparison with the elegant and colourful Maasai, I felt pretty ordinary really, so I didn't speak to Robert and his friends.

A week later, towards the end of our two-week safari, something happened to change my perception of how the Maasai viewed westerners. It had been a long day's riding, about six hours in the saddle. We had journeyed down the Loita Hills and onto the vast Loita Plains, which are adjacent to the Maasai Mara Game Reserve. We rode through herds of zebras and wildebeests. Because we were on horseback, they accepted our presence and continued grazing. There were also hundreds of Thomson's gazelle and the curiously coloured topi, a larger antelope with grey legs and a caramel brown body. At one point, three hyenas began to circle us cautiously before darting off. This was our only contact with predators. The sun was hot on the endless plain. I was riding by myself and became aware that no one in our group of fifteen was talking. (This was very rare!) It seemed that we had all been affected by the sultry atmosphere. I became aware of a rhythm, a palpable beat that rose up from the earth. I put my hand out and felt the energy pulsing up. I swear that what I felt was the heartbeat of Africa.

As we rode into camp, I saw that we had visitors. A large group of Maasai women sat in a line with their beadwork spread out in front of them. To cries of 'shopping!' my American friends dismounted and made a dash to the Maasai. I had very little spending money and was trying to resist temptation, but eventually I too wandered over. Standing behind the women was a group of warriors, aloof as always from the bustle of selling. In their midst stood the most beautiful man I had ever seen in my life. This was a jaw-dropping moment! I was knocked out by the sheer pleasure of looking at him. There was something almost Egyptian about him, something feline. It didn't take him long to notice that I was staring, and he obviously understood why I was hypnotised as he swaggered over to introduce himself (*moran* always either swagger or lope — they never just walk). This proved difficult as neither of us could speak the other's language, so he called in an interpreter. This man with languid, feline eyes and the brightest smile in the world was called Ntiapati. After flirting through an interpreter for a while, he suggested that we should get married.

Even if we were both just playing, it was flattering to be asked by this gorgeous warrior to be his wife — it would have meant being his third! It's not every day that such impulsive proposals come my way!

Being past milking time, the women had already left for their *enkang*. As dusk deepened, the warriors left too. I bade farewell to Ntiapati and watched, as one by one the warriors melted into the trees and vanished. I am always amazed that despite their red blankets, the Maasai just seem to appear out of thin air. One minute you are looking at the edge of a forest and the next minute tall men with spears materialise.

The following morning Ntiapati appeared again, this time with his mother and some other women. His mother held open a cloth bag filled with beaded jewellery and indicated that I should make my selection. I chose a bracelet. It was the first of many presents that the Maasai would give me.

I have a very clear memory of being surrounded by this group of women. I was immediately struck by the number of clouded, unseeing eyes and missing teeth. The next thing I noticed was that they were spatted with green cow dung which also crusted around their feet. Understandably, a thick veil of flies buzzed around us. If I am honest, I have to admit that I was repulsed.

I have come a long way in my understanding since then. Maasai women do all of the hard work and between caring for children and cattle they have less time to indulge in the luxury of a thorough wash. The women are incredibly modest. When washing clothes by the river they will wash themselves without removing their clothes, one section at a time. If they carry enough water to the house for washing, they wash their children first. Men, with so much free time, often pop down to the river to bathe. The women with Ntiapati had probably come straight from morning milking, which is why they were spattered with cow dung. It wasn't long before I learned to look beyond the cow dung and dirt to discover the beauty and warmth of Maasai women and their homes.

Ntiapati returned once more to our camp. I wanted to give him a gift too. Linda gave me a green t-shirt with a bear on it which I presented to him. The next morning we continued on our journey. Ntiapati was just a sweet memory, but one that had left an impression on me. Our flirtation had somehow changed my relationship to the land I was travelling in. It had opened a door and as a result I felt somehow more connected, more involved with Kenya. And I was left with a nasty case of Maasai-itis. This term was coined for European colonials who were enamoured of the Maasai. There is no cure and I had it bad.

Before I left Australia I had heard of the Maasai, but I was not the slightest bit interested in them, or any other African tribes for that matter. I think I had decided as a child that I didn't like people very much, and I was pretty sure that this was across the board, regardless of colour and custom. So I was more amazed than anyone by my 'road to Damascus' conversion. I was captivated and drawn to these people. And what people they were. Even from a distance, the Maasai exuded humour, playfulness, pride, dignity, astonishing beauty and grace. But their magic was more than that — and it seemed a kind of magic for surely I had been cast under a spell. I came to realise that the most powerful thing about the Maasai was that they were entirely happy being who they were. They believed that they were the best race of people on this earth; and it was hard to disagree with them. For the next few days I plagued the safari operator with a million questions about the Maasai. While out riding I kept watch for their red-clad figures as they walked across the savannah. I made a beeline to talk with every Maasai that wandered into our camp and spoke often with Daniel, who had accompanied us as our guide, and a Maasai *syce* who looked after the horses.

Within the outer reserve of the Maasai Mara, our camp was set up among a grove of acacia trees between two arms of a stream. A big family of baboons lived in a tree at the top of the camp. This was an ideal place to rest the horses and view the abundant game by vehicle. I was fortunate to see a rhino and her calf on our first morning. They were under the protection of the Rhino Surveillance Unit. We met one of the rangers working with the unit, a young Maasai man named Joseph. He was very proud of his work. With the characteristic hospitality of Kenyans, he took us to his small house near the main gate to meet his new wife.

The sight of a dozen *wazungu* women on her doorstep was too much for the girl, who shyly retreated inside, but not before slipping a beaded bracelet from her wrist and pushing it onto mine. I wasn't sure what this meant. Was it a gift or was I meant to pay for it? A total stranger had taken a shine to me and impulsively presented me with a beautiful gift. This was way out of my league. Joseph gave me no hint on what to do, so in the end I asked him if I should return the bracelet. 'Oh no,' he laughed. 'That is a present for you!' I have never seen Joseph's young wife again, nor did I ever learn her name, but I still treasure the blue bracelet she gave me. I have always considered it a good omen.

The bracelet was not my only gift that day. Linda presented me with a photographic book on the Maasai. Later that afternoon, Robert turned up again. He came to the camp to visit Daniel, who was in fact one of his older brothers. He was resplendent in a bright pink and red striped blanket, black plastic sandals and red socks. He saw the book and joined me to look at the photographs of his people. As he talked with me, I learnt that he was around twenty-five years old, though he couldn't be sure as the Maasai do not take much notice of birthdays. He was a senior warrior and not married yet. He told me that he had a girlfriend, but that she was to be married to an older man soon. Robert's English was quite good, but he was very shy. One photo in the book was of a group of naked *moran* painting each other for a ceremony. He quickly turned the page saying that I should not be seeing such things!

The next time Robert came to our camp I asked for his permission to take his picture. He posed obligingly, turning this way and that with an awareness of the camera that made him seem like a fashion model. His lopsided smile and brown eyes smiled shyly at me. All of a sudden a photo didn't seem like enough to remember this gentle young *morani* with. I offered to buy his blanket from him. He agreed to sell it for 400 Kenyan shillings (about $26 in Australian money), but asked if he could give it to me the next day when he had found something else to wear.

He arrived carrying my blanket early the next morning as we were eating breakfast. I asked him more questions about his culture and told him how much I wanted to return to Maasailand. He wrote his name and contact address in my notebook in a slow, shaky script and explained that Robert was his 'school name'. He also wrote another Maasai word, *enhorit*, which I discovered later meant friend. Then he invited me to come and stay with his family before I returned to Australia. I now know that most Maasai enjoy teaching westerners about their culture, and Robert's invitation was an example of the traditional hospitality that is found in many parts of rural Africa. A thousand such invitations must have been offered over the years. Thousands more pledges to write, or to send a copy of that photo. I guess most people would have politely declined, but Africa and the Maasai had woven just enough magic around me to make me say yes. Certainly the grace and spontaneity of the Maasai had inspired me. I had just over a week until I was due to join a camping safari in Tanzania over the Christmas period, and could think of nothing better than to stay here with the Maasai. The thought of leaving had already begun to wrench at my heart and if I am entirely honest, I must also admit that I entertained hopes of running into Ntiapati again too. Would he come to Nairobi to fetch me? Robert asked. No, I would hire a vehicle and return to Narotian.

When I told my plan to the members of the group, they responded in two ways. Linda and a few others thought it was great and encouraged me to embark upon this adventure. Others, with the best intentions in the world, counselled caution. You don't know the culture they warned, what if *something awful* happened to you? I thought a bit about *something awful*. What was the worst thing that could happen to me? I could be gang-raped by a pack of fierce warriors or beaten by hordes of jealous women or eaten by a lion. Somehow I couldn't reconcile these wild horror stories with the Maasai I had encountered who seemed to be above all else so gentle. Some of the group hinted darkly that they had heard that Maasai men beat their women as a matter of course; one man had even thrown his wife into the fire. What about female circumcision? What will you eat? What happens if you get sick?

I was more concerned with the practical and financial considerations of how to actually keep my promise and return to Loita. Though I had flirted with Robert, I had no serious romantic intentions. I wanted to visit Robert and Daniel and their family for a few days to learn about their way of life, and then maybe drive back via Ntiapati's *enkang*. I talked to Tony, our safari operator, about my plans for revisiting the Maasai and he agreed to hire me a car, driver, tent, equipment and even a cook for a week for $1300.

After twelve days our wonderful horse-riding safari sadly came to an end. Though expensive, it had been the very best way to discover the sights, sounds and smells of East Africa. Walking safaris also give you a very genuine and intense experience of the African bush, but to ride through herds of game and experience the wildlife from the back of another living creature — now, that is magical. It gives you a wondrous sense of intimacy with the natural world, and highlights your connection to it. I was indeed fortunate to have had such a physical introduction to Kenya and no doubt this experience, and the open atmosphere generated in our group by Linda, were instrumental in leading me to my next adventure with the Loita Maasai. If I had sat in a minibus for two weeks with a group of tourists intent on harassing lions and getting drunk each night, I would have missed out on the most precious aspects of our journey.

Our final camp was along the banks of the Mara River. In the brown water, hippos snorted, splashed and fought, while indolent crocodiles lay along the sunny banks. On our last evening, a lone bull elephant honoured us with his presence as he strolled along the opposite bank. The next morning I walked to where the horses were tethered to say goodbye to my friend Kisima. I silently thanked him for taking care of me, while he continued eating grass. Just as I was to turn to go, Kisima lifted his long face towards mine. He blew warm air gently on my face, and then returned to his grazing. A horse's farewell.

It was physically painful to drive away from Maasailand and back to Nairobi. That same day our group flew to the coast where I spent two awful days in a tourist resort full of aging, over-tanned Germans, pining for red blankets and the sound of cattle bells. One afternoon we went sailing out past Shimoni Reef south of Mombasa. Dolphins came swimming alongside our boat. Their shining presence had made the whole detour to the coast worth-while.

We returned to Nairobi on the 'Lunatic Express', the Mombasa to Uganda railway which is so steeped in history.

Back in Nairobi, the American women embarked upon a day of frenzied shopping while I fronted up to American Express to try and get $1300 for Tony Church. By sheer luck or divine interven-tion, they allowed me to write a rubber cheque and paid me in traveller's cheques. I had no money in my bank account in Australia. I had already borrowed six thousand just to get to Kenya and go on the riding safari. I held my breath during the entire process and had to forcibly stop my legs from running out of the office when they handed over the cheques. I now had enough money to get back to Maasailand. I would worry about mundane practicalities like my bank balance later. I had the rest of my life to worry about money, but for now my instinct told me, no, it screamed at me, to follow my heart and return to Maasailand.

MORAN *(Warriors)*

D e c e m b e r   1 9 8 9

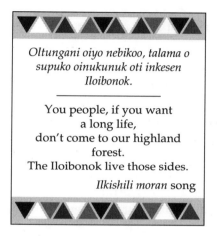

*Oltungani oiyo nebikoo, talama o
supuko oinukunuk oti inkesen
Iloibonok.*

You people, if you want
a long life,
don't come to our highland
forest.
The Iloibonok live those sides.

Ilkishili moran song

TWO DAYS LATER, ONE OF TONY'S VEHICLES COLLECTED ME FROM THE Norfolk Hotel. Our small safari team consisted of Raymond, the driver, Wilson Sitobi, a wonderful, wizened old cook, and Musolia, an experienced safari hand from the Kamba tribe and greatly liked by the Maasai. I think Tony sent him along to keep an eye on me. We stopped in Narok to buy supplies and again at the dilapidated trading centre, Narosura. Here I was able to buy a bright red and blue blanket for Daniel, cotton cloth for Robert, a *kanga* or cloth for Daniel's wife, and a few extras to give as presents to other family members.

Driving up into the Loita Hills felt as though I was going home after a long absence. My heart skipped a beat when I saw the first red blankets walking with their cattle. The drive up into the hills takes all day. The dirt track is impassable during the rains, but even at other times it takes an experienced driver to negotiate the steep and dangerous journey. As the sun set, I saw the pasture land with zebra and wildebeest grazing. The Maasai cattle were all safely in their *enkangs* by now.

We arrived at our camp site at Narotian after dark. It was so good to feel Africa's protective arms around me and hear the noises of the night. Soon Musolia had a big fire going and was busy putting up our tents. In the darkness I saw the flash of a torch and I knew it was Daniel.

'*Supa siangiki*', Daniel said as he stepped into the firelight.

'*Supa* ', I replied.

It felt like greeting a very old and dear friend. Daniel introduced me to a *morani*, Moseka ole Potot, who was around the same age as Robert. We sat by the fire talking for a while before Daniel excused himself and left me to eat my dinner prepared by Sitobi: fresh chicken soup with chunks of vegetables, bread and an orange, beautifully cut up and arranged in a dish. Sitting by the fire in the African bush made this simple fare taste like the most delicious feast. I then snuggled into my little camp bed, deeply happy.

I awoke at 5 am and lay still, listening to the morning. I soon heard Sitobi quietly moving around the camp and next the crackling of the fire. Then the swish of his shovel as he scooped the hot coals to one side. In the nearby village or *enkang*, one of Daniel's cows mooed and a cow bell rang softly. Musolia brought hot water to my tent and I silently thanked Africa for letting me be here.

Our quest this morning was to drive to where a safari group was camping a short distance away to collect Robert. He had agreed to walk with this safari group until I arrived. Daniel had already found a replacement for Robert and told me that his younger brother would be staying at Narotian for the next few days to help look after me.

I wasn't sure what to expect when I saw Robert again, but was reassured by his big smile. It was pretty presumptuous of me to have just arrived on the strength of our brief conversations. But I couldn't stop to worry about that now. On the way back in the vehicle, Robert sat close to me. I could feel the simple flirtation we had enjoyed growing into a stronger attraction. As we drove back I was very aware of him when our arms and legs bumped together.

We stopped at another *enkang* so that Daniel could ask permission for us to attend an *Emorata* (circumcision) ceremony the next day. Permission was granted. Then we stopped at another *enkang* to visit some of Daniel's friends. As soon as we arrived a smiling woman greeted me and led me by the arm into her house. This was the first time I had been inside a Maasai house and I was a bit nervous. It was the traditional flat-roofed 'igloo' style, made with cow dung plastered onto a frame of wood and branches in a wattle and daub fashion. In the centre of a dozen or so houses was an open space for the cattle at night. The ring of houses and a thick thorn fence provided a protective enclosure for the cattle at night.

Maasai women are responsible for the building and mainten-ance of their home. The materials — wood, branches, vines and cow dung — are plentiful and cheap. A woman can build an average sized house in around a week. They start learning the required skills as young girls, first building miniature houses for fun, and then later assisting their mothers for real. Houses are considered to be a woman's property. No man in Maasailand owns his own home, his wives do. (The only exception to this might be when a man builds a western style house, which seems to lack warmth and soul in comparison to the indigenous style.) The traditional home of a Maasai woman, and especially her enclosed sleeping area, is sacred. No one may enter without being invited.

To reach most Maasai homes, you must first negotiate a mine field of fresh cow shit, however as the Maasai say, 'He that steps on cow dung does not die'. Once past the cow shit, even I had to duck to enter through the low doorway. Inside it was very dark. There were no windows, and the light from the doorway was blocked by a sort of s-shaped corridor leading into the house. I felt my way around for a seat and discovered a bench. Slowly my eyes grew accustomed to the darkness. There were several women sitting inside, all smiling at me. I could see their teeth shining through the gloom. No one spoke any English, so we just all sat and smiled at one another until Daniel joined us.

There was a tense moment when I was offered a drink of milk and, full of westerner's fears, I refused it. Now I know milk is the lifeblood of the Maasai. It is their most precious food which was given to them by God (*Enkai*) when He put the Maasai in charge of all the cattle on this earth, or so the legend goes. How I wish I could have that moment back and I would gratefully drink the milk so generously offered me. But I didn't know any better then. I refused because I thought that if I drank unboiled milk I would die of brucellosis. Daniel asked if I would like to leave as I was obviously angry — it was beyond his comprehension why anyone would refuse a drink of milk. I managed to persuade him that I wasn't angry at all. I think he accepted this and began to think of me as a sweet girl who tries very hard, but has the manners of a monkey. (I doubt whether he has changed this opinion of me over the years I have known him.)

When we got back to camp, Robert and Daniel sat around talking and I offered them a soda. Musolia whisked me away to my tent for a wonderful lunch, complete with a bowl of fresh strawberries sprinkled with sugar. The food was wonderful, but I felt strange eating by myself in my own little tent. For the second time that day, food had made me feel uneasy.

After lunch Robert and ole Potot took me for a walk. I will remember this afternoon for the rest of my life. We rested by a grove of acacia trees. Ole Potot drifted off a way and started to snooze in the afternoon sun. Robert and I lay on the grass and talked of life, death and relationships — all the important things. During this conversation something changed between us. In that afternoon our lives changed forever. I felt the heady feeling of falling for a boy, but this boy was so different there was a sharp tang of excitement and a sense of discovery that I had never known before. As we each described our own culture's customs and attitudes, I actually felt that we weren't very different from each other at all. It was like talking honestly to someone for the first time in my life.

Robert explained to me that there was no taboo against associating with a *mzungu* girl. He knew of a second cousin who had had a three-year relationship with an American girl, so it was not totally unknown, just very rare, and certainly new to Robert. I wanted to know if there were any other rules and taboos in Maasai society that I should know about. Robert said that there wasn't really much else I should know. (I later discovered that there were heaps of things, but we didn't fully realise just how different our attitudes and expectations were. Like most of us, Robert just naturally assumed that everyone thought the way his own people did.)

I was totally straight with him and asked if he wanted to sleep with me. He was totally straight back and said he did. So we made a plan to spend the night together in my tent the following night. (I had already been invited to sleep in Daniel's house with his wife that night.) Having articulated that, there was a moment when we didn't know quite what to do, then all of a sudden we were holding hands. With the sun on our backs and ole Potot snoring nearby it was exquisitely innocent and wonderful. After a while, Robert said we had better return to the camp, which we did.

That evening, Daniel escorted me up the hill to his *enkang*. The cattle had settled for the night and lay all around the house. I was more than a little nervous. It was one thing to visit inside a Maasai mud and dung hut, but another thing to sleep in one. What if I didn't know what to do, or gave offence as I had earlier in the day over the drink of milk? What if they offered me something to eat? What if *something awful* happened? His children came outside to greet me. Previously Daniel had started to teach me how to greet people of all ages. I was thus prepared when all but the smallest children came up to me one by one and bowed their head. This was my cue to place my hand lightly on their head and greet them. '*Entito, Supa*', to a girl and '*Laiyoni, Supa*', to a boy, though in the dim light I probably got it wrong. '*Supa*' is pronounced 'saw-pah', with a soft 'b' sound for the 'p' (think of Zorba the Greek).

The children led me inside, past the *olale* (small pen) where the young calves slept and into the main room. Apart from the entrance area and the *olale*, a Maasai house is just one big room. It was cosy and gently lit by a small fire in the centre. Daniel's wife rose to shake my hand in greeting. The Maasai do not grip hands in the style of westerners, but rather just lightly touch palms. I settled down on a bench that ran alongside a wall. As I sat there, I felt a deep breath spill out of me. It took me by surprise for it was the sigh of someone who had finally arrived home after a long and arduous journey. Inside this warm, dark room I felt safe and comfortable.

As my eyes became used to the light, I began to notice the layout of the house. One side of the fire was the woman's side. Daniel's wife, whose name I later discovered was Narygunkishon, sat there on a low three-legged wooden stool. On the wall beside her was a rough cupboard which I could see contained pots, tins and other items. Behind her was the 'mother's bed'. This area was partially enclosed by a screen woven with long thin sticks. This is the woman's sanctuary which no one may violate. In the centre of the room, directly behind the fire was a stack of firewood that Narygunkishon used sparingly throughout the evening, demonstrating total control over the heat and flame in the same way that I can adjust a gas stove. The fire is used for cooking, warmth and light when required. On the other side of the fire was the visitor's bed, where the man of the household and his guests slept. This bed was not enclosed in any way and also served as a seat for guests. To the side of the visitor's bed was another small pen, usually for keeping young goats in at night. However Narygunkishon used this as storage space and kept her goats in another house.

I sipped a mug of sweet black tea as I slowly took all this in. This was one way to avoid drinking the milk. When it came time to sleep, it turned out that I could not sleep in this house after all because Narygunkishon had no room in her bed, especially as she was nursing and needed to be comfortable during the night. Instead she led me through the sleeping cattle to another house. I was not used to being so close to cows, especially ones with such large horns. My hostess found my hesitation most amusing (imagine a girl being scared of cows!). At the entrance to the house, she called out and another woman replied. It was a lovely big house with a huge bed for visitors. Robert and ole Potot were inside. Robert smiled and said I was welcome to share the bed with them. He had explained to me earlier that day that the golden rule in Maasai homes is 'When we are many in one house, we just sleep'. I was introduced to the woman whose house it was. She also was Robert's sister-in-law and slept in the mother's bed with her children. The house was very warm from the fire, so I spread one blanket underneath me on top of the cowhide bed and rolled a second one for a pillow. Despite the fire, the house was not smoky. I cuddled up to Robert, and we whispered to each other into the small hours. Needless to say, lying there next to each other meant that we spent a restless night, painfully aware of each other.

I was beginning to learn about the complex Maasai rules for who can sleep in which house. Each age group of Maasai men are clearly delineated, and in an *enkang* there is a house for visitors from each age group. When a visitor arrives in an *enkang* the first thing he asks is to be directed to his age group's house. This was not Robert's home *enkang*, therefore he had to sleep in his age group house. He could not sleep in the same house as his brother Daniel, who is from a much older age group. It gets even more complicated; for example, a man may not sleep in the same house as his sister. Newly circumcised initiates may not sleep in the same house as established warriors. I also discovered that married couples rarely share the same bed. The women sleep with the younger children and the man shares his bed with any male visitors. As the Maasai are so social, there are guaranteed to be visitors most nights. I began to wonder how Maasai babies were ever conceived as there seemed to be limited opportunity.

We rose before dawn. This was the morning that the *Emorata* ceremony was to be held. The operation is always performed in the early morning when it is coldest. It was still dark as I followed Robert and ole Potot out of the *enkang*. They wore red blankets and carried spears. I too was wrapped in my red blanket. We walked the short distance to the camp site.

We took my hired vehicle to the *enkang* where the *Emorata* ceremony was taking place. There would be two circumcisions today, a brother and sister. I was permitted to witness the male circumcision, taboo for Maasai women. However, as a *mzungu*, I occupied a sort of twilight zone when it came to tribal custom. Daniel was very keen for me to see the entire operation, and introduced me around to his friends and to the circumcisor or *alamoratani*, an elderly Okiek man. The men who perform male circumcisions are rarely Maasai themselves, but experienced practitioners from neighbouring communities who earn their living plying their trade. The Okiek people are the original hunter-gatherers of East Africa. The Maasai call them Ndorobo, which means those without cattle or those who keep bees in their *enkang* — a reference to the Okiek tradition of honey gathering. The Ndorobo and the Maasai share a long, symbiotic relationship. In the Loita Hills, descendants of the Ndorobo identify themselves as Maasai, explaining that 'Ndorobo' is just the name of their clan.

The male circumcision was performed outside, in the cattle enclosure. More than fifty Maasai were gathered around, in addition to a full complement of cattle. I first saw the boy, aged about fourteen, standing outside his father's entrance to the *enkang*. He was naked with a freshly shaven head. He had just come from the river, where the past wrongdoings of his youth had been symbolically washed away. The cold water may also act as an anaesthetic, though admittedly only a very minor one. In the middle of the *enkang* was a specially prepared cowhide and upright branches of the sacred olive tree that the Maasai call *olorien*. The boy was led towards the hide, and I could see that he was already in a trance-like state. He sat down, with his legs spread and his back supported by an older man, who was probably an uncle.

The rest of the men crowded around, and Daniel pushed me to the front. The boy's face was totally relaxed, his jaw slightly open, his eyes softly focused on the ground in front of him. As required of him during this initiation into manhood, he did not flinch or utter a sound. His face betrayed nothing during the operation. He did not even blink. The surgeon performed the operation quickly and cleanly, neatly slicing off three-quarters of the foreskin. I saw no blood. Once he had finished, the boy was dragged, still in his trance state, back into his mother's house. He was very brave and brought honour to himself and his family, and I'm sure will be a courageous *morani*.

Next I watched two *moran* bleed an ox. One held the ox in position, with a leather strap around the neck to make the vein bulge. The other shot a specially prepared arrow into the jugular vein in its neck. The arrowhead is fitted with a small block of wood just behind the tip, so that it cannot penetrate far and injure the ox. The blood is collected in a calabash made from a gourd that has been hollowed out. The blood was then taken to be made into a nourishing drink mixed with milk and fed to the circumcised boy.

Then I realised that they were about to circumcise the girl. She also looked about fourteen years old. Her head was cleanly shaven and she stood smiling shyly, dressed in the black robes of an initiate among her girlfriends. Several of the girls had already been circumcised, as was evident from their beaded headbands decorated with cowrie shells. Men are forbidden to watch. The procedure for girls is very different. Stoic silence is not demanded of them. The surgeon is usually an older Maasai woman, and girls are operated on inside their mother's house. In order to let in enough light, part of the roof is torn away.

I stood among a crowd of women near the door as they positioned the girl on the floor and stretched her legs behind her. Four women held her down. The circumcisor knelt in front of the girl, her instrument was a double-sided razor blade. I couldn't look any longer. A moment later the girl screamed out. In any language the shock was plain. I looked towards her again and saw nothing but blood. The girl continued to scream and plead. I must have stood there for ten minutes, keeping my eyes on the ground. I couldn't walk away for fear of offending. I could do nothing but pray that the girl would survive. Eventually I did walk away. The procedure still continued. I listened to the screaming from 20 metres away.

I was reeling from the shock of what I had just witnessed and needed to retreat into my own space. Raymond drove me back to our camp, leaving Robert and Daniel behind to join in the celebration that would continue for the rest of the day. We planned to go back and collect them later. I had no way to interpret or understand what seemed to me a barbaric practice. The male circumcision didn't bother me. It was a relatively minor operation, and the boy undergoing the procedure seemed to be in control the entire time. There was an undeniable sense of power and pride around him. By contrast, the genital mutilation of the girl was, to my mind, an act of senseless violence. This confused me greatly, because the Maasai I had met were nothing if not gentle.

As you can imagine, I have discussed the issue of female circumcision hundreds of times with Robert and other Maasai, men and women, traditional and college educated, since I witnessed that first *Emorata* ceremony. No one has been able to give me any reason for the practice except to say that the Maasai have always done it. I am totally convinced that it is not performed with the express purpose of enforcing chastity, or of diminishing sexual pleasure, though to a western way of thinking it would no doubt end up having that effect. (Western expectations of sexual relationships simply do not apply in Maasai society.) The male *Emorata* ceremony, such a fundamental and important ritual in Maasai society, is a tough initiation into an even tougher life. It publicly marks the change from child to man. So too the female ceremony makes a girl child into a woman. This is the key — child to adult. For an uncircumcised girl to fall pregnant is a disgrace. It is not possible for a child to beget a child. Traditionally, the girl would be circumcised immediately and married off with haste, or she may even be cast out from her family. Circumcision is the process by which the Maasai differentiate between a child and a woman. It is a clear and public ritual that decrees exactly where a member of that society stands and what is expected of them.

When we drove back in the mid-afternoon, the senior *moran*, Robert among them, were singing and performing *adumu*, the spectacular leaping dance. Twenty or more *moran* were in a group just outside of the *enkang* proper, singing a deep, rhythmic chant. Over the top of this, in a falsetto, one *morani* sang the story. *Moran* songs are generally about cattle, brave warrior exploits, more cattle, and not-so-gentle digs at the junior elders — the generation above them now retired from warrior duties. One song described how the junior elders can no longer jump when dancing because they have grown fat and lazy from sitting around talking all day. In the centre of the singing, swaying group, two or three *moran* jumped in unison, three or four high leaps in succession and then were replaced by the next couple and so on. The dancers leapt effortlessly with their bodies held straight, arms stiff by their sides as they shot up and down like pistons. The best dancers managed an almost imperceptible sideways movement of their shoulders as they reached their highest point as if to say 'This is so easy for a brave *morani* such as I'. I was mesmerised by the sound and the swaying mass of colourful *moran*. I must tell you honestly that Robert was the best dancer. He jumped the highest and looked the most handsome in the bright orange blanket I had given him.

Sitting outside the houses, elders sat drinking. Women sat in their own groups and children ran around. We found Daniel quite drunk from the home-made honey beer. He led me around introducing me to other elders and members of his family who all fussed over me and made me feel welcome. All Maasai ceremonies involve the brewing and consumption of large quantities of honey beer. It is made from water, sugar, honey and the fibrous fruit of the *suguru* tree. These sausage-shaped fruits help ferment the brew. I was offered a cup and hesitantly sipped it. It was a pale straw colour, and tasted like flat ginger beer with chunky bits floating in it.

Drinking beer is the prerogative of elders. Senior women are also permitted to drink, as long as they are discreet and don't take too much. However *moran* and other women are not. I was also offered my first taste of roast goat which was well cooked and very tough. An ox and two goats had been slaughtered earlier in the day in the bush away from the *enkang*. Throughout the afternoon, shifts of men went up the hill, and into the bush to eat their share of meat. These 'shifts' were in fact age groups or generations of Maasai who had been circumcised during the same time.

Some explanation is required here about the age group system, which is a fundamental aspect of Maasai culture. The life of a Maasai male is a well-ordered progression through a series of life stages, which are determined mainly by age, introduced through ceremonies and accompanied by specific duties and privileges. The males of every section (more about these sections later) pass through three main stages: *ayiokisho* (boyhood), *e-murano* (*moran-hood*) and *payianisho* (elderhood).

Moran are subdivided into junior and senior warriors. In Loita, the first wave of boys to reach adolescence and be circumcised are known as *Tatene* or the 'right hand' age group. When, after approximately seven years, the right hand age group graduate at their *Eunoto* ceremony into senior *moran*, the next group of adolescent boys are circumcised and become *Kedeyni*, the 'left hand' age group. Eventually, both right and left hand age groups are joined together to form a complete generation or age set at a ceremony known as *Olngesherr*.[1] Each age group and generation is given a name by their elders, being a symbolic wish or blessing to grow up to. For example, Robert belongs to the right hand age group known as *Ilkishili*, meaning 'those who go to see new things'. The boy whose ceremony I attended was being circumcised into the left hand age group known by the nickname *Ilmarjeshi*, which refers to soldiers.

Sometime in 1994 or 1995, if the rains are good, these two age groups will be joined as one generation at *Olngesherr* and will receive a new name from the elders two generations ahead of theirs.

They will then become junior elders and after a few years a new generation of *moran* will replace them. All the age groups ahead of them take a step forward, thus the current junior elders, *Ilkitoip*, will replace the powerful senior elders, *Iseuri*, who will be 'demoted' to the status of retired elders. *Ilkitoip* will in turn 'kindle the fire' for the next generation of *moran*. In a rapidly changing world where education is the new initiation and landrights the new challenge, it is hard to say just how many young men will have the opportunity to go through a period of traditional *moran*hood.

Men then continue to identify with their generation throughout their lives from junior and senior elderhood, through to retired elderhood and then finally venerable elderhood. The Maasai say *'Erisio olparror o Enkai'* — the age group is equal with God. The groups of men I saw disappearing into the forest that day to eat meat were organised strictly according to seniority, with the venerable elders and the retired elders being offered the choicest parts first. Each generation then has its share of the meat, with certain parts being reserved for particular groups. The right shoulder is generally reserved for the oldest men, the venerable elders. Daniel's generation, *Iseuri*, the men who are currently at the height of their patriarchal influence, were given the right ribs and side. The heart on this particular day was given to the workers, the young men who had done all the slaughtering and roasting. The women are usually sent the liver, feet, intestines and head. Particular parts of the animal are also used in ceremonies, for example, the heart is used in *Olkiteng lorrbaa*.

Maasai women have no such age groups, but instead are identified first as a daughter of their father's age group, then with the age group of *moran* with whom they danced as girls, and finally after marriage with their husband's age group. One of the first questions I am asked by an older Maasai man or woman is *'Ira engai?'* meaning 'Whose am I?' At first my response would be *'Ene Oddie'* — literally I am the daughter of Oddie. As my relationship with Robert progressed and was openly recognised, my response changed to *'Ene Rerente'* — I am ole Rerente's. Only an older person may ask this of a younger one; to do the reverse would be considered very impolite. As *'ene'* means daughter of, so *'ole'* means son of.

The singing was to continue till dusk, and the drinking long afterwards. In the late afternoon we drove back to camp again, this time with Daniel and Robert. When we arrived, I found a visitor waiting for me. It was Kikuyan, the woman whose house I had visited yesterday. She had brought me a gourd full of fresh milk and offered it to me. For a second I was nonplussed. I really did not want to drink any milk but I also did not want to risk offending this woman for a second time in twenty-four hours. Quick as a fox, Musolia sensed my uncertainty and came to my rescue by offering to make 'African tea' for the Maasai men. I breathed a sigh of relief; this was the polite solution. I discovered that 'African tea' is made with milk and a drop of water and 'English tea' is made the other way around.

Later Robert and I walked to the top of a small hill not far from the camp. It was one of the few times that we were alone without one of his age mates. I told him that he had made me forget Ntiapati and that I would rather stay here with him than drive to Olare Lamun. He made it clear that he would escort me to Olare Lamun if I wished, and that I could also be with Ntiapati. I tried to explain the western notion of, well, not so much monogamy, but just how I could not be attracted to more than one man at a time. With a smile and a shrug, he seemed to accept that.

I later learnt that the *moran* have a little more sexual freedom than the other men. Sex, however, is only discussed between couples. To discuss such relationships with any other person is totally unacceptable.

I had thought that communicating about personal issues would be difficult between two such different cultures, because believe me in my experience in Australia it is never easy. Nobody says what they mean, or are too shy and just end up saying whatever the latest *Cleo* tells you to say. I learnt quickly that Robert and I could discuss anything with complete openness — there was nothing that made me feel uncomfortable. Because Robert's English was limited and we both put such tremendous effort into explaining our thoughts, stripping them down to their most essential level, we didn't waste time on trivial subjects like the weather and star signs. As a result I have always expressed myself better to Robert than to anyone else. With hindsight, I now know this is true intimacy.

There is no need to say much about our night together. It is not the Maasai way to share information meant only for a man and a woman. That night is now a wonderful mix of memories and emotions. I would not have been at all surprised if Robert had been transformed into a black swan and flown away at dawn.

The next day, while Robert went to attend to a sick cow in another *enkang* about eight kilometres away (a mere stroll for a Maasai), Daniel offered to show me where he got his wild honey from. I set off into the forest with Raymond the driver, Daniel, ole Potot and a very, very tall *morani*. His nickname was Marefu, which means tall in Kiswahili and he must have been close to 200 centimetres. His appearance was accentuated by very dark skin and a prominent brow bone — a bit like Lurch from the Addams Family. We walked through the forest, past a stream where clouds of white butterflies sucked at the moist ground, and up higher into the thickest bush. The Maasai name for the Loita Hills is *O-Sapuko loo Loitai* — the highland of the Loita Maasai. The hills start at about 1800 metres and the highest point reaches 2682 metres, so it is usually quite cool in the morning and evening, though hot in the middle of the day.

This is not the steamy tropical jungle that most people equate with Africa, but more like parts of the Victorian high country. The pasture land has a distinctly alpine feel, dotted as it is with tiny blue, white and orange flowers. Here in the forest it is buffalo country, but I was assured that there were no fresh signs. Daniel pointed to a tall tree, and halfway up I could make out the knot where the hive was. The men made a fire at the base of the tree, rubbing two fire sticks to get the spark going. To do this they used a piece of wood with a notch cut along it. Into this notch they stuffed a pinch of dry grass, and then, holding a stick at right angles to the notch, Marefu twirled it furiously between his palms until the grass and kindling smoked and, with breath, the smoke was encouraged into a flame. Using wood from the *olorien* tree, the fire soon smoked the bees out of their hive. I heard them buzzing angrily from where I stood upwind a few metres away from the action lest I was stung. Next a large branch was propped against the trunk, and Marefu used this as a ladder to reach the hive. He used his blanket to cover his head and body while reaching into the hive to pull out great chunks of dark honeycomb. He did this several times, calmly shaking the bees off his arm. They must have been stinging him like crazy.

When Marefu had collected enough, he climbed down and began to eat. Daniel handed me the palest, most delicious piece. I felt like a bear cub as I licked at my fingers which were covered in honey. Afterwards, going back down the hill, I marvelled at how neatly the Maasai moved. The men skipped down a steep pathway, spear in one hand and their blankets a splash of brilliant red in the dappled green and gold of the forest. I crashed along behind like a baby elephant.

When we arrived back in camp, I treated Marefu's swelling bee stings with tea-tree oil and calamine lotion. The others watched the impromptu clinic with interest. From that moment on, Marefu treated me like a sister — instructing me in his language (he spoke very little English, which I have discovered makes for the best teacher), returning my mock punches and praising me every time I spoke correct Maasai. Robert and the others of his age group were always very respectful and never touched me, but Marefu seemed quite at ease and would throw his arm around my shoulder in greeting. I am only 152 centimetres tall and barely reached his armpit, so it must have been quite a sight to see me with this gentle giant.

I had been invited to stay that night in Robert's *enkang* in Morijo, where he lived with his mother and youngest sister. We decided that I should eat my evening meal in camp before setting off by vehicle at 4 pm. This would avoid any potential food problems. Morijo is approximately 15 kilometres from Narotian. All of the Loita Hills are beautiful, but Morijo is surely the jewel in the crown. The region is set in a valley with large expanses of sweet pasture, fringed in on all sides by purple hills. Robert's *enkang* was built on a rise and offered a stunning all-round view. Much larger than Daniel's *enkang*, with at least thirteen houses, it was built in the traditional Maasai style with the cattle in the centre and houses around the cattle enclosure.

Inside the house, I was introduced to Robert's sister, Nasango. She looked to be in her mid-twenties, with a plump face and shy smile. I sat on the visitor's bed and watched as she organised the fire, cleaned the tin mugs and fed her children without haste. Nasango was in an unusual position; she is in her twenties with three children but is still unmarried. I asked Robert how this could be, knowing that the usual practice would be for a girl to be married and move to her husband's *enkang* not long after circumcision. Robert explained that Nasango will not be married until after he is, so that there is someone to look after his cattle and home. Robert's mother is 'retired', and divides her time between visiting each of her children and grandchildren. She was away at this time with Robert's next brother, Ilampala. Under these circumstances, Nasango would have been circumcised as usual, but then allowed to have her own children. The children will automatically be recognised by her future husband and will come to the marriage as an extra bonus.

It seemed to me that Nasango had the ideal situation. She continued to live with her extended family, but could also raise her own children. I wondered how she, a mature and capable woman, would feel when she was eventually married to a stranger, a much older man chosen for her by her father and brothers.

Nasango was incredulous when Robert requested that she make me black tea with no milk. As she cooked, she started to sing in a sweet, high voice. Soon ole Potot joined in. He may have been shy, but he too had a fine voice. When Robert came inside from seeing to his cattle, Marefu and his older brother, Kirragei, were with him. The four *moran* and Nasango sang together, the *moran* moving together as one in rhythm to the song. Robert had told me previously that 'My age group is serious for singing'. Now I understood what he meant. In the firelight, listening to the steady bass sound of the *moran* and watching them sway back and forth, I felt like a snake hypnotised by its charmer. I was also captivated by the deep comradeship evident between the four age group brothers. It was so genuine and natural that I could not fail to be touched. What a wonderful society it is that allows men to express their love and brotherhood for each other. The Maasai declare that the true essence of *moran*hood is a balance of courage and gentleness. A *morani* should not have more of one than the other. In addition he must be strong, clever, confident and wise. But above all, courageous and gentle. No wonder the *moran* seem to embody the true spirit of masculinity.

I remembered the Maasai saying, '*Erisio olparror o Enkai*' — the age group is equal to God. This proverb has been explained to me thus: the age group is held in very high esteem. The ritual head of the age group, chosen at the *Eunoto* ceremony and known as *Ollotuno*, keeps a string of beads, each bead representing an individual member. If one commits an unpardonable sin, the leader removes one of the beads and throws it away saying, 'I have thrown you like that bead'. Comparing the age group to God goes to show the importance of the age group.

When it was time for the four *moran* to eat, I watched as Nasango carefully poured fresh milk into four tin mugs. Next she placed a large tin plate of *ugali* (maize meal cooked with hot water) on the floor in front of the *moran*. They ate slowly and with concentration, each taking a handful of *ugali*, working it into a ball and popping it into their mouths. I did not once observe a Maasai woman eating during the entire week I stayed with Robert's family. I later learnt that children are not permitted to be present when men eat. Nasango would have eaten with her children earlier, or she could also send them to a relative's house to eat. If a child accidentally walks into a house where men are eating, the child will turn around immediately and leave. This doesn't include toddlers, who are above the law. Women prefer to eat with their children rather than with the men.

A beautiful woman came inside and invited me to one of the elder's homes where they were singing and drinking. We all crammed into the house, where twenty or so elders were having a fine time. Daniel had arrived unexpectedly and was getting stuck into the home brew. They sang the songs appropriate for their age group, *Iseuri*, and I sipped from a cup of honey beer with the beautiful woman.

When it came time to sleep, I was disturbed to learn that I could not sleep in the same house as Robert. Our original plan had been to sleep in the house of another sister-in-law, but as Daniel had turned up, this house had to be made available to him. Robert could not sleep in the same house as his sister, Nasango, and his age group house was already full. He went to sleep with Marefu in their age group house in another *enkang* and I shared the visitor's bed in Nasango's house with Kirragei and ole Potot. Even Marefu could not sleep in the same house as his older brother, Kirragei. Robert assured me that 'there would be no problems' (as he put it) with the two *moran* I was sharing the bed with. There weren't. I pulled my blanket around me and fell asleep. I found the rules about sleeping arrangements very complex and very confusing at the time. While this information seems fairly innocuous to a western mind, it is offensive to the Maasai to openly discuss such matters. My so-called honesty, I'm afraid, is in the poorest of Maasai taste.

Robert returned early the next morning to see how I was, and then went out to check on his hundred or so goats before they went out to graze. Goats form an important part of the Maasai pastoral economy. They are far more likely to be sold for cash flow or slaughtered for food than a cow. Inside I watched Nasango stoke up the fire and make sweet black tea for me. She had lost some of her initial wariness and smiled at me directly. I had some hotel soaps in my bag which I gave to her as a thank you gift.

The morning activities went on all around me. I loved seeing the baby goats being let out to suckle with their mothers for the first time (goats and kids are separated at night). They run out into the sun, crying pathetically until their mothers respond. Then they race to them frantically and get stuck into breakfast. Inside the *enkang*, the cows were going through the same procedure with their calves, except that the calves are let out one at a time so that the women can milk on one side while the calf suckles on the other. The milk is collected in hollowed out gourds, known as calabashes or in Maasai as *olkukurto*. Each cow only gives a litre or so a day. This seems a small amount, but these Boran cross cattle are not a pure dairy or beef breed. Rather, they are what I call a 'survival' breed, hardy and capable of existing on poor pasture for months at a time and resistant to the local ticks.

During the morning Raymond came to collect us and we returned to the camp in Narotian. In addition to my problem with food, I was also beginning to feel uncomfortable being whizzed around in a vehicle like Lady Muck when everyone else walked. In the afternoon, Daniel escorted me up the hill to his *enkang*. I knew that he and Narygunkishon were planning to dress me up as a 'siangiki' — a young Maasai woman — so I took all the beaded jewellery I had bought or been given.

Narygunkishon dressed me in four pieces of coloured cloth, one around my waist as a skirt, two crossing over my upper body and tied at the shoulder and the final piece tied loosely around my neck as a cape. Then she added the huge round beaded collars, *oltirpe*, that all Maasai women wear at ceremonies, and the *entende* (the traditional wedding necklace with long strings of beads hanging down to the knees). Finally she hung her earrings over the tops of my ears and a beaded circlet around my head. I felt strange in all this finery, but they pronounced me 'sidai' (beautiful) and 'siangiki capisa' (a true Maasai girl). Daniel used my camera to take photographs of me with Narygunkishon and also with Robert, who looked vaguely embarrassed.

In the evening I returned to their house for my final visit. I gave them the food that I had left over, and some of the shoes and clothes that the American women had left with me to give to the Maasai. The shoes, especially the smaller sizes for women, were greatly appreciated. I also gave Narygunkishon some shiny purple cloth that she had admired. They presented me with a beautiful choker. Later that night, Robert gave me his necklace and his beaded wrist band. He also promised me one cow which I could pick out on my return. I gave him my blanket and some clothes. Though we never discussed it, it seemed understood that I would be back.

I was sad to say goodbye to Narygunkishon and her children when they came down to the camp early the next morning. I was also sad to leave Marefu, who was fast becoming a good friend. Daniel was catching a lift with the vehicle as far as Narok, and Robert was accompanying me all the way to Nairobi. Both were dressed in their western style clothes for town. Robert had a pretty impressive wardrobe cobbled together from the cast-offs of American tourists. His jeans were Levis, his shirt Cardin, and his runners were Nikes. I though he looked awful, like a peacock with his plumes cut off. There is nothing more aesthetically distressing than to see Maasai men and women devoid of their bright and graceful robes, and instead stuffed into an odd assortment of creased, ill-fitting and less comfortable cast-offs from modern western fashion. The government has long discouraged the Maasai from wearing their own clothes in Nairobi as part of the campaign to detribalise them. Where the Zulus of South Africa parade proudly in their traditional garments, and shake the ground with their warrior roars, the Maasai meekly assume the appearance of 'modern', 'developed' Kenyans in a suit and tie. For a preliterate people such as the Maasai who communicate their roles, history, symbols and imagery through clothing and body decorations, the spiritual and cultural impact upon their identity must be profound. In fact, the ultimate symbol of the Maasai dilemma must be a warrior in a dirty safari suit.

Six hours later we were back in the city. It seemed another planet to me after the peace of Maasailand. I was booked into the Norfolk Hotel, one of the best in Nairobi. I wondered how Robert would feel about staying in a hotel, but with the confidence of a true *morani* he sailed into the Norfolk Hotel, from one century to the next without batting an eyelid. He had been to Nairobi many times before, I discovered later, staying in the hotels with safari groups he some-times worked for as a guide.

This was our last night together for I didn't know how long. I certainly had strong feelings for Robert, but I couldn't understand all I felt. It had happened too quickly and I had just followed my heart without analysing what I was doing. Looking back on my correspondence now, a letter to Linda and the rest of the American group still seems to sum it up best: '... more than ever my breath choked in my throat when I saw how beautiful he was. The only thing I can compare it to is the surge you get in your heart when you see a horse gallop across a field. This is how I feel with Robert but even stronger. In retrospect, I think this is partly because he is the first man who has not judged me or compared me, he just accepts me and has no expectations. Horses are like this too.'

Already I missed the sounds of Maasailand: the singsong language of the Maasai; the hollow clang of cow bells; the bleat of a baby goat; the soft crackle of the fire; the grunting of a lion and the barking of a zebra. Somehow the sounds are the richest memories I have of Kenya. It is as though I discovered my sense of hearing for the first time. I asked Robert if he missed the sounds of his home when he is away and he replied, 'When I am not with you I miss them'. We said goodbye the next day and I promised to return within six months.

I find it hard to remember the feelings of the girl I was more than three and a half years ago. That was the beginning of a journey that has taken me a long way. I turn to my correspondence again to honestly record what I felt and thought: '... I don't entertain any fantasies about marriage. Robert will choose a Maasai wife in two years time. I know I cannot live there or even stay there for more than a few weeks at a time because the elders may not approve and it would be too unsettling for Robert. I know I can never take him out of his world into mine, and I wouldn't want to either ... I have no doubts or fears about our relationship, but I am aware of my responsibilities. I know I can never recapture that first wonderful week, but I can have new and different experiences. So there is no need to worry unless you fear the unknown — which I don't.'

[1] Not all Maasai sections follow the right and left hand custom. The Kisonko in Tanzania have one continuous age group.

C H A P T E R   F O U R

CATTLE OK GRASS OK
I LOVE YOU

Australia January to
April 1990

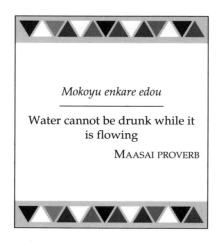

Mokoyu enkare edou

Water cannot be drunk while it
is flowing

MAASAI PROVERB

I STARTED WORKING OUT HOW TO RETURN TO KENYA AS SOON AS I WAS ON
the plane back to Australia. I was now in debt from my first trip, so
it called for some creative accountancy and a total disregard for
conventional money management. How much could I get for
Granny's diamond ring, I wondered, as she turned in her grave.
How much could I sell my bomb of a car for? Would a bank be
crazy enough to give me another loan? I was encouraged no end by
Beryl Markham's biography that I read on the plane. Apparently
she had spent most of her life in debt and had never let it stop her
having a good time. More to the point, she had had most of her
good time in Kenya.

Back in Melbourne I continued working with the Melody Lords,
who were releasing their first EP of glam rock classics and performing live three nights a week. I worked constantly: from 8 am to
10 am for the Melody Lords, promoting their gigs and EP, then I

would cross over Brunswick Street and work at the Melbourne Comedy Festival office helping to co-ordinate a major tour by Archaos, an *avant garde* French circus, until 6 pm each night. Three or four nights a week I worked taking the money on the door at the Melody Lords' live gigs. I also made some major adjustments in my life. I moved out of the beautiful (and expensive) flat I shared with my friend Carolyn and became a lodger in a house closer to work. I sold my designer clothes to a 'seconds' boutique in Toorak, and sold my car to the wreckers. That was really quite sad: even though the body had rusted, the engine was good and the little car had a lot of heart.

All the time a huge question remained unanswered in my mind. Were my feelings for Robert real or was it all a dream? Had it just been a slightly exotic holiday romance?

The reaction from my friends was either one of amusement or cynicism. Either I would get over it and return to my senses, or I was the victim of a confidence ring led by Robert that tricked white girls out of their life savings. I don't think anyone, including my mother, took my situation very seriously. She'll come down to earth, they agreed with each other, safe in the knowledge that this sort of thing never lasts very long. No one I can think of expressed anything remotely resembling surprise. I guess this reaction from my friends tells you more about me than anything I can say. One even said, 'Well, of course you are in love with a Maasai warrior, Catherine. What else would you do? We didn't expect you to marry a lawyer and renovate an inner city terrace for the rest of your life.'

What brings two people from different countries and immensely different backgrounds to a point in time where they begin a relationship? Three years later I learnt the Maasai answer to this question when it was posed to one of Robert's mothers, Mumai. She replied that it was *Enkai* (God). God had sent Catherine to be with Robert. I have thought about this often, and endured countless questions from friends and strangers all trying to understand why I made the choice I did. Mumai's answer still seems to be the best and most complete. However, if you care to search my psyche for early evidence of a predisposition to fall in love with a Maasai warrior, all you will find is a fairly standard unhappy childhood and angry adolescence. These had instilled in me self-reliance and independence from an early age, as well as a strong belief that I could do anything I set my mind to. I also always seemed to be searching for a 'big family' I could lose myself in. In a way, I guess I have just continued this pattern and found for myself the biggest family of them all — the Nkidongi subclan of the Loita Maasai.

I knew at the time that the only way I could resolve the situation was to return to Maasailand. I was sure that my feelings for Robert were deepening day by day, but I found it hard to believe he felt the same way about me. I could not phone Robert of course, but I could write. Week after week I sent him letters. Not passionate love letters, but restrained, conservative, friendly letters that would not embarrass him if read by someone else, for I wasn't sure how well Robert could actually read. I received no reply, until one day my doubts were dispelled by one line written in a shaky, childlike hand that arrived in a dirty airmail envelope. It read 'Cattle is OK Grass is OK I love you.'

After a couple of months working and saving, I phoned Tony Church (he had run the horse-riding safari) in Nairobi to find out when the rains started in Kenya. He poured cold water on my dreams with a dose of realism. He made it quite clear that a relationship with a Maasai was impossible, and suggested that I may do Robert irreparable harm by involving him further. This sent me reeling into doubt, until I got a hold of myself and decided to do what my heart dictated rather than be limited by the fears of others. Where was it written in stone, I wanted to know. Why is it impossible?

By April 1990, four months after my return, I had my plane ticket, some savings and my trusty American Express card. I had also driven my friends crazy with my single-minded pursuit, but it was too late to worry about that now.

The final Melody Lords gig I worked on was a huge bash at the Palace in St Kilda, where we packed more than six thousand screaming girls in. Patrick the drummer dedicated his solo number (Alice Cooper's 'No More Mr Nice Guy') to Kimba the White Lion. He also gave me two pieces of advice: 'Remember Tom Cruise's tattoo, "Be Fearless", and, during take off, always watch for the flames.'

CATTLE OK GRASS OK I LOVE YOU

When I said my goodbyes, I really didn't know how long I was going for. I didn't have any fixed plans or firm dates — I would just take it as it happened. I thought I could stretch my money to last about five months.

The flight I had purchased to Nairobi was very long, and very cheap. From Sydney to Singapore with British Airways, then with Pakistan International Airways from Singapore to Karachi via Bangkok, overnight in Karachi, and from there to Nairobi via Abu Dhabi. It would take me three whole days, but at only $2000 return, it was the cheapest way back to Kenya. Flying to Singapore with British Airways, a spare seat separated me from the chatty American girl in my row. The panic and nausea I had felt earlier in the day was gone. I watched inflight TV, read, ate and slept. The most beautiful moment of all was when we flew into a brilliant orange sunset somewhere over the vast Indian Ocean.

Changing flights, I discovered why Changi International Airport in Singapore picks up all the 'Best Airport' awards every year. If I ever get stranded at an airport, I pray that it is this one with its own gym, showers, day rooms, bars, restaurants, duty free shops, chemist and cinema. Three hours passed like a flash here, and I was back on a plane bound for Karachi. Looking around the shabby interior of the PIA plane, I remembered Patrick's advice about the flames. I hoped fervently that PIA had spent more money keeping the engine up to date than they obviously had on the upholstery.

I only had one night and a day to spend in Karachi. I arrived on the eve of a national religious holiday, Eed, so that all the shops and markets were closed. I tried to ask the driver who took me to my hotel what Eed was all about. He explained he was a Christian and couldn't really answer my questions. I spent my time here resting in the hotel and consoled myself with the thought that at least with all the shops closed, I couldn't spend any money. Outside my room, high in the Karachi Sheraton, large hawks wheeled in the grey sky. On my bedside table, a metal arrow was screwed into the wood, pointing to Mecca. I passed on the in-house movie, *The Man from Snowy River*. A fax arrived from my friend Patrick. It was a photocopy of a packet of Chocolate Chips Ahoy biscuits. His scrawl at the bottom promised to save one for me.

The next stage of my journey took me from Karachi to Kenya, with a duty free stop at Abu Dhabi airport, the capital of the United Arab Emirates. This turned out to be a really intense experience. Abu Dhabi Airport is a techno jewel set in the desert. A vast expanse of sand and then suddenly I was in the middle of a Star Trek set. Outside the plane windows, the heat shimmered. The terminal building itself was like a huge octopus with tentacle-like tunnels connecting the plane to the interior — a glittering, peacock blue and green duty free hall. Like a very bizarre Noah's Ark, people from every race, colour and religion seemed to be gathered here. African, European and Asian faces were absorbed in a shopping frenzy. The odd sheikh glided by like Caspar the Ghost. I bought only a red apple and an orange juice for about $2.70.

During the last leg to Nairobi, I felt alternately nervous and excited at the thought of seeing Robert again. I tried hard to expect nothing, but a feeling that something wonderful was about to happen kept bubbling up inside me.

CHAPTER FIVE
DON'T CALL ME MEMSAHIB

May 1990

Isipat engari, mengari iregiei

Truths are shared, but not so customs

MAASAI PROVERB

BEFORE I LEFT AUSTRALIA, I HAD SENT ROBERT A LETTER AND A TELEGRAM telling him to meet me at the Norfolk Hotel on 4 May. There is no post office in the Loita Hills. The mail service is provided intermittently by a rich cousin of Robert's, who has a vehicle and a post office box in Narok. This is a round trip of about ten hours. Letters can pass through many hands before reaching their addressee, so I had no way of knowing whether Robert had in fact received them. Even if he had, there was no guarantee that he would be able to find a vehicle to Nairobi once he had walked the twenty kilometres to Narosura, the nearest trading post. A daily *matatu* (the local form of public transport — a cross between a bus and a taxi) operates between there and Narok.

I had plenty of time to reflect on these thoughts while I sat waiting on the terrace of the Norfolk Hotel in Nairobi. On the way to my rendezvous, it took all my efforts to keep from turning around and going straight back to Australia. I didn't know if I could bear to face the disappointment of Robert not showing at all. During the first hour I sat waiting, my hands shook and I perspired. Three hours and two gin and tonics later, I was still waiting, albeit more calmly. I decided that he wasn't coming. It was infinitely easier to believe that, rather than to think of what might happen when he did arrive. Of course my big fear was that, when he arrived, absolutely nothing would happen.

I had chosen a seat which allowed me a clear view of the footpath. I kept searching, seeking out Robert's face amongst the crowd. A handsome face with a lopsided smile. Each time I saw a long, loose walk or a big smile my heart would stop dead. Is that him? I'd instantly look away, lacking the courage to see if it really was Robert. Then I'd painfully look up, only to be disappointed. My strangled heart would lurch into life again, with a tinge of relief. I felt relief only because once we were together we would have to face the next hurdle. I reasoned with myself. Maybe he hasn't got my telegram. Maybe the *matatu* has broken down. Maybe he doesn't want to see me again.

I ordered an ice-cream sundae, and then decided to wait just one more hour. It was six o'clock and I had been here since noon. Then, all of a sudden, Robert was standing next to me. He smiled at me shyly and shook my hand — the only acceptable greeting. The Maasai do not indulge in public displays of emotion, kisses, tears and hugs. However, his smile and the very fact that he had actually come all this way to meet me were reassurance enough.

The ice-cream sundae arrived and sat on the table between us. We both ordered tea and smiled at each other between slurps. 'Good to see you again', he kept saying. The sundae sat there melting, a symbol of our shyness, of not being in our best environment.

We spent the next couple of days in Nairobi, getting to know each other again. Despite the questions and uncertainty that were at the back of my mind, I kept on following my heart. It told me loud and clear that I wanted to be with Robert. So I quietened my doubts and took each day as it came.

If I had to pick one word to describe our first few days together again, it would have to be, above all, 'awkward'. However, even in the no man's land of the hotel, where neither of us quite knew how we should be with each other, there was a tremendous empathy between us. Robert assumed we would go to the Loita Hills, but I was less sure of my welcome.

As we planned our return to the Loitas, I knew that I couldn't just land on Robert's family. To give me independence, I hired a vehicle, tent and two staff from Tony Church. The day before we were due to leave, I went shopping for my supplies in Nairobi. Robert went to see a relative about a cow bell, and I floated down Mundi Mbingu Street to the city markets. I filled two straw baskets with fruit and vegetables from the Banana Hill Greengrocers inside the City Market. The baskets were sewn closed using twine and a huge needle. Next I went into Goodfares, a small supermarket, and bought passionfruit cordial, tea, longlife milk, sausages, tinned cheese, butter, biscuits and eggs.

From there, I headed down Biashara Street, past all the Indian shops full of cloth, cheap frilly children's wear and khaki safari fashions. I stopped at the hardware store, and then the bead shop to buy 'saen', the colourful beads imported from Czechoslovakia that have been used by the Maasai for decades since the Arab trading caravans and early European explorers travelled through Maasailand. Next I bought fine basmati rice from the spice shop. At another I purchased green cloth as a gift for Robert's father, and pencils and writing books for the children. I also chose a wooden jigsaw map of Africa. This was the closest thing I could find to an 'educational toy' in the toy shops full of pink-skinned baby dolls, space toys and books featuring western children doing western things.

Back in our hotel room, Robert and I compared packages. His were all variously bundled up in scraps of newspaper and old plastic bags. There was gingham cloth, a child's jumper, dress and shoes, a tin of cow fat, two cow bells and a small wooden suitcase. He explained that he would have to swap one of the cow bells, because they both sounded the same. He wanted each of his cattle to have an individual sound, so that people from far away could hear the bells and know he had many cattle. He knew exactly which oxen were going to be rewarded with a bell. If I had asked, he could have told me their names and pedigree as well.

That night, Robert started telling me about how life was for him when he was growing up. I say 'started', because the telling has taken more than three years, and is not yet finished. The story began when I asked Robert about his family.

Robert's father is a highly respected elder and son of the great Oloiboni Senteu. The Iloibonok are the prophets, ritual experts, healers and spiritual leaders of the entire Maasai nation. Iloibonok literally means 'those who make medicine'. Their clan, known as Nkidongi, are descended from the first Oloiboni, and could be considered the Maasai equivalent of royalty. The Iloibonok are not 'chiefs', or political leaders of any sort. No one Maasai bears this responsibility, for all decisions are made through the consensus of the council of elders. The Iloibonok are a sort of intermediary between the Maasai and God.

When Robert was born, his mother was in her forties and his father was more than sixty. When he was very young, though no one can say what age for sure, but probably around three or four years, Robert fell from a tree and was impaled upon a branch which went through his side. For the first few days, he was treated with traditional medicine. When the wound became infected, his family sought outside help and he was flown to Nairobi for surgery. Today his body bears the thick scar of the surgeon's knife around his middle, and also the more decorative scars where his tiny body was cut and forest medicine rubbed in the wounds.

Robert also suffered from another illness when he was little which sounds as though it may have been meningitis. He recovered from this without hospitalisation, though he has been left with a slight palsy on the right side of his face which is responsible for his beautiful lopsided smile. Partly because of these early traumas, and partly because he was the last baby, his father kept him close by when he was a boy and did not send him to school at the same age as his older brothers.

Robert spent his first nine years with his father. In the morning, they would leave the house and build a small fire to keep warm. Robert's father would then start to receive his visitors for the day: other retired elders and younger men seeking his advice. I can see Robert, serious and silent, crouched by the fire, feeding it sticks and running to fetch cups of tea for the old men. His formative years were spent soaking up their counsel, their stories, their hopes and fears for the future. At night he did not sleep with the other children, but instead shared his father's bed. No wonder that he is such a sober and responsible adult — he was a little old man before he was ten.

Robert went through all the normal stages that mark the progression of Maasai children. First the tops of his ears were pierced. Then his two lower middle teeth were cut out with a knife. Robert recalls both times his teeth were cut out (the first and second teeth are taken). It was very painful, but he was promised a cow if he didn't cry. So of course he didn't. The permanent gap is not only considered beautiful but it was also necessary in case you had lockjaw because milk could be poured through the gap. If these teeth are not removed, the Maasai will say that you eat 'like a donkey'. Unlike cattle, donkeys are not highly thought of.

On his cheeks, small circles were cut. Today the scar is coloured black like a tattoo. The cuts were made by his father for purely decorative reasons. There are other, smaller scars on his face from the cuts made by his father as a punishment for crying. It sounds a rather terrible punishment, but the Maasai abhor crying and fathers used to make these small cuts to teach their children to be strong.

Later on, when Robert was about eight, the final big holes were cut in his ear lobes. This cut takes out quite a large piece of flesh from the centre of the lobe with a razor or knife. The hole is then gradually stretched by inserting progressively larger wooden plugs. Only one ear is done at a time so that the child may sleep on one side while the other side heals. When I asked Robert if all this hurt him very much, he replied, 'I don't mind, I am a Maasai'. This is a typical response. When pushed, he finally admitted that having his ear cut did hurt, but that his father had told him not to cry, so of course he didn't. Robert also practised withstanding pain as part of the games that all little Maasai boys play in preparation for the day they are circumcised and become *moran*. The first 'game' the boys play is to pinch each other cruelly without blinking or flinching. The second game is to withstand self-inflicted burns. On Robert's legs are smooth, shiny circular scars, testimony to all the times he held a burning stick against his own skin.

When he wasn't with his father, Robert would be sent out to care for the calves and goats. He had his own dog, Kolompo, and they would hunt together. Another scar on Robert's leg is due to an enraged warthog that attacked him. Fortunately he was saved by Kolompo, who must have been very brave to face up to an angry warthog, which, despite its somewhat comical appearance, is a very fierce opponent.

Maasai boys love to hunt small animals like dik-diks, bush bucks, gazelles, zebras and birds. Robert says that he and his friends never hunted monkeys or baboons because 'They are like people'. Learning about the environment, the wildlife and, yes, even how to kill the animals is all part of a Maasai boy's early education. Older men do not hunt, and hunting for food is a practice abhorred by the Maasai. However an intimate relationship with the environment and a high degree of self-sufficiency are skills for survival in Maasailand. The Maasai are rarely sentimental about animals, though they respect a good working dog and award all wildlife their own intrinsic value. But Robert must have had a very special friendship with Kolompo, for when he died from a snake bite eleven-year-old Robert vowed never to have another.

At nine years of age, Robert was allowed to go to school in Morijo. Two of his older brothers, Daniel and Ilampala, had gone to school before him. Daniel for six years, and Ilampala for eight. His nickname was earned from the Maasai word for books, *impala*. Their father was something of a progressive and acquiesced to the government's demand that some of his children attend the local primary school in Morijo. The government had particularly appealed to the Iloibonok families to set an example for the rest of the Maasai. The Oloiboni at that time, Simel, also sent one of his sons to school.

During the 1950s, Maasai fathers were offered a terrible choice by colonial administrators: send one son to school or be fined one cow. Most men reluctantly allowed the government to take a son and some were forcibly taken away.[1] It must have been an agonising and utterly confusing time for the Maasai. What could school offer these children that God did not already provide for them in this perfect pastoral world? Some Maasai responded by sending a child of their least favourite wife, or by marrying Kikuyu wives and then sending these children to school. (The Kikuyu have since become the most powerful tribe in Kenya, masters of bureaucracy.

Many make no secret of the fact that they wish to chase all the Maasai into Tanzania and take over their lands. Some have used their Maasai connections as a perfect foil to cheat their less sophisticated 'brothers' out of land — all in the name of development and progress, of course.)

In order to go to school, Robert left his mother's house and went to live with his father's first wife, Mumai. My automatic response was 'How sad, to have to leave your mother's home to attend school'. But Robert corrected me. Mumai, he explained, is just like his 'own' mother. In fact he calls all his father's wives *yeiyio* — mother. Beyond this, all the wives of his father's age group, *Ilterito*, the mothers of his peers, are classificatory mothers. All *Ilterito* elders are his classificatory fathers. All siblings, cousins and even second cousins are considered brothers and sisters. In Maasailand, cousins, half-brothers and brothers are all considered one and the same thing. A full brother may sometimes be referred to as *'Olalashe ongar kina'* or a brother who shared the breast. Warriors of the same age group are brothers, friends and comrades.

I was raised on the western nuclear model with exactly defined relationships, each one with its own correct level of love and affection. For example, everyone knows that you should love your own mother more than your best friend's mother. Not necessarily so for the Maasai. Love and respect is offered liberally and unstintingly.

I liked Robert's enormous extended family, but I found it confusing at the same time. As I tried to organise the family tree in my head, I constantly asked him for clarification on the precise relationship. Did he mean 'same mother/same father' or 'same father' or 'son of your father's brother'? Numerous 'brothers' were in fact cousins. I think he found my preoccupation with blood ties amusing.

In addition most Maasai are known by several names — a combination of formal, stock and pet names collected over a lifetime. Robert's brother Ilampala, for example, is variously known as Nkaroya, Lesafari, James, Menya Lendoiyan and ole Mengoru, as well as all his stock and age group names. After his *Olkiteng lorrbaa* ceremony, he will be given yet another name. It certainly makes recording family trees a challenge!

At school Robert learned to read and write a bit and to play soccer and other sports. He also became Robert. That is, the teacher wrote a list of boys' names on the blackboard: John, Joshua, Joseph, James, Daniel, Paul, Moses, David, Mark, Peter and Robert. Each boy was told to go and pick the name he wanted. Oloimooja stood back, listening to his schoolfriends call out their names. He wanted a name that nobody else had. No one had picked Robert, so he finally chose that name for himself. Later that same day he announced to his mother that he now had three names, and his third one was Robert. She thought he was playing a joke and refused to believe him until years later when he started working with safari companies, who, like the Bantu teachers, found it easier to call him Robert. Good English names were still the order of the day in post-independence Kenya.

In another show of marked individuality, Robert also chose his own surname. His elder brothers were all 'Mengoru', however Robert chose another of his father's names — Rerente. At school the teacher also forbad him to wear any Maasai decorations, and under no circumstances was Robert to stretch his left ear. It had already been pierced, but the lobe had not yet been stretched. The teachers were very successful in brainwashing Maasai children to equate traditional practices with being inferior. After four years at school, Robert's father bade his favourite son to 'come home to start warrior work'.

On the morning that we were to return to the Loitas, we piled all our shopping and my luggage into a taxi and drove to Tony Church's property, 'Keepers', in the white ghetto of Langata. We swapped the taxi for a 4WD and two of Tony's Kenyan staff. Robert and I were keenly aware of the complexities of our relationship inside the privileged gates and under the bemused smile of 'Keepers'. When it came time to depart, Tony suggested that the 'Memsahib' should sit in the front. I climbed into the back seat next to Robert. 'Don't call me memsahib', I muttered through gritted teeth as we drove off.

When we arrived at Narotian, Daniel invited me to pitch my tent next to his house in the *enkang* and eat with his family. He said, 'I want you to learn to cook and eat food like a Maasai.' He instinctively put his finger on one issue that allowed me to remain an outsider last time. So I left the vehicle, the staff and camp paraphernalia at the camp site, and moved up the hill. In retrospect, this was the ideal situation. I was taking a step towards the Maasai, but at the same time I had the camp to retreat to if I couldn't handle it.

Although Robert and I spent some time together, it wasn't appropriate for us to be seen spending all our time together. Also Robert had things of his own to do during the day. So I was thrown on my own resources. I gravitated towards the women (especially Narygunkishon) and children who drew me into their lives. I had my first experiences of carrying water, eating Maasai food and milking cows.

The two staff guys, Kimanthi and Kariuki, thought my behaviour very strange. They couldn't understand why I would want to leave the familiar comforts of the camp and stay with the Maasai. My new policy was to walk everywhere, as the Maasai did, so I left the vehicle idle. Kimanthi and Kariuki were from the agricultural Kamba and Kikuyu tribes respectively. They were modern, educated Kenyans who considered themselves superior to the 'backward' Maasai, and were unable to understand why tourists were so fascinated with such 'primitive' people. The colonial era had been successful in teaching people to equate tribal traditions with being inferior and, as a result, most Kenyans have moved squarely into the twentieth century and lost contact with their traditional culture. In Nairobi, people call you a 'Maasai' if you do something stupid, like crossing the road in a careless fashion. This was my first intro-duction to tribalism in Kenya. If I had harboured any illusions about black brotherhood, then I wasn't going to find it here.

On the other hand, the Maasai are contemptuous of the agricultural tribes. As Daniel laughingly puts it, 'The Maasai are number one, then *wazungu* are next, the rest are just Kikuyus'. The Maasai preference for whites, rather than 'fellow' Africans is understandable. The white people they usually meet, namely adventurers, missionaries, administrators and tourists, are generally competent, successful men and women with their own power base and great technological knowhow. Europeans have long been interested in the Maasai, endowing them with the mystical properties of the 'noble savage'. Westerners usually express a great interest and curiosity in

Maasai culture. The historical contempt of the Maasai for all things western only serves to pique the respect accorded to the most famous tribe in Africa.

Olashumpai is the Maasai word for foreigner, but it has also come to be the common term for white people. A foreigner is anyone who is not a Maasai; brown, yellow, white and black — if you are not a Maasai then you must be a foreigner. What exactly defines being a Maasai? The word Maasai literally means 'speakers of Maa'. Roughly speaking, there are many ethnic communities who speak Maa. This would include the pastoral Samburu in northern Kenya and the Warusha, who practise agriculture on the slopes on Kilimanjaro in Tanzania, as well as the Baraguyu, some Okiek and the Njemps fishermen of Lake Baringo. However, most people divide the Maasai into two very broad groups: the semi-nomadic pastoral sections and the more settled, agricultural communities. Even this division is not as rigid as has been thought. The boundaries that define who is a Maasai, and who is not, are constantly changing. For example, a Maa-speaking Okiek man may acquire cattle and adopt a pastoral lifestyle; a 'pure' Maasai man may settle permanently, farm crops and reduce the number of cattle he keeps, in the process becoming more of an agriculturalist, or he may lose all his cattle to disease and be forced to seek refuge among his farming neighbours. It is a fluid system that has been going on for centuries, reflecting the harsh realities of life in the Rift Valley.

The pastoral Maasai are divided into many separate sections, or *iloshon* (singular *olosho*). Some people have translated the word *iloshon* to mean 'tribe', while others prefer 'subtribe', 'tribal section' or 'nation'. Each *iloshon* is an autonomous unit, with its own name, territory, style of dress, variations on ceremonies and age grouping, and differences in pronunciation. My own experiences are with a certain subclan (Nkidongi), within a clan (Ilaiser), within a particular *olosho* (Iloitai). They are not representative of Maasailand as a whole. The more I learn, the more I come to realise that there is no such thing as an expert on the customs of the Maasai, not even the Maasai themselves, who would at best know about two or three different *iloshon*.

Upon my return to Robert's home, uppermost on my mind was

the question of how I would be accepted. I assumed that my romance with Robert would be frowned upon and cause trouble within his family at the very least. It seemed that I was wrong. Robert explained over and over to me that there was 'no problem' with our relationship. I found this hard to believe at first, being from a culture that not only deeply mistrusts all outsiders, but has a taboo against mixed race relationships. Later on, Robert would sometimes call me *enkashumpai*, or white woman. I thought he was mocking me until he explained that it was meant as a compliment. I have heard Maasai call a woman who is freshly bathed and dressed *enkashumpai* or a house that has just been swept *enkaji o enkashumpai*. A favourite white heifer or bull might be called *enkashumpai* or *olashumpai*. Besides, said Robert, it is the truth, you are *enkashumpai*, so why worry about it.

The Maasai in general, and the Nkidongi dynasty in particular, have a long history of adoption. In past centuries, during wars, men and older boys of a defeated tribe might be killed, while their women and children were absorbed by the Maasai.[2] However, men captured in war might also be absorbed by the Maasai and undergo a ceremony of naturalisation that bestows full rights upon them, including inheritance. Such a ceremony is also available to a man from a neighbouring tribe who might, after staying with various families and learning the way of life, decide to seek naturalisation. Women from other tribes do not need to go through a naturalisation ceremony, for once they are married to a Maasai man, their citizenship is finalised. It is not uncommon for a Maasai man to marry a woman from another tribe, especially where both tribes share a common border, trading arrangements and knowledge of each other's language and customs. Though I was hardly from a 'neighbouring tribe', perhaps this helps to explain my immediate acceptance by Robert's family. To the Nkidongi Maasai, who have such a healthy superiority complex, nothing seemed more natural than an outsider wanting to learn their ways. Also, I believe it is relevant that the founder of the Nkidongi, Kidongoi, was himself an outsider adopted by the Maasai. Perhaps because of this, the Nkidongi have a long history of adoption.

I stayed two weeks in my tent at Daniel's *enkang*. Encouraged by the graciousness of the Maasai, my fear of their food began to dissolve. I tried milk tea, roasted maize and *ugali*. Narygunkishon showed me how to milk a cow, cook *ugali* and clean a calabash. Fresh and soured milk are served direct to *moran* from a calabash. To clean one you must take a burning stick from the fire and ram it vigorously into the bottom. Any milk scraps are absorbed by the charcoal, which you then shake out. The process must be repeated several times until the calabash is clean. Traditionally, a calabash was the only acceptable receptacle to collect milk in, though nowadays, the Maasai are not above using a plastic jug or tin mug.

When it came time to learn how to milk, it took the combined efforts of Narygunkishon and Daniel to convince their most docile cow to stand still for me. Cows are milked twice a day in the *enkang*, in the morning and again at dusk. Unless they are very bad tempered, they are rarely tied up to be milked. Sometimes their young calf is tied to a post or doorway, and this keeps the cow in one spot. The cattle know the Maasai very well. Probably their first days of life were spent inside the house of their owner, sharing the warmth of the fire with the other children. I say 'other children' on purpose, for the Maasai love their cattle deeply. As they grow, the poddy calves sleep in the *olale* inside the house, and during the day are tended close to the *enkang* by the children. Each Maasai cow, bullock and bull has its own name and is loved as an individual.

The cow I was meant to be milking knew straightaway that I had no idea what I was doing, and kept turning her head (with large horns) towards me, and also tried to kick me. My desperate pulls on her teats produced no milk. In the end she walked away in disgust. For my next lesson, Daniel introduced me to Soiyaan. She was a young, dark grey cow with no horns. Soiyaan too, pointedly ignored me and walked away to graze. So I scratched her beautiful hornless head with a stick instead, which she enjoyed. I decided to give up my ideas of learning how to milk, and devote my efforts instead to collecting hornless cattle.

Towards the end of the visit Daniel gave me Soiyaan. This was a solemn and important gift, for the Maasai have a deep regard for their cattle. In addition to the extended family, the age group and classificatory relationships, there is another type of bond in Maasailand, best described as a 'stock relationship'. When one person gives another a gift of livestock, they are forever after known to each other by the name of that animal. Daniel had given me a young heifer, so from now on we called each other *'Paashe'*. Stock names are usually spoken very tenderly, and used with great respect. Once you have given or accepted a gift of livestock, you must never use the usual name for your stock relative again, or you will deeply offend your animal.

Sometimes in the afternoon, I would sit in the sun with the women and their younger children. It was hard to believe that I could feel so content sitting on an old cowhide among the dirt with dung, grubby children and flies all around. I was learning to make the simple beaded necklace which is worn by both men and women. The beads are strung on string made from strands taken from waxed nylon bags, like the ones used for horse feed in Australia. The bags are used to transport dry foodstuffs in Kenya, and are then traded and bought. The women carefully pull out a single strand, and then divide it into three or four separate strands. Two of these are then rubbed on the top of their legs. With a quick backwards motion, the strands are twirled together to make a strong piece of twine. I was hopeless at doing this, not the least because my chubby white stumps of legs are covered in hair, and to rub string on them hurts like crazy. Maasai women have practically no body hair, but whether this is a natural state, or a direct result of their string-making, I couldn't say.

My favourite time of the day was at dusk, after milking. As the sun began its descent behind the Loita Hills, the cattle would settle for the night inside the *enkang* and the area around the houses known as the *boo*. With a deep sigh of contentment, they would fold their legs underneath their bodies and sink to the ground. Children played around the *boo*. Inside the houses the evening meal was being prepared. Sometimes I would sit outside on a low stool beside Daniel and other elders. The children would bring out steaming mugs of milk tea. It was a wonderfully peaceful way to finish the day. At night, after sharing a simple meal like potatoes and rice with Narygunkishon, the children would follow me into my tent and sing until it was time for them to sleep. Bedtime for everyone is rarely later than 9 pm in Maasailand, though no routine is strictly enforced with the children who are left to find their own rhythm. The exception occurs when there are visitors or there is some serious business to discuss, in which case Maasai men can talk into the early hours.

I had not yet met Robert's mother, who seemed to be constantly on the move visiting her various relatives. Robert's father lived at Narotian with his third, and favourite, wife. She was a beautiful brown-skinned woman with cheekbones to die for. Robert and his age group called her *Yeiyio*, mother, but she introduced herself to me as Kokoo, meaning grandmother. Kokoo, always calm and smiling, was the epitome of elegance. I had first met Robert's father in December 1989 and now continued our growing friendship. Papa spoke no English, so we communicated mainly with smiles and gestures. A good common talking point was our jewellery, which we often compared. By the time I met Papa, he was an old, old man in his nineties. His cheeks were sunken and the skin was loose around his jaw and neck, but his eyes were like bright black diamonds. His other striking feature was his smile, with a full complement of strong, white teeth. What a *morani* he must have been in his day! Now he moved slowly but still managed to get around. I would sometimes find him sitting in the sun at our camp, where he would take tea or soda. He had a penchant for green cloth and eccentric hats. As a venerable elder, he was retired from active management of the community. His advice was still sought, and his memory consulted. He supervised the affairs of his large family and his cattle with the help of his seven sons and numerous nephews. He would address me as '*enkerai ai*' (my child) or '*pasanai*' (my dear). Robert told me that to others, he called me his '*mzungu* baby'. When I expressed surprised at being called a baby, Robert laughed and explained that his father was so old and had seen so much in his life that even someone in their forties would be considered a child by him.

The Maasai have many beautiful endearments that they know their children by. Robert's mother calls him '*Kaiyai*' (the one sent by God), and the next son, Ilampala, '*Olongututi*' (the one I like to kiss a lot). It is not uncommon to hear women call their children '*enkoshoke ai*' (my stomach), or '*enkutuk ai*' (my mouth), or '*Enkai naishoo enkerai*' (the child that God gave me). Parents become known formally as the mother of or father of their first child. Thus Narygunkishon is politely called *'Ngoto Sintiman'* (mother of Sintiman). Daniel is *'Menye Sintiman'* (father of Sintiman). The first child is therefore often referred to as *'Enkai naishoo enkarna enkerai'*, (the child from God that gave me a name).

During my two-week stay in Narotian, Robert became ill. He had a swelling in his lower left side and felt pain when he walked. I though it might be a hernia. He had no name for the swelling, but said he knew the medicine to take for it. This involved going deep into the forest with a friend, slaughtering a bullock and preparing a special soup from the roots of a certain plant. He said this made the swelling grow bigger, and then it could be lanced. I wanted him to see a doctor, but he refused. In preparation for his retreat, he went to Morijo to arrange for a bullock to slaughter and ask a friend to accompany him. It meant leaving me for a couple of days. No self-respecting warrior wants to be around a family settlement when he is ill; he must go into the forest to treat himself.

On the second day that Robert was away, he sent me a surprise. It was my tall friend Marefu, with one of Robert's goats for me. The goat wasn't meant as a pet, but as dinner. I knew this was a generous act and a great compliment — the Maasai equivalent of six dozen long-stemmed red roses. The goat met his end in a fairly low key manner. I like to think that it was all over before he knew what was happening. I had never seen my food slaughtered before, but I figured that if I was going to eat the goat, then the least I could do was pay it the respect of watching it being killed. First Marefu covered the goat's mouth and nose with his hands to suffocate it. After a few minutes it was barely conscious. Then its throat was slit with a knife. The blood gurgled and spouted out bright crimson. The life went out of the goat with a rush of air and a sloppy sound. I left Marefu to skin and cut it up under the tree and returned when he had the barbie going. The meat was skewered on sharp sticks and roasted over hot coals. Goat tastes delicious cooked this way and everyone enjoyed the rare chance to eat meat. Papa's dog, Simba, waited patiently for the bones.

The day after we ate my goat, Narygunkishon dried the hide in the sun. She stretched the hide out to its full size and used the flat side of an axe to hammer small wooden pegs around the edges to hold it in place. The skin was then left to dry for a couple of days. Large cattle hides are scraped of hair and used to cover beds, or can be made into pack saddles for donkeys. Small hides are often sold to a skin trader who visits all the *enkangs* on his bicycle. He buys the hides for about 30 shillings ($2) and sells them onto a local development project which has its own tannery.

One evening a man arrived in the *enkang* who was a dead ringer for Robert. I knew immediately that this must be his brother Ilampala. He grinned at me and asked if I knew who he was. I did, for Robert had often spoke of his brother four years older than himself, and in the next age group, *Ilrandai*. Ilampala's English was excellent, for he had spent eight years in school. As time passed I learnt that he understood the western mind far better than anyone else here. He had spent only a short time as a *morani*, and instead had experienced a different side of the world, first as a cattle trader and second as a shop assistant in a Maasai trading *duka*. Apart from looks, Ilampala was as different from Robert as could be. Where Robert was reserved and serious, Ilampala was gregarious and a joker. Robert had four brothers, two half-brothers and innumerable cousins. As the last child of his father, he was subject to the sovereignty of his older brothers and occupied a lowly position on the totem pole. The Maasai have a saying — a boy is not a man while his father is still alive. You might also say extend it to his older brothers as well. For example, Robert was not permitted to sell or swap any livestock without the permission of all his brothers. When I told him that I thought this was a bit rough, he just shrugged and explained that it was the way of the Maasai.

I was glad when Robert returned to Narotian after two days. His arrangements were now in place for his meat camp in the forest. I hadn't been able to have a good chat with anyone since meeting Ilampala. Life could be a bit lonely without proper conversation, I discovered. Then the two weeks were over, and I had to get the vehicle and equipment back to Nairobi. At the same time, Robert would go into the forest to cure himself.

When I had first arrived in Nairobi, I had no plan beyond wanting to see Robert again. Now, our relationship had survived the 'make or break' days in Nairobi and had been confirmed by the weeks we had spent in the Loita Hills with his family. The time had come for me to move closer to his world and to be able to express myself to him in his language. I was sure language was the key to a deeper understanding of Robert and his culture. Although Swahili is the language of East Africa and has a reputation as being relatively easy for English speakers to learn, I wanted to learn Maasai — a far more difficult language spoken only by the 500 000 or so Maa speakers in Kenya and Tanzania. I had heard of a language school for missionaries in Nairobi that taught Maasai. My plan was to enrol for one term.

[1] I quote from a letter written by the District Commissioner of Narok on 24 December 1947: 'Since the Engidongi [sic] had not obeyed the order to produce two school children to date, I had all available children brought before me and chose two little Laibons for the Loita School. Their names are 1. Oloshega ole Ngabwal (aged about 7 years) and 2. Kapete ole Simel (aged about six).'

[2] The Maasai have a strict taboo against killing women. It is the ultimate disgrace. If a man kills a woman accidentally, then he must undergo a ceremony of expiation to be purified. If he does not do that, he will be cursed and ostracised. The traditional fine payable for this crime is forty-eight or twenty-eight sheep, payable to the woman's father or relatives. The fine is only payable when a Maasai woman is killed. If a woman from another tribe is killed accidentally, a man must still undergo the purification ceremony.

C H A P T E R   S I X
AINGORU *(Searching)*
J u n e   t o   A u g u s t   1 9 9 0

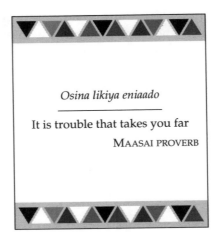

Osina likiya eniaado

It is trouble that takes you far

MAASAI PROVERB

I WAS ACCEPTED AS A MAASAI LANGUAGE STUDENT AT THE CPK·
Language School run by the Church Province of Kenya in Nairobi,
just outside the city centre. The students were mainly missionaries
from all over the world who had come to learn Swahili. Because I
was enrolled as a student, I could stay at the Anglican Guesthouse
next door to the Language School. The Guesthouse was a rambling
sandstone building set in a small but lovely garden. I arrived on a
Sunday.

The girl who greeted me at the reception desk had jet black
extensions that started out as braids, and then halfway down burst
into hundreds of tight, glossy ringlets that shimmied down to her
petite shoulders. Hairdressing is big business in Nairobi. In the
suburbs or 'estates' as they are called here, it seems as if every
second house is operating a hair and beauty business. The two main
styles are perms or 'curly kit' (an almost forties style full perm) and
extensions or braids, where hundreds of tiny plaits made from
synthetic 'hair' are joined at the scalp and shaped in just as many
styles.

AINGORU (SEARCHING)

The girl introduced herself as Susan and showed me to my room on the second floor, where I would live for the next three months. It was small, clean and simply furnished, as you would expect from an establishment run by the Anglican Church. There was a generous window that looked out onto trees, some of which were already displaying the golden red leaves that appear during the cooler months of June and July.

Downstairs near the reception was a big old-fashioned lounge room with bay windows that overlooked the garden. There were bookshelves filled with an odd assortment of novels, bibles and mission newsletters. I found a Maasai translation of the New Testament, and even more exciting still a hardback copy of Enid Bagnold's *National Velvet* which I promptly pinched. The other guests began returning from their various church services. There was an Anglican Cathedral nearby, a Seventh Day Adventist Church and a modern Pentecostal Church, plus I was to discover hundreds of others throughout the city and estates. If Adelaide is the City of Churches, it ain't got nothing on Nairobi. This place is Christian City. If Kenya came late in the piece to Christianity, then it seemed to be making up for lost time in a very big way. Church-going was an accepted part of the weekly social calendar, even if it meant you went half-drunk straight from the nightclub.

Lunch was served in the dining room. I sat down on a chair at a corner table for six, then noticed that everyone else in the room had remained standing, so I quickly stood up. I discovered that this was in order to say grace. I had only ever seen this happen before on television shows like 'The Waltons' and it was the start of a big learning experience for me. The other guests were a mixture of black and white, clerical and secular, plus a few big guys wearing great purple robes. These, I found out later, were bishops. Before I had even finished my soup, a Kenyan man sitting opposite (who turned out to be a plain-clothes minister) politely inquired, 'Are you saved in the name of Jesus Christ?' No, but can I still stay for lunch is what I wanted to tell him, but instead I got sucked into the first of thousands of meal-time conversations about Christianity. However the roast chicken was excellent and was followed by fresh fruit salad with cream.

At the next meal I got stuck with an aging English couple who were going 'home' after seven years 'in the field' — the mission field, that is. The woman wore her dark hair in a beehive bun, had thick-rimmed glasses and a mouth that was permanently pursed into a tight little catsbum of disapproval.

'And precisely what', she wanted to know, 'are you doing in Nairobi?'

My explanation that I was studying Maasai at the Language School did not seem to satisfy, because she then went on to ask me, 'But what for? Which church are you from? Why are you studying?'

I toyed for the moment with the idea of telling her that I was bonking one of the natives and needed to know how to say 'don't stop' but chickened out. Instead I muttered something about wanting to work with a development agency such as World Vision.

'But you can't', she practically screamed at me from across the table. 'You're not a Christian!!'

By this time she was leaning so close I could smell the brimstone on her breath, 'They would never employ *you*.' I made sure I never sat near her again.

I learnt not to sit with English missionaries. They seemed to be the worst and certainly the most judgmental — not a good Christian attitude as far as I understood it. The Americans were more easy-going, and the Africans were the best of all. If I timed my arrival in the dining room right, all the white missionaries would have sat next to each other and I could then sit at an African table. The African clergy and evangelists had a far more reasonable attitude, which made for less stressful meal times.

The CPK kitchens served plain, old-fashioned cooking — plenty of it and usually very good. The Guesthouse had originally been established by Australian missionaries and it showed in the menu which featured roasts with golden crunchy potatoes and other veg, casseroles and baked puddings. One nice old bishop from Uganda told me that 'We can all work towards light, each in his or her own way, but not everyone has to preach for God. Even bishops need people who perform other tasks in this world.' I liked his god a whole lot better.

By this time I had started at the Language School. I was the sole student learning Maasai. My teacher was a dignified Maasai elder, Mr Stanley ole Kinana. He had grown up in a mission school and later qualified as an English teacher. He taught at the first school in Morijo in the 1950s and recalled that Daniel ole Mengoru, Robert's older brother, was one of his pupils. Because he had grown up in a mission, he had none of the usual physical markings of a Maasai elder. His ears were not stretched, he had his bottom teeth and his face was unscarred. His manner was reserved and formal. Though I burned with curiosity about his past (had he ever been a *morani*, for example), I kept my questions to myself. If I had learnt one thing from the Maasai, it was to show good manners and not be too familiar.

We worked each morning on grammar and conversation. After lunch I worked by myself with language tapes, practising the pronunciation and intonation of words and sentences over and over again. It is a difficult language to learn because it is highly tonal. The grammar and sentence structure are very different from English, so, unless you are gifted with languages (which I definitely am not), it is almost impossible to learn it by just listening to Maasai speakers. You really need a thorough grounding in grammar, and this is what I learnt with ole Kinana.

Traditionally, Maa is an oral language, not a written one. Within their beautiful singsong language I knew I would discover the history, traditions and attitudes of the Maasai. Being with Robert and his family was teaching me to see through Maasai eyes and I now needed to be able to think in their language and symbols. Most of all I wanted to know and understand Robert in his own language. It was not going to be easy though. Robert, like most Kenyans, speaks three languages: his mother tongue and Kiswahili fluently, and English quite well. In addition, he could greet and exchange pleasantries in another five languages. I, on the other hand, had grown up speaking only one language and I suspect that the part of my brain responsible for learning new ones atrophied through lack of use years ago.

The pastoral society of the Maasai is well reflected in their language. They have no word of their own for money. *Empisa* is from the Kiswahili word *pesa* and *irupiani* is from the Indian word *rupee*. The closest word is *enkoshola* which literally means a piece of land. However they have thirty-one different words to describe the colours of their cattle, twenty-eight words to describe various types and states of grass, and sixteen different words for rain. They have no word for bribery, saying that in Maasai society they do not know the act of corrupting someone for ulterior motives. Their language has no words for school or shop or car, which are again all borrowed from Kiswahili. There is no Maasai word for please, for it is implied in a polite request. The word for thank you — *ashe* — is applied liberally.

Maasai language is very rich. The elders in particular place much importance on oratory skills. Their graceful speeches impressed the early explorers and British colonial authorities. As a warrior should be brave, so an elder should be eloquent, and a particularly fine speaker will be greatly admired by his peers. A simple point will take hours to discuss, with each person involved reiterating the discussion so far and then adding on their own view. This being the case, I was not surprised to discover the depth of Maasai oral history. There are numerous narratives including myths, legends, ogre tales and animal stories. Then there is another part of oral literature known as proverbs or *Ndungeterashe*, which literally means 'the cutters of fine, thin leather'. This refers to the precision and brevity of the proverbs, which summarise the collective wisdom of the Maasai. Some are universal, such as *Meishaa ilmoruak aare kishoni'* (a cattle gate is not large enough for two elders to go through — a combination of too many cooks and a man's home is his castle); *'Mikurru enkukuo naishu'* (do not not pick up a live piece of coal — don't go looking for trouble); and *'Mepal oloitiko isirat'* (a zebra cannot shed its stripes). Others are more obscure and require a thorough understanding of Maasai lore, such as these beauties: 'The reason why the dog ate excrement is not because he missed a relative to advise him, it is because he ate the deaf ear' and 'The birth fluid of one's child is not drunk, what matters is the one who emerges in a good way' (meaning that blood relationships do not count for anything; it is the performance of the child that matters). Proverbs are employed by elders and used to instruct the younger generations as well as reflecting their poetry and philosophy. The third form of Maasai oral literature is the riddle. The Maasai distinguish between two types, simple and complex. Before a complex riddle, the audience will be asked *'Ira ngen?'* (Are you clever?) Here are two simple riddles. What moves across the world but leaves no trace? The butterfly. What acts as an alarm to awaken all people? The morning.

Ole Kinana also recommended books for me to read about the Maasai. When I became fed up with my language tapes and books, I would head off on foot into town and have a chat with the Maasai *askaris* who stood at the entrance to the African Heritage shop on Kenyatta Avenue. These guys were employed to add a little bit of authentic Maasai colour to the shop, but underneath their red blankets they wore western clothes. From there I would walk around the corner to the MacMillan Library and pore over their small collection of books on the Maasai, most of which contained conflicting information, but none the less helped me to build up a potted history of the Maasai.

Some writers believe the Maasai to have been one of the Lost Tribes of Israel. Some believe that their earliest oral traditions pre-date the Old Testament. Their earliest legends (the ascent from a place of drought to a new land), some of their social customs (male circumcision), and food taboos (no pork, fish, fowl, game meat or mixing meat and milk on the same day) do echo stories and prescriptions written in the Old Testament. Other writers have alluded to the similarities between Roman warrior dress and that of the Maasai *moran*. It would be fascinating to fly back in time and trace the origins and influences of the Maasai ancestors. If I could make one magical journey, that would be it. Perhaps new information about Maasai art, newly 'discovered' and presented by Gillies Turle in his exceptional book, *The Art of the Maasai*, may reveal some of the missing pieces to the puzzle. The religious artefacts exposed for the first time ever in this book are used by the Iloibonok for divination and healing. Several pieces suggest Egyptian hieroglyphics.

The precolonial history of the Maasai has been the subject of debate by scholars and linguists for decades. The German administrator Moritz Merker in 1908 went so far as to link the ancestors of the Maasai with the Babylonians and Hebrews of Arabia. However their origins and most of their history still remain shrouded in myth.

It is generally accepted that the Maasai came out of the region to the north of Lake Turkana. As a race, they are classified as Nilotics, people from the Nile region. Linguistically they are considered closest to the Bari of Sudan. After migrating south, dispersing and absorbing other tribes along the way, they reached Nakuru and the Ngong Hills in the seventeenth century. The vanguard of the Maasai went on to the slopes of Kilimanjaro in northern Tanzania. By the eighteenth century, the Maasai commanded the heart of the Great Rift Valley and the surrounding highlands. Their territory extended about 320 kilometres from east to west and about 800 kilometres from north to south — an enormous area that stretched from Lake Turkana in the north, to the south end of the Maasai Steppe in Tanzania.

The first Oloiboni, Kidongoi[1], is believed to have been discovered by the Maasai during their southward migration in around 1640. They say he descended from God, as told in the following version of the story. Two Maasai warriors came upon a small child in the forest of the Ngong Hills. One warrior, from the Ilmolelian clan, saw the child first and wanted to leave him behind. But the second warrior, from the Ilaiser clan, picked up the child and took him with him as the Maasai continued their migration southwards. He brought him up as his own son, which is why the Iloibonok dynasty is part of the Ilaiser clan to this day. As he grew, the boy proved to have unusual powers. In the dry season, he always brought his cattle home well fed and watered. Some say he had a long tail like a cow that caused water to form wherever it touched the ground. Others say he possessed the power to make rain fall in front of his cattle to make grass grow instantly. Realising his special powers, the people made him their spiritual leader. He became the first Oloiboni, and the position has been hereditary ever since, handed down through the male line of the Nkidongi dynasty.

The two outstanding Iloibonok of the nineteenth century were Supeet and his son, Mbatiany. Mbatiany and his family lived in the fertile Sanya Plains between Mounts Meru and Kilimanjaro in present-day Tanzania. For a long time the Iloibonok family had lived in that area, creating their own spiritual community, though presumably the early Iloibonok had spent some time in the area around the Ngong Hills, which are closely associated with them in name and legend. Mbatiany had several sons, and when he died in around 1890, a bitter dispute arose between two of them, Olonana and Senteu, as to who should inherit their father's position. Both sons it seems had the power to prophesy, but Mbatiany had allegedly chosen Senteu to take over from him as the major Oloiboni for all pastoral Maasai.

As the story goes, lying upon his deathbed, Mbatiany instructed his wife, Karaine, Senteu's mother, to send their son to him the next morning in order to receive his father's blessing and also the sacred *enkidong*, an ox horn that contained the divining stones. (In some accounts, the *enkidong* is referred to as a 'magic box'; it is in fact a lustrous black and white horn originally owned by Kidongoi and handed down since the 1600s.) However, Olonana's mother over-heard this exchange and warned her son. Very early the next day, it was Olonana who presented himself to Mbatiany instead of Senteu. Because Mbatiany was very ill, practically blind and senile, Olonana tricked his father into giving him the special blessing. On his way outside, he ran into his brother Senteu who realised what had taken place. Unfortunately, what had occurred in the hut that dawn could not be undone for, as Mbatiany explained, 'You are both my children'. However Mbatiany still had his sacred *enkidong*, and this he handed over to Senteu.

Truth is stranger than fiction, and usually less glamorous. This story, with its echoes of the Old Testament tale of Jacob and Esau, may simply have been invented by elders to explain the cause of a deep rift between two brothers who hated each other — a terrible thing to happen in the closeknit Maasai community, when brothers, half-brothers and cousins are called by the same name. In another version of the inheritance story told to me by an Nkidongi elder[2], Mbatiany had another son, his oldest in fact, who was mentally retarded. This son had a huge, misshapen head, and so was called Elukunya, which is Maasai for head. When he was an old man, Mbatiany rejected normal family life, went quite mad and spent most of his time roaming the forest. He died without making a proper will, and is rumoured to be buried near Namanga. According to Maasai custom, the sacred *enkidong* therefore went to the oldest son, even though he was retarded. Senteu forcibly took the *enkidong* away from Elukunya.

During the final decade of the nineteenth century, after Mbatiany's death, a succession of disasters swept Maasailand: smallpox, rinderpest, bovine pleuro-pneumonia and famine. The pastoral Maasai lost over eighty per cent of their livestock and fifty per cent of their people. The 'Decade of Disasters' was probably responsible for many of the Iloibonok leaving their community in the Ngosua region and the Sanya Plains in northern Tanzania. Senteu spent time with the Loita Maasai, who roamed the area around Narosura, the Loita Plains, and what was to become the Maasai Mara. Olonana spent most of his life near the Ngong Hills, where he practised his profession. A good many of the Maasai sections throughout Kenya, including the numerous Purko, recognised him as the major Oloiboni. Olonana negotiated with the colonial administration about Maasai land rights, though he was not entitled to do so, the position of Oloiboni being purely spiritual and not political. The British cared little for such a distinction, and exploited the trusting nature of Olonana.[3] In 1901, the colonial administration appointed Olonana (or Lenana as they called him) Paramount Chief of all Maasai. In exchange for his co-operation, he received £6/13/4 per month as a government chief and a lifetime's supply of beads and blankets. He was also invited to judge cattle at the Nairobi Show.

After years of raiding and harassment between the rival brothers and their factions, peace was made in 1902, when Senteu travelled to the Ngong Hills and settled for two years close to his brother. But the peace was short-lived. Senteu left under a cloud, accused by his brother of practising black magic against him. When Olonana died in 1911, his young sons were still uncircumcised. His family's fortune and prestige have never recovered to this day[4]. Olonana's followers blamed his death on Senteu's supposed black curse.

Just after the turn of this century, while Senteu was still in the Ngong Hills, a son was born, Mengoru Lekuta Rerente Ololoreeshe, to his fourth wife, Intereshet. Sixty or so years later, this son of Senteu would hold his last son, and name him for another great Oloiboni — Oloimooja.

Senteu finally settled his family and Iloitai followers in the Loita highlands, where he accumulated more than fifteen wives and had many children. Ever since that time, the Loita Hills have been the home of the most powerful and respected branch of the Nkidongi dynasty. The chosen successor to Senteu was Simel, the sole son of his favourite wife. All the clans and *iloshon* recognised him as the major Oloiboni, and the rift created by Senteu and Olonana was finally healed. When Simel died in 1987, his successor was his second son, Makombo ole Simel, who is the major Oloiboni for the entire Maasai nation today. He now holds the sacred *enkidong* which was given to him by his father, who in turn received it from Senteu. Makombo's *enkang* is about six kilometres away from mine, in Kisokon, also known as the Valley of the Laibons. Senteu, who died on 2 June 1933, is buried nearby.

Even today, the Oloiboni still officiates over all major cere-monies. He prescribes medicine, provides charms and amulets and foretells the future by reading the stones thrown from a calabash or *enkidong*. The stones are part of a complex numerology system. Every male of the Nkidongi dynasty may choose to enter the pro-fession, so to speak, if he feels the calling. It is not always the first son who is chosen to follow the ways of the father. Robert, like his father before him, will probably practise in his old age. Robert's father is what you might term a minor prophet who uses his own special *enkidong* to interpret *Enkai's* messages and treat his private patients. Robert has been blessed by his father and authorised to work as an Oloiboni with his own *enkidong*.

Secular Maasai greatly respect and even fear the Iloibonok family, who have a great many customs that set them apart from other Maasai. In relative isolation in the Loita Hills, they have become the cultural and spiritual guardians of the pastoral Maasai nation. The Maasai assure me that their Iloibonok can see into the future. They say *Enkai* speaks to the Maasai through the Oloiboni's dreams. As Robert puts it, 'The Oloiboni dreams nicely.'

Robert was told about one of these 'dreams' a year after we were married. He was visiting an old, old man who had been a warrior alongside Robert's father, and he told him this story. When he and Robert's father were young *moran*, they paid a visit to their father, the great Laibon Senteu, who was near the end of his long life. They each wished to know what the future held for them. Senteu told the first *morani* that he would be very rich, and that his family would own vast herds of cattle. This has come to pass, and his family's cattle are too numerous to count. When it came to be the turn of Robert's father, Senteu told him something even more amazing: 'Your children will come to live with white people.' It is unlikely that at this time Robert's father had ever seen a white person, but this prophecy too has come to pass.

The Maasai came to the attention of Europeans from around 1840, when the first missionaries arrived in East Africa. Their writings were often used as a basis for accounts of the Maasai written by explorers who arrived from the late 1870s onwards. Up until this time, the Maasai were thought to be a blood-thirsty, murderous tribe — a theory which explorers such as Joseph Thomson and Gustav Fisher helped to debunk. The rumours were spread first by Arab traders who controlled the lucrative ivory and slave trades. They had a substantial vested interest in deterring Europeans from venturing too far into the interior. But venture they did, and in the process ended the slave trade and changed the face of East Africa forever. In 1894, the Berlin Treaty to decide the British and German 'spheres of influence' sliced a border between Kenya and Tanzania, effectively cutting the Maasai nation in half.

By the time the British arrived, the 'Decade of Disasters' had devastated the Maasai. European settlers demanded part of Maasailand to the north, and the administration set to negotiating with Olonana. He agreed that the Maasai would vacate their lands around lakes Nakuru and Naivasha and the Rift Valley corridor, and that they would instead occupy two reserves, one to the north of the railway line, which had by this time been completed, and one to the south.

This agreement, signed on 9 August 1904, was to be valid for 'as long as the Maasai endure as a race' and was deemed by all to be 'in their best interests'. The treaty included several clauses that were never fulfilled, including the construction of a road between the two reserves for the movement of stock, and the perpetual preservation of the Kinopop region (sometimes referred to as the 'Promised Land') for the sole use of the Maasai for ceremonies, in particular *Eunoto*.

However the road and other promises became academic, for soon the white settlers were demanding more land in the northern reserve. The colonial administration agreed that this land should be made available to the 'superior races', and in 1909 renegotiated with Olanana, suggesting to him that he would have more power if all his people were together in one reserve in the south.

The evidence available today suggests that there was a lot of coercion and manipulation by the British officials, which is no great surprise. Olonana died in 1911 before an agreement had been reached. It was claimed by some that Olonana's dying appeal to his people was to move to the southern reserve and obey the British. The other Maasai leaders (who, I might add, were not representative of all sections of the Maasai), capitulated and signed.

In a further sad twist of irony, when Maasai leaders appealed to the British Court of Law, the court declared that the Maasai could not bring a civil case since they were not British subjects, even though their land had become British land! After two years of passive resistance, the Maasai in the northern reserve were forced to move with their stock to the southern reserve — into the land of other Maasai sections. None of the land lost in the two treaties was ever returned to the Maasai at independence in 1963.

I discovered all this from books, as the Maasai themselves do not know and are not interested in such things. They live in the present, not the past.

After a month, as I began to get to know Nairobi, I started to feel more comfortable. It was no longer the swirling mass of 'black' people that it had first seemed. Instead, as I walked daily around the streets, I saw Nairobi as an eccentric and bizarre crossroads. I began to enjoy its chaotic and cosmopolitan atmosphere. Rural and urban Kenyans from all tribes shared the broken pavements and muddy gutters with Asians, Europeans, Ethiopians, Somalis, Arabs and a variety of tourists. In the midst of all of this, it was the Somali and Indian women who stood out. The Somali women in their flowing robes and veils were some of the most beautiful women I had ever seen. They held themselves with great dignity as they waited outside Uhuru House (Freedom House), headquarters of the Department of Immigration for news about their own applications, or those of their families. The Indian women wore sumptuous saris, and glossy, fat braids of black hair swung as they walked through the crowded streets with a regal air.

I started to form a small group of friends, and got to know many of the staff at the CPK Guesthouse. I'd met Susan on my first day at the Guesthouse. She was a Kenyan girl in her early twenties. Her boss (known as the Warden) was increasingly annoyed as Susan and I became friends. She felt Susan spent too much time talking to me and not enough time typing. Susan introduced me to her boyfriend, Martin, who became a good friend. I also got to know a few of the missionaries who impressed me with their quiet faith. One was David, an Australian evangelist, who worked for an organisation called the Church Army. He came every week or so for meals when he was in Nairobi. His spiritual conversation was so interesting that I was inspired to go off and read the New Testament for the first time. He told me he felt that God had brought me to Africa to show himself to me. Another was an American woman, Joan. She was very much in the classic American fundamentalist vein, and her speech was full of 'Praise God', 'Amen' and talk of the Spirit. However, unlike a lot of the other missionaries at CPK, Joan wasn't a snob. She didn't mind mixing with the 'unsaved', and she wasn't judgmental. In fact, she accepted that there were other ways of looking at the world. Joan had 'come to Jesus Christ', as she put it, late in life after raising a family. Her tolerance made her a very warm and understanding person: Joan and the laidback Aussie preacher seemed to me to be true Christians in the sense that they expressed many of the finest qualities of Jesus Christ that I had read about.

Around the time that I was meeting people and beginning to acquire a small social circle outside of the Guesthouse, I met a brash young Kenyan who made an immediate impression upon me. Whitfield typified the modern young Kikuyu man on his way up, from his pompous Anglo name, to his trendy flat-top hairstyle and baggy trousers. So secure in his word-perfect English, western attitudes and European clothes worn with such contrived flair. Arrogant, ambitious and flashy. The total opposite of Robert. Which is probably one of the reasons I had an affair with him. Whitfield introduced me to an aspect of Nairobi I had never seen before. Smart, young and modern, he whirled me into an exciting world of clubs, bars, discos and parties. I was intensely attracted to him. We had a brief fling before Whitfield left Kenya forever to make good in Europe (the ambition of every young man in Nairobi).

This was a pretty tumultuous time in my life. The affair led me to examine over and over my feelings for Robert. Did I really love him? Was I worthy of him? Did I only want an exotic black boy-friend?

The episode left me feeling lost and troubled. I had lost contact with where I had been and was unsure of where I was headed. In my despair, I remembered Joan's invitation to visit her in Bungoma, where she ran a bible school for aspiring Kenyan evangelists. With the clarity with which I had known that I must go to Kenya, I now knew that I must get out of Nairobi and go to Joan.

I imagine that I am not the only lost soul to have gravitated to Joan. She replied to my telegram without any hint of surprise (though she admitted later that it had taken her a while to remember who I was). Bungoma is in Luyaland in western Kenya, not far from Uganda. The train stops there before going further on across the border. I was met at the train by Sarah, a young Ugandan woman working with Joan who was hoping to immigrate legally. As it was Sunday, she took me to church at the local primary school. Each classroom contained a different charismatic religion, and I'm still not sure what exact version Sarah belonged to. The service was more like a three-hour dance workout, interspersed with lessons that were simultaneously translated into English for the sole benefit of the only *mzungu* in the place, me. This service had absolutely everything. There were people speaking in tongues and having fits; there were the road to Damascus testimonials; and the preacher had a handy line going in casting out demons 'in the name of Jesus Christ!' And then there was virtually non-stop singing, clapping and dancing among the schooldesks. I now know how people reach the heights of religious ecstasy — it is through sheer exhaustion.

It was a lot more fun than the only other church service I had attended when I was nine years old. On that occasion I nagged and nagged my mother to take me to church. She finally agreed, but craftily took me to a High Church of England service. This held as much interest for a nine-year-old girl as a salted cracker, in fact less. A cat innocently walked into the church and saved me from death by bordeom. I played with the cat quite happily for the rest of the service. During high school, my mother wrote a note saying that we were agnostic, so I was not forced to attend the weekly Scripture class. I used the time instead to read in the library. Needless to say, religion was not my strong point.

Out of the urban madness of Nairobi, I sank back gratefully into the simple rural life. Joan had a big family of young people around her, made up of her students, members of the church community and other missionaries. They were all good people who shared a commitment to their God, community and each other. They had a few strange habits though. For example, when I was introduced to people, they would never say 'Hello' back. Instead they would furiously pump my hand exclaiming, 'Praise God!' Joan went on with her work, and I found myself with plenty of time to think about and question my relationship with Robert. The gentle, spiritual atmosphere of Joan's home and her own accepting way provided the ideal space to heal and refocus my energies.

During this time I began to consider Christianity. I thought long and hard about what it would mean if I committed my life to Jesus Christ, and joined that exclusive club of 'saved' souls. Considering the circumstances, it would have been surprising if I hadn't. Later my friends in Australia admitted that this was the only time that they had truly been worried about me. Living in Kenya, marrying a Maasai warrior, giving up my job was cool with my friends, but upon receiving a letter warning her that I was considering Christianity with a capital C, my friend Carolyn almost jumped on a plane to rescue me from being saved. A product of the Catholic education system, she now has a strong aversion to all things religious.

Joan never once asked me what had led me to seek her out or what I had been doing. I was welcome to stay as long as I liked and she offered me a rent-free room in exchange for typing her work. It was tempting to stay here, away from the 'real world', and I thought about it seriously. In the end I returned to Nairobi after two weeks. My life was enriched from having begun to grapple with my spiritual nature, but organised religion was not for me.

Africa is a very spiritual place, and I wanted to explore and learn from her without being limited by all the do's and don'ts. It is not hard to be inspired by Jesus Christ, but after a long, hard look, I still had serious misgivings about some of the attitudes of the church. I also had reservations about the sheer arrogance of a group of people who declared that they alone were right and everyone else was wrong.

With the benefit of hindsight, I now understand that this period was a kind of self-imposed test of my commitment to Robert. Just as I had tested myself during my affair with Whitfield, I had put myself through a different sort of test with ... whom? God? My childhood beliefs? I was not really sure. Did I think God would punish me if I married a black man? Absurd, I know, but maybe part of me had absorbed those crazy beliefs at some time in my life. I gave myself every reason I could come up with to break with Robert, but he withstood them all. In the end, I looked God in the metaphorical eye and told Him that I was staying with Robert and if He didn't like it then it was just tough.

The Maasai are very spiritual. They are not animists, or Islamic, but believe in a single divine being they call *Enkai*. Their reverence for *Enkai* is tied up in every small task they perform, such as when the women milk, and when the *moran* go on forest retreats. If I live to be a hundred, I will still only understand a fraction of traditional Maasai spirituality. As a member of the western capitalist world, I have lost my connection to the earth. If I understand anything at all, it is only by virtue of my association with the Nkidongi. The Maasai are still connected and have no need of evidence or theological debate about *Enkai*, for *Enkai* is a constant, enriching presence. Proof of their deep spiritual nature is all around. It is in the grass, the sky, the forest, the cattle; the new rays of morning light and the dark mysteries of the night; the first spark of fire from the *olpirron* sticks, and the lifeless body of a slaughtered ox; in each and every ceremony, and each and every time an elder gently touches the bowed head of a child in greeting/blessing. *Enkai* is with the Maasai when they give birth, and when they lay out their dead to face the setting sun. *Enkai* is both the great unknown creator and an intimate friend who knows and guides the Maasai; the nurturing mother who brings life and the incomprehensible father who visits famine and disease on his people. Their understanding of timeless renewal is evident in their reverence for rain and their calm acceptance of death. Prayer is not a special request, but a continual dialogue from the moment of awakening to the time of sleep.[5]

Maasai conversation is liberally punctuated with references to *Enkai*. It is interesting to note that the prefix for *Enkai* is the feminine 'Enk' rather than the masculine 'Ol'. In their beadwork, the Loita Maasai say that the colour black represents *Enkai* at night, while blue beads symbolise *Enkai* in the day. Naturally schooling and Christianity have interferred with traditional Maasai beliefs. Robert gets all mixed up about the first Maasai man (in some accounts known as Maasinta) and Adam.

While I was sorting myself out at Joan's place, I had plenty of time to reflect on Robert's childhood and how very different it had been from my own. I tried to imagine Robert as a snotty-nosed Maasai kid with flies drinking from his eyes, his skinny body barely covered by a scrap of dirty cloth. But it was — and still is — impossible. I can think of him as nothing but a glorious young warrior. My thoughts are not mere fantasy. I was soon to learn that Robert was indeed a celebrated *morani*, as these two examples from his life illustrate.

At fourteen, he was the first of his generation to be circumcised and opened the way for the rest of his age group. He had to face this enormous task without the support and encouragement of other boys. He had no peers to reassure him or spur him on. The boy chosen to be circumcised first must be of the strongest character, for he will be a leader for the rest of his generation. After circumcision, Robert spent six weeks as an initiate or *olaibartani*. At the end of the six weeks, Robert went through another small ceremony called *Ashumaki kule* ('taking up the milk'). This was a special blessing by elders which enabled Robert to drink milk alone, normally taboo for *moran*. But Robert had no other warriors to drink milk with, so a special dispensation was granted until some other boys were circumcised and had caught up with him.

Once his period of healing was over, Robert had his head shaved, washed his body and donned the red cloth of a *morani*. The shaving and washing are symbolic of rebirth into manhood. Until their hair grows long again, the young warriors are known as *imbarnot* (singular *olbarnoti*). The young *moran* are now free to build their *emanyatta*. This is a special settlement where the *moran* gather to learn from their elders and generally have a good time together. They slaughter cattle and goats daily in the forest close to the *emany-atta*. They may live there for months at a time, together with mothers of the members of their age group and young, uncircumcised girls. Such is the fear of and respect for members of the Nkidongi subclan, that Robert could only visit his age group's *emanyatta* located in Naibala near Entasekera. The warriors from other clans do not like to settle with members of the Iloibonok family.

The second significant episode occurred three years later, when Robert's bravery and mental strength came together spectacularly and he joined the warrior elite by killing a lion. Lion-hunting is now banned by the government, and the Maasai have to call in the rangers if a beast moves in on their cattle. However ten years ago the spearhead of Robert's generation, *Ilkishili*, experienced one last taste of how their fathers and grandfathers had lived. To put this practice in perspective, there are more than two thousand warriors of the *Ilkishili* age group in the Loita Hills and less than twenty have killed a lion. As Robert puts it with his usual flair for understatement, 'to kill a lion is not easy'.

The Maasai have the ability to live in harmony with the wildlife; they are in fact East Africa's original conservationists. Despite their practice of hunting lions, the fact remains that wherever Maasai have lived, the wild game has remained. The major game parks and reserves have all been annexed from Maasai land. The Maasai do not hunt other wild animals for food. All wild game is considered to be 'God's cattle', and there is a strict taboo against eating the flesh of any wild animal, with the exception of eland or buffalo, which are most like cattle, and then only during times of extreme hardship. Young boys and *moran* will kill animals as part of their training. Most of all, the Maasai loved to hunt lions. Lion-hunting is not an exercise in stealth. To prepare for this ultimate test, the *moran* retire for several days to the forest where they slaughter a bullock. They also prepare a special 'medicine'. Forest plants are prepared in different ways, but most often as a potent narcotic soup. Robert will not be drawn on the details of these drugs, for they are a secret of the *moran*, but he did say that they make you 'very dangerous'.

I can picture Robert and the other twenty *moran* as they leave the meat camp to find a lion; painted as for war in red ochre, their bodies shiny with grease, their long, plaited manes immaculate. They each carry a buffalo hide shield in one hand and a heavy spear in the other. Strapped to their thighs are heavy metal bells stuffed with grass to muffle them. They start off quietly, moving in groups, following the early spoor of a male lion. When the lion is sighted, the *moran* stop to take the grass out of their bells and, to the accompaniment of their ringing, they start to chant as they pursue the lion. The lion will run for a while too but, like the *moran*, he knows this is serious stuff and sooner or later he will stand his ground for battle.

The *moran* close in and circle the angry lion, who roars and rumbles. The lion is a big male, in his prime, as much a *morani* in his own right as the men who now surround him. The circle moves in slowly, chanting all the while, enraging the lion, hypnotising him, their shields held in front of their bodies. There is no escape for the lion, no gap to run through. As the *moran* continue to advance and the circle tightens, they all know that one of them will make a move to spear the lion. They also know that the *morani* who moves his shield and throws his spear will break the lion's fearful trance, and the lion will charge this man.

With Robert's group, it was Robert who lifted his shield and threw his spear, and the lion charged towards the movement. His heavy spear hit the lion in the face between the eyes and down into its neck. As he threw his spear, Robert yelled his father's name, claiming this deed in honour of Mengoru. The lion kept coming and Robert fell back underneath his shield. The other *moran* did not let their comrade down, for almost as soon as the first spear had been released, four others were placed in the lion, robbing him of his force before he had time to revenge himself on Robert. Once the lion is down, no one else may throw a spear.

Not all *moran* are so fortunate. Many of the bravest have died of gross infection from a mauling. The *morani* who throws the first spear may keep the lion's mane to wear as a busby. He may also cut off the tail and place it atop of his spear so all the world will know that he is the 'One'. The *morani* who throws the second spear may cut off one paw and put it on his spear. A frenzy of celebration then must follow as the *moran* move from *enkang* to *enkang*, starting with that of the first *morani*, which in Robert's case was Morijo. The girls sing their praises and they are feted with gourds of milk and given animals to slaughter. They dance in a total of nine *enkang*s before throwing away the tail and the paw. Their names are immortalised in songs and stories, and they will forever be acknowledged as the bravest of the brave, the finest warriors to walk the plains.

Revived and emotionally fortified after my time at Joan's, I took the train back to Nairobi. Robert came to meet me there. We then travelled to Narok by bus. This time I would be travelling like a local. It meant I couldn't take very much with me. Apart from my renewed clarity, clothes and some presents, I had only a few kilos of rice and flour. Buses and *matatus* to Narok leave from an area called Nyama Kima (Swahili for meat), deep in the bowels of the non-tourist side of Nairobi. The maze of narrow streets around here was a chaotic confusion of vehicles, kamikaze pedestrians, bars and shops. *Matatus* were faster and more expensive but I felt nervous travelling for long distances in them, so instead we entered a big, colourfully painted bus with its name emblazoned down the side, Marura. Inside, most of the other passengers were Maasai, some in western clothes but many wearing tartan togas topped with red blankets or else a grey storeman's coat much favoured by elders. Spears are not allowed in Nairobi, but all the men carried their *orinkas* and some had shiny silver tins of cow fat with them.

Groups of men would squash up on one seat so they could be with their friends and all talk together. I saw five men squashed into a seat built for only three while the seat in front remained vacant — they just can't bear to split up. The concept of personal space counts for nothing with the Maasai. Women gathered small mountains of cardboard boxes and bright *kyondo* bags around their feet. The few small infants strapped to their mothers' bodies were peaceful amid the bustle, for it was just as hectic inside the bus as out. Getting Marura ready to go was no small thing. Five or so young men were involved in touting for customers, collecting money, issuing receipts and hauling goods up onto the roof rack.

At the same time, a never-ending stream of salesmen thrust their goods at you through the windows or as they walked up and down the aisle. Everything from ice-cream and sweets to cheap watches, mirrors, books, cassette tapes and calculators were on sale. I felt sorry for these salesmen, because no one seemed to buy anything and it must have been a long and depressing day for them. However they did at least have some sort of job, even if it was on one of the lower rungs of the employment ladder, and thousands of people in Nairobi had no hope of earning an income. Robert bought me vanilla ice-cream in a round cardboard tub.

The problems created by urban drift were obvious for all to see in Nairobi. Entire families from rural areas who had come into the capital seeking work resorted to begging on the streets. Street kids survived on their wits and by working as 'parking boys' who guided drivers to parking spots and watched over their cars for a few shillings. Others strapped infant siblings to their backs and begged in the streets, risking death by running alongside moving cars. Many of my newly acquired Kenyan friends — educated, urban city-dwellers — were scornful of beggars and complained of their growing numbers. If a child clung to them, they would hit them and shoo them off. They warned me against giving money, saying the kids only wanted to buy cigarettes and that it encouraged them. However I found it difficult to believe that many people would beg from choice. Robert and other Maasai impressed me with their compassion and generosity, for they never walked past a beggar without giving something, their traditional commitment to others often shaming me, as I had so much more to give.

Eventually Marura lurched into life and we left Nairobi. Halfway down the Great Rift Valley escarpment road, Marura broke down. When it became obvious that the bus would not start again without a spare part from Nairobi, we placed our belongings by the side of the road and waited for another vehicle to give us a lift. A *matatu* stopped, and ten or so of us managed to cram in. After an uneventful three-hour drive, the *matatu* finally arrived in Narok mid-afternoon. I was beginning to know Narok a little bit by now. Maasailand is split into two districts — Kajiado district and Narok district.

Narok town itself is the capital of Maasailand, where spear-carrying warriors walk hand in hand with educated Maasai in shabby blue suits and secondhand ties. I have since come to suspect that Narok is in fact the centre of the universe, with its mishmash of cultures and south-meets-north mayhem. We headed straight for the Spear Hotel. It is the only hotel in town that does not serve alcohol, guaranteeing a relatively quiet night's sleep. The next day Robert tried to find a *matatu* driver who was willing to negotiate the track into the Loita Hills.

There is no organised public transport beyond Narok, so these death traps on wheels have a monopoly, and they know it. There may or may not be a set price for the distance you wish to go. A lot of the time it depends upon how many people the tout can squeeze into the vehicle, which is usually a battered old station wagon or utility. This time, we waited an entire day for the vehicle to fill up. Robert did all the negotiating, while I stayed out of sight inside the hotel dining room re-reading the newspaper. I was learning fast that when using public transport in Kenya always carry a book. I stayed away because the colour of my skin would push the price right up. There's something wrong with the logic here, because if I did have money I would not be travelling in a *matatu*, however the touts never pause to consider this. They think white equals rich, and most of the time they are (relatively) right.

By late afternoon, Robert had struck the deal and we squeezed into the vehicle. I was in the front seat, wedged tightly between the driver and a young Maasai woman nursing her baby. On the far side next to the door was another woman. Robert sat with two other men on metal benches in the back. There was a mountain of cargo on the floor between them. The journey through Narosura and up the Niyandi Inkujit escarpment into the Loita Hills in a 4WD is challenging, but in a *matatu* it is positively hair-raising, though the scenery was great. The outline of a herd of zebras appeared in silhouette across the dirt road. Impalas and Thomson's gazelles, surprised by our vehicle, stared at us before bounding away. Wildebeests rorted and kicked on the plain.

We let the two women and one of the men off in Narosura. The vehicle broke down less than three kilometres further down the track, and the driver had to walk back to buy a wire. It was bitingly cold. Because I was next to the driver my right leg was bruised badly from all the gear changes.

Despite such a long day, the freezing cold and the extra patience required of me, I would not have wished to be anywhere else in the world. This was my third return journey to Loita and my heart was tight with excitement. There were no headlights, so once it got dark, a teenage boy sat on the bonnet to navigate. At one stage a ghostly white shape appeared out of the dark and then disappeared — an old buffalo bull gone grey with age caught lumbering along the road

At around midnight the engine conked out for about the tenth time and no amount of mechanical persuasion could induce it to start again. Two teenage boys were sent back to Narosura about ten kilometres away to get some more spark plugs. Strange as it may sound, finding spark plugs at this time of night was not an impossible task as shop-keepers in rural areas are used to being wakened at all hours and are very helpful. The cold was worse now that we had gained a little altitude. We stood by the car. Soon a group of children from a nearby *enkang* appeared to watch as the driver fiddled about under the bonnet.

Robert and I were invited into one of the houses. The woman whose house it was made us milk tea and after 'eating the news', as the Maasai say, she brought out a cattle skin for us to lie on. She was speaking Maasai, but with a strange accent. The village was not in true Maasai style, but square thatched cabins with newspaper lining the inside walls. All the people we saw were dressed in western clothes. Robert thought they might be Kikuyus who had been absorbed by the Maasai. I marvelled at how adaptable I had become as I lay down next to Robert on a cowhide in a strange house stranded in a remote corner of Kenya. I felt nothing but peace. It was deeply satisfying to be with Robert again. After the trials and so-called civilisation of Nairobi, it was good to relax in his calming steady companionship.

I had just fallen asleep when we heard the sound of the car coughing into life outside. The journey continued. After more than twelve hours travelling, I was exhausted, physically and mentally. Just when I thought I would actually vomit from nausea through sheer exhaustion, we stopped. We had arrived at Robert's mother's *enkang* in Morijo. I was led into a house and for the second time that night I lay down on an unfamiliar bed in an unfamiliar house and fell into a dead sleep.

I woke early and then dozed until around 8 am when Robert came in to see if I was OK. As usual, it was impossible for us to sleep under the same roof, so he had spent the night in the house for his age group. It felt wonderful to be back in Maasailand. Breakfast was a huge cup of sweet milk tea. Then Robert took me outside to show me his cattle. The other times I had been to this *enkang*, his cattle had been out grazing so this was the first time I had seen them.

Robert presented his gift to me — a poddy calf. She was black and white with splashes of brown on her legs. Her pretty face was mainly black and marked by a sworl of white hairs in the centre of her forehead. Her name was Lenyorra.

Next I watched as Robert treated a sick cow, and for the first time began to appreciate what skilled herdsmen the Maasai are. This cow had an infected eye and she definitely did not want to be caught. Robert slipped a leather strap around her neck and leg and in a single, swift motion put the fighting cow down on her side. The examination of her eye obviously caused her pain, and she kicked and tried to thrash around, but was held by the hobble and Robert. He washed the eye with water and then applied some white powdery stuff. When I quizzed him on what the medicine was, he explained it was 'medicine from the forest'. The whole exercise was impressive from start to finish. These guys really know how to handle their cattle! Just as I was beginning to relax around these beasts, the largest monster of all came running towards Robert and I. His horns spanned six feet easy, so I beat a hasty retreat out of the danger zone. However Robert stood his ground and laughed at me. This was no charging bull, but rather his favourite pet, a speckled behemoth of a bullock, also called Lenyorra (he was my calf's uncle). He ran up to greet Robert like an enormous dog, snuffling and butting gently against Robert's back — searching for salt, Robert explained.

With their rainbow of colours, startling horns and decorative brand marks, Maasai cattle are very beautiful. Much more beautiful to my eye than a herd of Aberdeen Angus or Poll Hereford clones. Robert told me that he owned 'around sixty cattle and more than one hundred sheep and goats'. A Maasai man will never be exact about how many head of livestock he owns. I thought there might be some superstition about this, but Robert had never heard of one.

ROBERT'S CLAN & FAMILY CATTLE BRANDS

CLAN: Ilaiser - right side

SUB CLAN: N'kidongi - right side

FAMILY: mengoru - left side

His father had simply taught him that it was always polite to under-estimate the actual number of livestock that you owned. There are many proverbs that teach against boasting, such as 'Eat, but remember to wipe your mouth'. In Maasailand, nobody minds a rich man, but everyone loathes a braggart. Traditionally the Maasai believe that they have a Godgiven right to own all the earth's cattle.

There are a number of variations on the theme of how God came to give the Maasai cattle, but the story as told to me by Robert is this: In the beginning, the Maasai did not have any cattle. One day *Enkai* called Maasinta (the first Maasai) to him and instructed him to make a big enclosure. He then told him to wait by the enclosure the next morning for he was going to give him something wonderful, but not to be surprised by what he would see and hear. Maasinta did as he was told, and soon heard a loud crack of thunder. *Enkai* then sent a leather strap down from heaven and it was along this that the cattle descended into the enclosure. Maasinta was afraid but did not move or make a sound. While all this was going on, the first Ndorobo, who lived with Maasinta, woke up and upon seeing the cattle descending cried out loudly. When he heard this sound, *Enkai* took back the strap and the cattle stopped coming. *Enkai* thought it was Maasinta who had cried out, so he said, 'Are these cattle enough for you? I will never do this again, so you had better love these cattle the same way I love you.' That is why the Maasai love cattle so much.

Robert's cattle and those of the other families in the *enkang* usually grazed together on the Morijo Plains, cared for by a young boy from a poorer family. However, their herder had recently been circumcised and was still recuperating, so it fell to Robert to take the cattle out to graze. I wanted to accompany him, but he reckoned that the cattle walked far and I wouldn't be up to it, so instead I stayed in the *enkang*. After lunch of *ugali*, beans and potato, I visited a woman named Kanasaa whom Robert had said 'would be a good friend for you'. She was the third wife of one of Robert's cousins. I found her nursing a new baby. There were many children in her house, curious to see me close up. My Maasai was still too slow and stilted to have a real conversation, but we made do while she made me tea. Afterwards she took me down the hill to visit my friend Marefu, his sister Naserian and mother, Interekei. Marefu was sweating out a fever. 'Malaria', he assured me, though there are no mosquitoes in the Loita Hills. The Maasai call any fever malaria. Naserian was eight months pregnant with her second child. She took me with her when she went to get firewood. I watched in awe as she nimbly climbed up a dead tree that had fallen against another trunk and hacked off four large branches with a panga. Back on the ground, she split the branches lengthways, bundled them at either end with a leather strap and swung the whole lot on her back to carry them home. All the while she kept up a continuous conversation in Maasai and adamantly refused to let me even carry a piece of wood for her.

The next day I walked the fifteen kilometres or so to Narotian. Robert arranged for me to walk with his sister-in-law, Nolkipenperia Mary, who was the first wife of his half-brother, Ngaiyo. The Maasai tend to walk men with men and women with women. Robert complained that I walked so slowly it made him tired. He and another *morani*, Seketo, would follow us later in the afternoon. Mary had to walk to Narotian to help with a big double ceremony that was to be held at Daniel's *enkang* the next day. With her new baby snugly slung across her back in a warm blanket, Mary set a steady but comfortable pace. We stopped at the *dukas* where I bought us sodas and then we had three short stops along the way so that she could feed her daughter and I could catch my breath. When we reached the rise above Narotian, Mary pointed towards Daniel's *enkang*. Could I see it? she asked me in Maasai. Even from that distance, the hill top was awash in red. Many elders had already arrived, swathed in their red blankets. The sound of conversation buzzed from below us. I had never seen so many Maasai in one place before. I felt nervous as we started to walk down the hill towards the giant party.

When we arrived at the *enkang*, the honey beer was flowing freely. Narygunkishon greeted us and bustled Mary and me into her house where she was flat out washing cups, cooking tea and serving honey beer. There was a relay team of women carrying water back from the river. As each one wrested her jerrycan off her back to the ground, they paused to greet me and welcome me back.

There was to be a double ceremony the next day. Robert's older brother, Daniel, was to go through the *Olkiteng lorrbaa* ceremony, which translates to 'ox of the injuries'. This ceremony is the final confirmation of elderhood upon a Maasai man, and consequently one of the most important days in his life. It is a purification ceremony that each elder must go through before he can circumcise any of his children. The ritual slaughter of the ox cleans away the 'wounds and injuries' that he may have caused to his family and society. Daniel's oldest girl, Sintiman, was almost old enough to be circumcised, therefore it was time for his final confirmation of elderhood. The other requirements that a man must fulfil before the ceremony can take place include having paid up the dowry for his first wife in full and ensuring that any older brothers have paid up their own. If a younger brother undergoes this ceremony and an elder brother is not fully paid up, then the younger brother may 'buy off' this obligation with one ox. The other part of this double ceremony was the circumcision of Robert's nephew, Loldudula.

With so many visitors in the *enkang*, sleeping space was at a premium that night. I managed to squeeze into Narygunkishon's bed with three women and assorted children. We were packed in like sardines, and there was no way that you could turn over or even stretch your legs out. However, we were relatively well off as most of the men had to make do with the floor. Some chose to keep on drinking and talking, forsaking sleep altogether.

Robert's three-year-old niece, Mesianto, was cuddled up next to me, and in the early hours peed all over me. In my sleep I felt a warm liquid drench my clothes, then it turned cold and I woke. It took me a few seconds to work out what had happened, but there was no mistaking I was lying in a puddle of pee. I took off my skirt, which had copped most of it, and then sat upright, not knowing what else to do in the dark, cramped bed. Narygunkishon came to my rescue with some rags to mop it up — the hide bed does not soak up much fluid. Mesianto must have been holding on all day with all the excitement!

A few hours later I watched as the men gathered outside in the dawn light for the *Emorata* or circumcision ceremony. I had seen Loldudula before of course, but rarely spoken to him. My impression was of a gangly youth too tall for his skimpy robes who shyly tended the cattle. I understood more about what was happening this time than I had at the first ceremony I had attended in

December 1989. Inside the cattle enclosure, green *olorien* branches had been placed upright in the earth. Loldudula appeared from his mother's house, flanked by Ilampala, who would act as his 'sponsor'. Loldudula was naked and walked proudly to take his place seated upon the cattle skin in front of the green branches. The men crowded around, Daniel — as usual — pushed me to the front. A pot of cold water was splashed over Loldudula. All of a sudden an anguished wailing rose up. It was Loldudula's elder brother, Pariken, giving vent to the emotion that his brother was not permitted to express. His crying died down, and I could see his mother looking on anxiously from her doorway. The mood was solemn and intense. The operation proceeded and was over in a few minutes. Loldudula was, of course, supremely brave. Now it was over, he allowed Ilampala to drag him back into his mother's house.

Next I saw Daniel catch a large black ox and wrestle it to the ground. It was then hobbled and led away into the forest to be slaughtered. After an hour or so, Robert's friend Seketo led me away into the forest where all the men had gathered. Maasai women are not permitted to attend the site of the slaughter, however Daniel insisted that I be there as he wanted to show me 'everything for Maasai culture'.

My first impression was of the vivid red of the blankets and meat splashed against the cool green of the forest. More than two hundred elders and *moran* were gathered in one spot. (These days I would rather die than walk into a male gathering such as this one, however my ignorance protected me and I blithely tripped in.) At one end of the clearing, a circle of *olorien* branches and leaves had been set to to represent the *enkang*. Only Daniel, Papa and members of their own age groups were permitted to sit inside this circle. No other age group was allowed to enter it. Daniel and the elders from Papa's age group were painted in red ochre. In another area, large chunks of meat were roasting over a wood fire. Raw meat was piled on a bed of green branches. The head, hooves and black hide were neatly arranged together. A mass of intestines oozed nearby. A huge balloon like thing sat nearby, taller than a young calf. This, I was told, was the ox's stomach!

I sat at the edge of the clearing and let Seketo feed me the choicest pieces of meat. I noticed that an elder had a wooden skewer with chunks of raw meat on it. He explained that his daughter was pregnant and craving meat. Women usually have to be content with the leftovers from a feast such as this one; however, a man may freely request meat for a pregnant relative. After a while, I heard the distant sound of women singing. The men left the meat camp, and walked towards the singing.

The women were standing in an open grassy area. Prominent were Narygunkishon and Daniel's mother, Mama (she is also Robert's mother). They were both decorated ceremonially with red ochre and wearing their finest beads. The men and women ran out to do mock battle, each hitting the other with branches. They were fighting for possession of a skewer of meat stuck in the ground. The lively game went on for a time, and I received a few switches on the bum from one of Robert's cheekiest friends, Asai. The women claimed victory of the meat. Next the stomach, head, one hoof and a slab of raw meat were brought out. Daniel, his wife and mother all sat on the stomach, which thankfully could take the weight without bursting. Everyone else gathered in a large group around them. There was a blessing and then Daniel was given a new name, Obiki, which roughly means 'he who does not die easily'. After this everyone walked back to the *enkang* singing.

The rest of the afternoon was a joyous confusion of singing, dancing and feasting. Hundreds of Maasai dressed in their finest is a dazzling sight. The elders honoured Daniel with honey beer. The *moran* danced and celebrated the entrance of a new *morani* to their ranks. I helped serve tea and then sat in the sun with a group of women to watch the celebrations. The day was significant in another way, for I finally met Robert's mother, Mama. She greeted me shyly but warmly, and then went back to her duties. She was small with a slight build, and around her shaved head was a single strand of coloured beads.

At the end of the day, my friend Kikuyan invited me to sleep at her house, which was in another *enkang* about 40 minutes walk from Narotian. I was happy to accept because I knew that I would get no sleep in Daniel's *enkang* that night — the celebration was set to go on for a while. Robert escorted us to the *enkang* at dusk and then left to try and find another house where he could sleep. Inside her house, I found Ilampala and an age mate drinking tea, so we spent a pleasant evening talking. Kikuyan roasted some maize for us and her children. I had forgotten to bring a blanket, so Ilampala gallantly left me his before he left to sleep in his age group house in the same *enkang*.

The next day I returned to Daniel's *enkang* and stayed for another week or so. It is strange how I can remember certain details about this time so clearly, and others hardly at all. The *Olkiteng lorrbaa* ceremony was so enormous and overpowering that the rest of my visit fades in comparison. All I can say is that I stayed with Daniel's family, sharing the bed with Narygunkishon, her infant son Melubo and daughter Mesianto, who had stuck fast to me since I arrived. I continued to learn how Robert's family lived as everyday incidents occurred and the gentle rhythm of Maasai life unfolded naturally and simply around me. I had become part of the *enkang*, and if the Maasai thought I was strange they were too polite to show it. I was always made to feel welcome, especially by the women who delighted in the little of their language I could now speak.

My visit came to an end when Robert went on safari with the National Outdoor Leadership School (NOLS). This is a sort of Outward Bound course for American tertiary students. Part of their training included a ten-day hike in the Loita forest, learning to live in the bush with nothing but what they could carry in their packs. Robert loved these trips best of all the safaris he escorted. Instead of just acting as a spear carrier, literally, to add a bit of local colour to a safari camp, NOLS employed Robert and some of his English-speaking friends as guides and co-teachers, albeit at a pretty paltry rate. Their skills were really stretched, and it seemed that Robert gained as much from these expeditions as the students no doubt did.

Before he left, Robert had asked our friend Marefu to help me get back to Nairobi, where he would meet me in ten days' time. The first part of our journey was easy, because Robert had already arranged for a NOLS vehicle to drop us at Narosura, where we could probably get a lift onto Narok. Once Marefu and I arrived in Narosura, we scouted around for news of a vehicle. 'Narosura' means the place of the black wood, but there are few trees in this arid dust bowl now. It is a depressing place to spend a Sunday. I bought a soda and some boiled sweets and settled in for a long wait.

Once it grew dark, it was obvious there would be no lift and we faced the prospect of having to spend the night in this soulless shanty town, so Marefu arranged for a room in one of the 'lodgings'. There was a blackboard menu in the bar, but nothing was available on a Sunday so I settled for a stale chapatti and a soda. Our bare room made the Spear Hotel look like the Ritz. Four stained walls, two torn mattresses, a small table and a couple of dirty grey blankets. On the bright side, the door could be locked from the inside, there was a candle stub and matches and, incongruously, a clean, folded towel on the foot of each bed. Marefu was doing a valiant job of looking after me. Again I noted how comfortable I felt sharing a room with a man I hardly knew — not something I would have been able to do in Australia. Necessity — and the Maasai — make for interesting bedfellows.

After a surprisingly sound sleep, I woke early and managed to organise a bucket of hot water to wash with. There was a small room for washing right next to the pit loo, so the smell wasn't the best, but the cake of soap and warm water was very welcome. Rather than use the loo, I preferred to walk out of town where I found a nice patch of bush.

We found a shop that sold us tea and stale *mandazi* for breakfast. *Mandazis* are triangles of sweet fried dough, an African donut. Because it was Monday there was more life in Narosura. All the shops opened and women arrived with produce to sell. Chooks scratched around and school children passed through. A big lorry pulled in, and Marefu ran over to see if the driver would take us to Narok. There were several other people in our position, all waiting for lifts. Marefu and I got to sit in the back of the open tray. The tray was bare metal, so we fashioned padding out of my luggage. We shared the space with hundreds of crates of empty soda bottles. The four-hour ride was bumpy, dusty but most of all noisy from the rattling of thousands of empty Coke, Fanta and Sprite bottles.

Four hours later, looking very dusty and feeling very stiff, we arrived in Narok. This was the end of the line for Marefu, he had delivered me to 'civilisation' safely and was clearly happy at the prospect of returning to Morijo. In the tea shop where we ate some samosas and drank soda, the radio played a Rick Astley song about a modern girl who rules the world. I felt anything but modern after my time with the Maasai, and I was not happy at the prospect of returning to Nairobi. For the last leg of my journey, I travelled by myself in Marura, the colourful bus that I travelled down in. The combination of white skin and Maasai beads drew a few quizzical stares in the bus, but not hostile ones.

While waiting for Robert to join me in Nairobi, I turned to my diary. I hadn't written anything at all about the last few weeks. In the same way that I stopped using my camera after my first trip, I now also ceased writing. I wanted to be immersed in Maasai life; I didn't want to stop and record it. It is too easy to hide behind a camera or a diary. It is far more challenging to just get in there, boots and all, and do it. The Maasai didn't scribble notes about their lives; they just lived them. My notebook felt to me like an intrusion and branded me an outsider, an observer rather than a participant. I decided that anything I recorded would have to be with my heart and my mind.

I thought about my relationship with Robert and how it had deepened and grown. Travelling together had been very good for us. Before we just had a desire to be together, now after our experiences we had a shared past and a wealth of new information about each other. Robert had opened up to me and let me see past his formal, reserved outer shell to his shy, sweet, gentle core. The gentleness was not a surprise, for anyone with an ounce of perception can see straight away that Robert is a very gentle man. His dark, gazelle-like eyes say it all. I love watching him with small children, who instinctively run to him for protection from an angry parent or sibling. I realised that I admired him enormously, and most of all for his quiet, considered manner. He never says a bad word about anyone, never offers a harsh judgment. He considers everything thoroughly, and never speaks or reacts on the spur of the moment — which is of course the complete opposite of me. This makes him much in demand as a leader among his peers, and he is often called away to consult on this matter or that matter affecting his age group. He is serious about his responsibilities, dedicated to his family and community. I had once worried that my influence would corrupt and unsettle him. I overestimated my own power. I now knew that nothing or no one could persuade Robert to do anything against his own wishes.

While I was in Nairobi, my friend Susan from the CPK Guesthouse invited me to spend the weekend at her mother's farmlet in Kambaland. The Kamba are the fourth largest ethnic group in Kenya. Decades ago they were skilled hunters who also kept livestock and cultivated the land. Today Kamba men and women make a lot of the souvenirs that tourists from all over the world know Kenya by. The popular woven bag known as a *kyondo* is woven by Kamba women. Traditionally they used sisal, then wool was introduced and now even brightly coloured plastic bags are used. Many Kamba women seem permanently connected to their weaving! Kamba men make bows, arrows and spears. Kamba carvers are renowned for their soapstone and wood carvings. These days the Kamba have given up hunting and concentrate on farming. Also many work as tradesmen and artists.

Almost everything grows in Kambaland. In the Kangundo district, high on a hill, Susan's family grow coffee as their cash crop and maize, beans, pumpkin and potatoes to eat. This was a new part of Kenya for me to discover. Not the open plains and forests of Maasailand, but dense cultivated small farms. Western ways had replaced Kamba tribal culture, but had not affected the closeknit community built around extended families that is the very heart of rural Kenya.

Susan's widowed mother, brothers and younger sister lived on a few hectares of good farming land. The family compound had four dwellings, each one progressively more modern as the family had grown more prosperous over the years. The oldest one had a thatched roof, the newest one corrugated iron. As Susan boasted to Martin, her Kikuyu boyfriend, the Kamba have always built square, cornered houses with mud brick. One building was the kitchen and this was the hub of the compound. The wood fireplace was a traditional one, with three cooking stones.

As I discovered over the weekend, the Kamba are excellent cooks. The first night we ate *githeri* — beans and maize kernels cooked slowly in a clay pot. The flavour was exquisitely sweet and by far the best *githeri* I had ever eaten. Pumpkin also cooks beautifully in the clay pot, and the Kamba serve wedges of sweet pumpkin with cups of tea as an afternoon snack. The second night Susan cooked meat stew with rice and chapattis. She also cooked up a green vegetable, *sukuma weeki*, which I was reluctant to try as it reminded me of spinach. Cooked the Kamba way, however, this was a soft, delicious green vegetable.

The whole extended family ate meals together, squeezed into the warm kitchen seated on a motley assortment of traditional three-legged stools (the most comfortable) and modern cane furniture. The chickens also liked to settle for the night in the warm kitchen, even though they had their own house next door. One plump hen had craftily laid her eggs in a corner and so was permitted to nest there.

We returned to Nairobi two days later. I had a beautiful *kyondo* from Susan's mother and a Kamba name, Mwikali, which she explained through Susan meant 'she who stays put'. I had planned to meet Robert that afternoon at the Norfolk but he didn't turn up. This didn't worry me greatly, because I knew what the transport could be like. The next day I waited all day, and again no Robert. I was bitterly disappointed and also beginning to worry that something was wrong. He arrived on Wednesday with bad news. He had heard in Narok, where his safari concluded, that his father was seriously ill.

It was painful to see Robert in silent agony about his father. We spent two days together in Nairobi, and then Robert left for Narotian where his father was waiting for him. It was typical of Robert to keep his commitment to me, even when his beloved father lay ill and waiting for his son. The morning he was to leave, I woke up crying on his chest, but stopped when I saw how much it confused and troubled him. He had more serious problems to worry about without me making it harder for him. I saved up all my tears until he said goodbye and walked quickly out the door, then I let them all out.

I steeled myself for another eventful flight back to Australia via Karachi. This time I left Kenya with a sense of calm and quiet resolve. I had come here to answer one question, were our feelings for each other true? The question had been answered, and then I got lost in the middle. My affair with Whitfield, which I now knew had been a holiday romance, and my dalliance with Christianity in

AINGORU (SEARCHING)

Bungoma had taught me a lot about myself and my feelings for Robert. Now I was leaving again, but this time I was sure of our love for one another. My plan was to return to Australia, organise my finances, work hard and get back here to be with Robert. Simple really.

[1] Some oral accounts claim that the first Oloiboni was ole Mweiya or Muya. This could have been another name for Kidongoi, or another Oloiboni. Robert believes firmly that the first was Kidongoi.

[2] Retired Major Raphael ole Loolpapit, Entasekera, October 1993.

[3] The Maasai lost more land than any other Kenyan tribe as a result of the infamous colonial treaties of 1904 and 1911, which forced them to vacate first the fertile Nakuru/Naivasha region, and then the Laikipia Plateau and Kinangop to make way for white settlers. At independence in 1963, these areas were never restored to the Maasai, but instead sold to the Kikuyu as small farming plots. Loss of land continued, with the creation of the Maasai Mara Game Reserve, Amboseli and the Tsavo National Parks — all carved from the southern Maasai reserve with no consultation and compensation. Even today it continues, under an insidious policy of group ranching, which 'divides and conquers' the Maasai. Excessive encroachment by agriculturalists has farmed to death large areas of Maasai land that provided dry season grazing and essential water catchment.

[4] Olonana's successor was his eldest son, Seggi, who was circumcised into an established age group and ruled by his uncles.

[5] Eugene Hillman, a Catholic missionary who has worked with the Loita Maasai, writes that 'the Maasai occasionally use the word *enkai* for "sky". It is hard to think of a more awesome symbol for the Originator of everything. "My God", the people pray, "you are surrounded by stars, with the moon at your navel; you last forever". What is symbolized here is surely that same ultimate horizon of hope which Jews, Muslims and Christians haltingly name *Yahweh* or *Elohim* or *Allah* or "God" (a term derived from pre-Christian Teutonic religious experience).'

CHAPTER SEVEN

ESIAI *(Work)*

Australia September to
January 1991

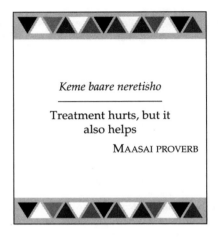

Keme baare neretisho

Treatment hurts, but it
also helps

Maasai proverb

I ARRIVED IN MELBOURNE IN SEPTEMBER AND PLUNGED RIGHT BACK INTO the madness of the entertainment world. I needed money to return to Kenya as soon as I could — that was my single aim in life. Keeping busy stopped me from thinking too much, and I didn't feel like thinking anymore right now. Ploughing into work kept me focused on my goal.

I started out helping my friend Carolyn Logan publicise a new jazz club that had just opened. Carolyn and her sister Lisa were living in a two bedroom flat in Balaclava, close to St Kilda Beach. With typical generosity, Carolyn put a spare mattress on her bedroom floor and, *voila!* I had a home. Next another great job appeared, co-ordinating the move to a new home for the Melbourne International Comedy Club. Another mate, Liz Baillie, invited me to set myself up in her office and then found me a freelance job as advertising co-ordinator for the Melbourne season of Circus Oz. These were fantastic jobs, and I was delighted to put the confidence I had developed in Kenya to good use in Australia. I was well supported by my friends, and I put my amazing good fortune down to more than a mere 'lucky streak'; I took it as the universe's seal of approval that I was on the right track. Work, a place to live, transport, and encouragement from people I cared about all fell into place around me. It was impossible to doubt when I was getting green lights all over the place!

The team at the Comedy Club were great people to work with, especially the manager Elena Martinez, a bubbly Cuban American with some giant-size dreams of her own. Once the Club had opened in its new premises, she invited me to stay on, working nights in the box office. This I did and have continued to do so ever since whenever I am in Australia. I buckled down to working days and nights, and remained very focused on my return to Kenya and Robert. My tunnel vision propelled me further and further along the track.

Everything else had to take second place to my obsessive drive to save money. That included my beautiful Anglo-Arab mare, Siska, who was agisted with my riding instructor outside Melbourne. Previously I had paid for private lessons every week, and spent most of my weekends with Siska. Now I no longer had a car for the 40 minute drive, or the money to spend on lessons. The long hours I was working left me exhausted. Sunday was my day off, and I needed it desperately to catch up on sleep, washing and housework. I had once promised myself that I would never be the sort of horse owner who stopped off once a week to hand an apple to their friend over the paddock fence. Now I found that I was worse than even that.

To know how I felt, you need to have spent your childhood desperately wanting a horse. As a child, I read every horse book ever published and covered my walls and school books with pictures of horses. There was one book in particular that I remember, called *Silver Snaffles*. It tells a magical story of a little horseless girl who visits an old pony in a dingy stable every week to give it carrot tops and apple peel. One day the old pony speaks to the girl and tells her to walk into a dark corner of the stable. She does so, and passes into another world where all horses can speak and they lovingly teach her to ride. Ever since then, I have been chatting up old ponies and looking into dark stable corners.

Every Christmas I asked for a horse, and every Christmas my family would joke that they had got me one, but it had run away so they only had a bag of horse shit. Ha ha, excuse me if I don't crack up with laughter. It's a hard-luck love story that only city girls who could never have a horse would understand. But my story had a happy ending. You see I grew up, moved out of home and started out on my career. The theatre world proved to be my compensation for the lack of a pony in my childhood. One day, it dawned on me that I could do anything I wanted.

Years of 'No, you can't have a horse,' are a hard legacy to shift, but shift them I did. I started out in a small way, just buying horse magazines and watching show jumping on TV. Then through happy coincidences, I found a wonderful riding instructor, who taught me how to ride and helped me find my own horse. And we should have lived happily ever after, winning first prizes in Adult Riding Club dressage competitions, but I spoiled everything by falling in love with a Maasai warrior and running off to live in Kenya. Occasional visits to my horse are out of the question, since I spend the entire time bawling my eyes out. So I have since wrapped that dream in mothballs and stored it carefully so that I can find it again, sending off regular agistment cheques. I can never forget that it was Siska and my desire to learn from Linda Tellington-Jones that led me to Kenya in the first place. So Siska is a piece of the puzzle I am yet to understand.

The money I had borrowed to travel to Kenya the first time around, plus other credit-card debts were haunting me. I had got myself into a horrible financial mess and had to face the music. I applied for a consolidation loan and paid off all my debts. I now had a $30 000 bank loan to pay back over four years. I consoled myself with the thoughts that I had had a good time spending it and that if all it cost was $30 000 to find my true purpose in life, then it had been cheap. Many people spend their entire lives and considerable fortunes searching for meaning and inspiration. I had found the initial key to mine at the relatively young age of twenty-six.

All the time I was in Australia, I was impatient to return to Kenya. I felt dissatisfied with my own culture. The cityscape now appeared ugly. My body and soul felt heavy and constrained within it. I was earthbound, and longed for the air that Africa represented to my soul. The Maasai knew how to live in both mediums, connected to the rhythm of the earth and the spiritual mysteries of the sky at the same time. I wanted to learn to do the same. At night I went to sleep thinking of Robert and woke up with a dull pain in my heart. Some mornings I just could not bear to tear myself away from my dreams of Africa and would be late for work as a consequence. My habits also changed; knowing how hard Maasai women work to bring water to their homes, I found it impossible to leave a tap running while I brushed my teeth. The act now seemed profligate. I no longer took pleasure in buying expensive clothes for I could not help calculating what that amount would buy in food or school fees in Kenya.

Christmas 1990 came and went. The spectre of the Gulf War loomed, then exploded into everyone's life. I had saved enough money to finally return to Kenya for about six months in February 1991, including enough money to pay my loan repayments for that time. Out of the overriding desire to get back to Kenya, a vague plan had begun to form. I could get a work permit and find a job in Nairobi. That way I could continue to pay off my loan while remaining in Kenya. This appeared to be the perfect solution to my problem. But were jobs available, and even if they were, would I qualify for a work permit?

The worst part about preparing to leave Australia each time was dealing with my mother. She grew progressively more anxious as the day of my departure again drew near. In between helping me wash and iron my clothes, my mum was prone to irrational emotional outbursts and none-too-subtle suggestions that I should see more of the world than just Kenya. On this particular occasion, it ended in Mum's tears and a declaration that she was going to drown herself in the ocean. Fortunately I was able to persuade her to have a midnight swim in the rockpool instead.

The Gulf War meant there were no flights to Africa out of Karachi, so I was spared another PIA flight. Instead I flew to Singapore on 5 February with British Airways and then connected with an Air Mauritius flight to Kenya. Air Mauritius is no Third World airline, and is run with all the efficiency and style of the majors, with an extra dash of *savoir-faire*. Despite a bit of a 'milk run' route with stops in Reunion, Madagascar and Mauritius, I enjoyed the service and especially the food.

The island of Mauritius looked enchanting as we flew in low over sandy beaches, bright green fields of sugar cane and misted mountains. I made a mental note that I must go back for a closer look one day. Today the most I would get to see was the Transit Lounge. The way I figure it, you can either fight the transit lounge experience or go with it. I actually enjoy it because, like flying, it is one of the few times that I can really get away with doing absolutely nothing. I read my book and breakfasted on a bar of Swiss chocolate, fresh bread and cherry jam, juice and coffee in the small transit restaurant. I noticed that I was starting to smell a bit, and so bought some duty free perfume to camouflage my travel stink.

Flying into Nairobi felt different this time round. Gone was the agonising ball of doubt gnawing away in my stomach. It is comforting to know that the more risks you take, the easier it becomes. I had weaned myself from the usual western expectation of being in control of each and every situation. I didn't even want to know what time it was any more, let alone what was going to happen to me every minute of every day. Faith and true confidence in my own abilities to handle anything that life was likely to dish up had liberated me from fear. And without fear, you can do anything. Everything would fall into place for me in Kenya — or so I thought.

ADUNG ILKEEK, ANAP ENKARE

(Chop wood, carry water)

February to July 1991

*Osupuko maarpe kiriama. Emincho
Ilkokoiyoi eya osupuko. Intai ilrikok
pooki aitanapa.*

Let us go to die together
in our forest.
Don't give the Kikuyus our forest.
(On this) all our leaders are sworn.

MAASAI WOMEN'S MAENDELEO SONG

ROBERT MET ME IN NAIROBI AND WE MADE THE LONG JOURNEY BACK TO Loita in a *matatu*. The short rains had fallen later than usual this year and the hills were green and beautiful. I was welcomed warmly by everyone at Narotian.

Robert, like all unmarried *moran*, had no house of his own. He slept in his age group house and moved around with his cattle. A small house had been vacated by a family in Daniel's *enkang* and was given to me to live in. Now I had a home, Robert and I set up house together. From this time on, everyone considered me to be Robert's wife. The house was old and falling apart in places, but it was my own space.

Baba and Mama Hannah and their three children had lived there previously. They were not Maasai but Kisii people who had immigrated to Maasailand, so their house was not in typical Maasai

MY FIRST HOUSE
(Originally built by a Kisii family)

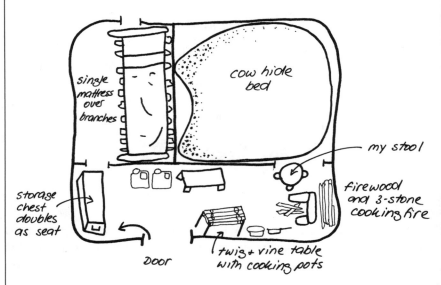

round window

single mattress over branches

cow hide bed

my stool

storage chest doubles as seat

firewood and 3-stone cooking fire

Door

twig + vine table with cooking pots

style. It was square in shape with a thatched roof and had been divided into three areas: a main living area with a fire at one end; a space with one large Maasai bed; and a second smaller space with a western style single bed which had a store-bought mattress on top.

Traditional Maasai beds are raised 30 to 60 centimetres off the ground and made of wooden planks. Over this base are piles of sweet smelling bush, called *sinone*, which also serves as padding. The final layer is an untanned cowhide scraped clean. If the household is wealthy, there will usually be three or four hides piled on top of the other. The beds are large enough to sleep four adults and are in fact very comfortable. Sort of like a futon really. In hot weather, the hides stay deliciously cool. They are also very easy to clean. The Maasai do not use pillows, though warriors with elaborate ochred hairstyles sometimes sleep with their head on a small wooden head rest.

My little house had a wooden door, and two small holes served as windows, which I would stuff with rags at night to keep the wind out. The position of the doorway in the centre of the front wall meant that the interior was not as dark as usual. I love lots of light — the lack of it was one of the most difficult things I had to get used to while living in Maasailand.

The main difference between this house and the others in the *enkang* was that there was no *olale* for young calves and goats. Baba Hannah did not own any animals. His people were agriculturalists, and he preferred to grow crops and swap them for milk rather than keep any livestock himself. This made my house much easier to keep clean and was also easier on my western sense of smell. Maasai houses usually have a smoky, leathery smell that permeates your skin after a while. They smell of wood smoke and goat piss and of good, strong work with animals. This may sound perverse, but when I first see Robert after a long absence, I love to breathe in the distinctive Maasai smell of his skin.

Narotian is part of Entasekera, an area in south-eastern Loita, known in local government language as a sublocation, or subcentre. It has trading *dukas*, a government school and a free health clinic (which has no drugs, but is staffed by a very cheerful and conscientious woman). There is a Catholic mission, which has its own clinic (not free but very cheap and well run), and American missionaries have established a small church.

There must be several hundred Maasai families scattered over the area, but you wouldn't know it as the *enkangs* are so spread out. My *enkang*, known as *Enkang o Mengoru* after Robert's father, is situated on a small, grassy knoll, dotted with yellow-green acacia trees and leads down to a creek. On three sides we are framed by forested hills. To the south runs a well-trodden and hilly path to the trading *dukas*, government school and Catholic mission two kilometres away. If you keep walking south, you would cross into Tanzania, where the mountain Ol Doinyo Sampu straddles the border, and the northernmost tip of Lake Natron lies. Further into Tanzania is the holy mountain of the Maasai, Ol Doinyo Lengai, the Mountain of God, which is an active volcano. A short distance to the east lies the Nguruman escarpment, a stretch of pristine forest that is sacred to the *Iloibonok* family. To the west are the Loita Plains that roll into the Siana Plains and the Maasai Mara which ends at the impressive Soit Ololol escarpment.

Traditionally the Maasai were semi-nomadic, accompanying their herds in search of fresh pasture and water. Possessions were few, being limited to what could be carried on the backs of women and in leather panniers on each side of the family donkey. Gourds for milk and water, cooking pots, rolled cowhides and personal adornments made up most of the load. Each family had access to dry season pasture and would build semi-permanent *enkangs*. The small dung-plastered huts would protectively encircle an enclosure where the cattle spent the night. The entire *enkang* would be surrounded by a thorn fence to keep out predators.

These traditional settlements still exist today. The giant circles, like some mysterious pattern made by the gods, are easily seen from the air in the Great Rift Valley. However, as the Maasai began to lose much of their land, first to colonial settlers and game reserves, and later to group ranches monopolised by elite Maasai and to encroachment by agricultural tribes, their nomadic ways had to change. These days the Maasai of southern Kenya do little but go droving in dry seasons, though it would pain them to admit it, for in their souls they are still wanderers and always will be.

When you stick in one place a long time, you begin to want

more than just shelter from your house. In the Loitas, the traditional circular style of *enkang* has gradually changed, and our *enkang* is an example of this. The six houses are larger and feature thatched roofs instead of the traditional flat 'igloo' style. The houses are not enclosed within the thorn fence, but sit in a semicircle outside of it. Each doorway opens to face the cattle enclosure, and each family has their own gate, *mlango*, that leads into it. My own house was situated about six metres behind the others; this saved it from the worst of the flies.

The head of the family was Robert's ancient father, who lived in a house with his third and favourite wife, Kokoo. On the far side of their house lived his first wife, the equally ancient Mumai, who had cared for Robert during his school years when she lived in Morijo. Mumai lived with her son Olkiliai, his young wife Meiyoki and their two children. On the other side of Kokoo's house was her daughter-in-law Nolmemeri and her eight children. Next to her lived Robert's oldest brother Daniel and his wife Narygunkishon. They had six children. The fifth house was in a pretty rundown state, and was used by Robert's eldest sister, Ntanin. During the day she sat in Narygunkishon's house, helping cook and care for the children. At night she slept in the old house with the eldest children. Nine adults and sixteen children made up my immediate family circle. Robert's family had lived in this *enkang* for almost ten years — a sedentary lifestyle made possible by good rains.

Though this group formed the basis of our *enkang*, individuals did move between here and the other family *enkangs* settled by Robert's other brothers in Morijo, about twenty kilometres north, and Imburapitia another fifteen kilometres south-west. The family's collective cattle also moved between the three areas, depending on where the pasture was best.

I started my household with a few borrowed stools, an odd assortment of pots, cutlery, tin mugs, plates, two jerrycans which could hold ten litres each, a red bucket, a plastic jug for milk and two large plastic basins, one for washing in and the other for clothes. There was a small supply of soap, shampoo, medicines and a first aid kit. I had a bag of clothes and three blankets. By Maasai standards, I was really set up.

There was no electricity, so of course at night Robert and I saw by firelight. Plus I had a torch and some extra batteries. I didn't find it difficult to live without electricity, running water and appliances. Life has a different rhythm in Maasailand; the trick is to adjust to it. And I did so slowly and gently, with a lot of help from my Maasai family. Of course it helps if you are in love, which distracts you from what might look like, on the surface at least, a life of drudgery and cow shit. I was not only in love with an individual, but in love with a community.

However fascinated I was by the Maasai, living among them presented me with great challenges of both a physical and emotional nature. The physical work was relatively easy. I learnt to get my water from the creek at the bottom of our hill. It is a running stream and the water is very good. I have never had to boil it. I learnt to collect it slowly, holding a tin mug or jug to the surface with the mouth facing upstream and allowing the flowing water to fill the container. I then poured it into my jerrycan until it was full. I had to bend down to do this and my back would get very sore from this unaccustomed work. Turning on a tap is definitely easier.

Maasai women can carry thirty litres or more in a large round container on their back, supported by a leather strap that goes around the container at both ends. They then hoist it up onto their backs and secure the loop of leather around their foreheads. This way they carry the weight on their middle back, and can control how much weight is on their neck by supporting the strap with both hands. If the *enkang* is a long way from the water supply, then the women will use donkeys with sacking bags on either side to carry the water home. In Morijo, the women in our family walk more than six kilometres to the river and back each day during the dry season. I cannot carry water on my back. The leather strap pulls my hair and leaves an ugly red mark on my forehead for hours. I prefer to fill two ten-litre containers and carry them by hand up the hill to my house. The other women cluck their tongues at me and say that I will hurt my shoulders and lungs like this. Using this method, on a good day (that is, when I am feeling energetic) I can make the round trip three times and have sixty litres of water. This is more than enough to drink, cook with, wash ourselves, utensils and a few clothes. Or viewed another way, the equivalent to ten flushes of a western toilet, or twenty if you have that nifty half-flush button.

I improvised a small clothesline to one side of my house. This proved very useful for airing blankets each morning. With a dirt floor and a thatch roof, you must shake your blankets vigorously every day or else they feel very gritty. Once the blankets were out in the sunshine, I turned my attention to the dirt floor. At first it seems like an exercise in futility to sweep a dirt floor, but you do see results, even when using a leafy branch as the Maasai women do. Once the floor has been thoroughly swept, Kokoo showed me how to sprinkle water on the earth to keep the dust down. Later on I developed the habit of saving the bath water from the night before and sluicing the floor with it. This makes the floor beautifully cool to walk on in the heat of the day and I am told that it helps reduce 'jiggers'. These are tiny opportunitistic insects which like to burrow into bare toes and fingers. I washed my dirty cups, dishes and pots using hot water, a pot scrubber and washing up paste I brought with me from Nairobi. Maasai women use hot coals from the fire on their pots, and this brings them up with a beautiful shine — much better than I could achieve with detergent. They break the coal direct from burning sticks and add water. Then they remove any hard pieces and crush the rest up with their hands to make a thick, gritty paste in the pot. They rub this until all the food bits are off and the pots gleam silver inside. The outsides are left black from the fire.

Narygunkishon, Nolmemeri and sometimes other women provided me with firewood. I did offer to help carry my bundle from the forest, but they refused my help. It was pointed out to me that I would be more of a danger to them in the forest where the buffaloes and leopards slept during the day. I did not know their sounds and could not move quietly through the bush like a Maasai. So I graciously accepted my daily ration and tried to consume as little fuel as possible.

More difficult than the physical work was dealing with the language barrier. I was accustomed to being able to express myself. I actively enjoy all the subtleties of the English language and especially love to lay on the sarcasm and humour. Now I found myself with language skills the equivalent of a three-year-old's. Robert had no patience when it came to teaching me new words and phrases.

He spoke English when he was with me. The CPK Language School course had given me a basic vocabulary and some of the grammar. This meant that I could exchange pleasantries, 'eat the news', as the Maasai say, but anything requiring more than two short sentences left me on the sidelines. I had thought I would be able to pick it up more easily, and was frustrated when I couldn't. The intense alliteration and tonality of Maasai left me confused about what words were being spoken, and if I understood that, then I couldn't catch the subject and tense. As I said before, language is not really my thing.

To rub salt into the wound, the Maasai would compare me to Tim the missionary who could speak fluent Maasai. The implication being why couldn't I? When I finally met Tim, I found him to be a charming man who was indeed fluent; he spoke the language with a beautiful soft rhythm. I also discovered that he had a wife and household staff to care for him and had devoted a solid year and a half to nothing but language studies. I bet that he would still be struggling if he had to carry sixty litres of water each day and cook and clean! After all my housework, I was often too tired to grapple with language studies.

Just as vast and confusing as the language was learning the complex social rules of the Maasai. I made lots of mistakes during the first days in my house. One was cooking a meal of rice for Robert and his friends. I had hoped to make an impression on them with my culinary skills, but I didn't yet fully understand all the food taboos that the senior *moran* must abide by. One of their taboos is against eating anything with fat in it cooked by a woman. I had used a little oil in the rice, so the *moran* could not eat any. I cooked them tea instead, all the time feeling awkward as I fumbled with the fire and tried to fill the mugs in the dim light.

Moranhood is marked by many food taboos, which are strictly followed until the *moran* become junior elders at their *Olngesherr* ceremony. The ideal for the Maasai is a purely pastoral diet, but this is impractical for most people. However, it remains the standard for the *moran*, as ordained by *Enkai*. Even when it comes to eating meat, there are rules. For example, the *moran* are prohibited from eating any meat seen, handled or cooked by women. This extends even to a cow or ox that might die inside the *enkang* from disease or accident

My brother-in-law Daniel and his family. Left to right: Leseamon,
Melubo, Daniel, Gunisai and his wife Narygunkishon.
(PHOTOGRAPH: SORREL WILBY)

My brother-in-law Ilampala with his wife Nosotua and their two children,
Lendoiyan (left) and Nashunyi (right).
(PHOTOGRAPH: SORREL WILBY)

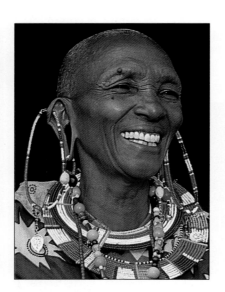

Robert's mothers: (top left) Mumai; (top right) Mama;
(bottom left) Kokoo; (bottom right) Paashe. (PHOTOGRAPHS: SORREL WILBY)

Robert's father. Born around the turn of the century, Papa saw many changes come to Maasailand. A son of the great Oloiboni Senteu, he was a celebrated warrior, who had four wives, raised eleven children, and acquired substantial livestock wealth. He was a respected orator, prophet and revered elder statesman. (Photograph: CATHERINE ODDIE)

Partial view of our enkang in Narotian. My house is on the far left.
(Photograph: NEIL HOLBROOK/Woman's Day)

Nolmemeri and family. Back row (left to right): Momposhe, grandmother
Kokoo, Pariken, Loldudula, Nolmemeri holding Matanga. Front row (left
to right): the twins, Napalell and Hannah, and Nataiya.
(PHOTOGRAPH: SORREL WILBY)

Left to right: Loldudula, Robert and Ilampala stand at the edge of the
Loitas, looking across to Tanzania. (PHOTOGRAPH: SORREL WILBY)
Opposite page: Three-year-old Ndoondo standing in the doorway of our
first house in 1991. (PHOTOGRAPH: CATHERINE ODDIE)

Robert with his favourite bullock, Lenyorrah. (Photograph: SORREL WILBY)

This is the easy part. Next I have to carry 20 litres up the hill!
(Photograph: SORREL WILBY)

Opposite page: Robert proudly wears his lion mane headdress — the prerogative of only the bravest moran.
(Photograph: SORREL WILBY)

If Shakespeare had been African, Oldorobo would have been his Puck.
The forest spirit incarnate with his daughter and Ndoondo in 1992.
(PHOTOGRAPH: NEIL HOLBROOK/WOMAN'S DAY)

Robert Oloimooja ole Rerente on our wedding day in July 1992. He wears
a blue cape, a colour symbolic of *Enkai* , and red ochre in his hair. He
carries a beaded ceremonial *orinka* and a wildebeest tail fly whisk, both
symbols of a respected family man and elder.

(PHOTOGRAPH: NEIL HOLBROOK/WOMAN'S DAY)

On the morning of our wedding day, friends help to arrange my decorations and clothes. (Photograph: NEIL HOLBROOK/Woman's Day)

Just a small part of my new extended family photographed on our wedding day. (Photograph: NEIL HOLBROOK/Woman's Day)
Opposite page: My girl, Ndoondo, and me.
(Photograph: NEIL HOLBROOK/Woman's Day)

My brother was a real hero on my wedding day. Here he is drinking
warm blood from the dewlap of a freshly slaughtered ox. Mark's
comment: 'It tasted like salty steak soup'.
(PHOTOGRAPH: NEIL HOLBROOK/WOMAN'S DAY)

Group portrait August 1993. Back row (left to right): Kokoo,
Narygunkishon, Meiyoki, Nolmemeri, Mumai and me. Front row (left to
right): Narotiai, Gunisai, Ndoondo, Matanga, Sembeta and Nataiya
(PHOTOGRAPH: SORREL WILBY)

Nolmemeri, my Maasai 'mum'. (Photograph: SORREL WILBY)

Morani Sapuk, friend and champion. (Photograph: SORREL WILBY)

Ndoondo in 1993, aged five and attending the local pre-school.
(PHOTOGRAPH: SORREL WILBY)

Another special friend, Momposhe. (PHOTOGRAPH: SORREL WILBY)

Mumai and her daughter-in-law Meiyoki framed by the doorway of the house Meiyoki built. (PHOTOGRAPH: SORREL WILBY)

Robert's brother Olkilia and his son Sembeta. Olkilia is married to Meiyoki (see above). (PHOTOGRAPH: SORREL WILBY)
Over page: Robert, Ndoondo and me in our house.
(PHOTOGRAPH: SORREL WILBY)

(which women milking will have seen). In this circumstance, other members of the *enkang* may skin and eat the animal, but the *moran* cannot. Instead they eat their own meat at special meat camps in the forest called *olpul* (plural *ilpuli*). Men from all age groups may attend the *olpul*, but warriors spend a great deal of their time in the forest.

They can disappear for months at a time, coming out only to retrieve another goat or cow to be slaughtered. Robert has admitted to me that he could eat half a goat by himself at one sitting! Over the years, I have come to understand the significance of the *olpul*, for it is much more than just a giant Maasai barbecue. In essence, it is a spiritual retreat, where the *moran* are free to concentrate on communicating with *Enkai* and the forest.

Robert has told me that every morning he and his friends would try to wake very early. They would then, one by one, walk from their camp into the forest and pray aloud to *Enkai*. They must do this before, say, 6 am which is about the time the women in the distant *enkangs* go outside to start milking. Maasai women often say a prayer before or during milking and the *moran* want to make sure that they get in first. It offends their warrior sensibilities to think that they are praying at the same time as a woman.

There are other prayers in the evening, featuring a ritual blessing invoked as the entrance to the *olpul* settlement is closed for the night. The *moran* also commune with the forest, which they consider a sacred place. Within the Loita forest along the Nguruman Escarpment, there are many sacred sites which feature during particular ceremonies, such as rivers, ancient trees and certain hill tops. However, the forest in its entirety is a holy site of paramount importance to all Maasai. It represents the heart and soul of their culture, and to no one group more so than the *moran*. From what Robert has explained to me, it seems that the *moran* enter a state of spiritual oneness with the forest during this time. This feeling is no doubt heightened by the 'forest medicine' or narcotic soup that the *moran* drink daily. They become hypersensitive to the sounds and smells of the forest. They are disgusted by the smells of the family *enkang*, the mundane conversation of married men and women, the barking of dogs and the crying of children, so they avoid visiting an *enkang* at all costs. One particular smell they cannot tolerate is that of soap, and so they especially dislike encountering *wazungu*. Robert says the *moran* can become 'very fierce' if they come across strangers in the forest.

Unlike the more glamorous physical exploits of cattle-raiding and lion-hunting which the Maasai are famous for, little is known about the spiritual aspect of *moran*hood.

Other taboos that apply to the *moran* include always eating with an age mate, never washing alone and never drinking the milk from your family's cows. Instead they are meant to swop the milk around with their age mates. In this way, milk is equally shared out between *moran* from rich and poor families. *Moran* must also choose which food they wish to eat each day, either milk or meat, for they may not eat both on the same day. To do so is considered to be taking food from the cow when it is living (milk) and also when it is dead (meat). Food taboos have the effect of isolating the *moran* from family settlements, thereby strengthening the brotherhood bond between the age group. A strong sense of communalism is fostered, and it is considered unhealthy for an individual *morani* to spend time alone. This is in contrast to the period of elderhood, where more individualistic pursuits are encouraged.

A large part of everyone's diet, including mine, was sweet milk tea. Making tea, or should I say 'cooking' tea as the Maasai do, is a fascinating and graceful ritual. Maasai women do all their cooking from their low seat by the fire on the 'woman's side' of the hearth. Everything they need is within reach, and all tasks, from pouring tea, to cooking, to breast feeding are performed with an elegant economy of movement. Forget all this pot to the kettle business, to make a good cuppa in Maasailand you must first stoke up the embers of the fire by blowing on them. Maasai women have perfected this art and can usually stir up a fire by blowing from where they are seated. I have to get down on my hands and knees.

Next, take a clean saucepan, add a cupful of water and put it on to boil. Take a small handful of leaves and throw them into the boiling water. Now add several cups of milk from a gourd. The gourds are cleaned daily with a long stick and a handful of ash. This imparts a smoky flavour to the tea, not unlike Earl Grey. You can add sugar to the milk mixture just before it reaches boiling point.

Most Maasai use a lot of sugar, around the equivalent of four heaped teaspoons per cup (minimum). You must never take your eye off the milk. The tricky part is next. Once it reaches boiling point, it will foam up immediately. At this point, just before it spills over the top, you are meant to casually and gracefully lean over and pick up the hot, handleless pot with your bare fingers and place it carefully on the floor. Years later, I am still trying to perfect this. My milk boils over and sends up clouds of ash and smoke from the indignant fire. Because cooking on an open fire coats the pots with a thick black crust, the women insist that it insulates the metal from the heat, and that the pots are not hot to the touch. I refuse to believe them and use the utmost caution when taking boiling pots from the fire. They laugh at me because I insist upon using oven gloves when I remove the pot. I also invested in a pot with a handle and this made life much easier.

Apart from milk tea, I mainly ate boiled rice, sometimes potatoes, roasted cobs of maize and chapattis. The roast corn was my favourite and it was also the easiest to cook. Being pastoralists, the Maasai make a good cuppa and do a great barbecue, but apart from that, they cannot cook. They do not have a tradition of cooking grains and vegetables. The staple food of Kenya, *ugali*, is usually served with a tasty sauce. The Maasai serve it plain, with a cup of milk to wash it down. Their rice is gluggy, and their chapattis slimy with too much grease. A Maasai woman who can cook is held in high esteem by men and children, who appreciate good cooking when they find it.

Some families in Maasailand are beginning to plant small vegetable gardens, mainly for maize, pumpkin and beans. Traditionally the Maasai have a religious aversion to agriculture. They consider the agricultural tribes such as the Kikuyu and Kamba to be the 'despised diggers of the earth'. One Maasai myth tells the story of Leeyio[1], who had two sons. When he lay dying, he called his sons to him and asked them what he could bequeath to them. The first-born son said he wanted a bit of everything. So that is what he got: a few goats, a cow, a piece of land to farm. The second son wanted only a memento of his father, and asked for his fly whisk. Leeyio was touched by his son's simple request and in return promised to give him wealth and make him great among all people. The firstborn son became the father of the agricultural tribes, sentenced to eke out their days scratching a living from the dirt. The second son became the father of the pastoral Maasai.

With much of their traditional grazing land gone, the Maasai these days rely more and more upon what they term 'Kikuyu food', such as maize, beans and potatoes. They buy food from the *dukas* when they have money, and now some families are also beginning to grow it for themselves. This work is usually handled by the women and so it has brought with it a new set of problems. Time spent growing crops or supervising the labourers who do the work is time diverted from caring for small stock and children. It leaves less time for chores such as collecting firewood and water. Children are often called on to guard the *shambas* (a plot or garden of food crops) from monkeys.

Collective gardens are unknown, for the Maasai prefer to raise cattle and therefore farm *shambas* as autonomous family units. A successful *shamba* with access to water can be a valuable source of food in the precarious dry season, but it does come at a cost to women, wildlife and water supplies. The cost will ultimately be borne by the entire pastoral Maasai and their environment.

Narygunkishon had a large garden where she grew maize, beans, potatoes, tomatoes and pumpkin, which she shared with me. Another part of the Maasai diet is *oloshoro*, a thin porridge made with maize meal, fat and milk. Fresh and soured milk is enjoyed by everyone, but especially the *moran*. Meat is eaten very rarely by families. The Maasai cannot bear to slaughter one of their animals unless it is for a good reason, such as a ceremony or if someone is sick and needs to drink soup. In this instance, a goat or sheep will be slaughtered, and a special soup made with the offal and medicinal herbs from the forest. The meat will be shared around the *enkang*.

Cows and bullocks are only ever slaughtered for ceremonial purposes. This is one of the reasons why commercial beef ranching does not work with the Maasai. They cannot bear to part with their animals, and would rather have a large herd of thin cows than a smaller herd of well-fed, high milk-yielding cows. Centuries of experience of the capriciousness of nature have taught them to keep a high number of cattle. In times of drought, half may die but they are still left with the nucleus of a breeding herd.

Another reason the Maasai keep excess cattle relates to community attitudes towards money. The Maasai say 'cattle are our bank'. If a Maasai man has cash, even if it is in a bank account, he will not be able to keep it very long. Soon he will be obliged to help one relative or another with medical treatment, food, school fees or ceremony expenses. It is much safer to keep money 'on the hoof'. Lastly, personal prestige is closely linked with a man's success as a pastoralist. The number of cattle a man has will determine his status and influence in Maasai society, and will have direct bearing on the position of his children – especially *moran*.

An American tourist who had come to see my house one day with a safari group exclaimed with considerable overstatement, 'But you have no bathroom!' She was right. I had no bathroom. In Maasailand, the bush serves as the toilet. Everyone goes outside the *enkang* to the bush beyond – the men going further than the women. Dogs and hyenas clean up the evidence. Soft *oleleshwa* leaves make for good toilet paper. Many Maasai are initially horrified when they discover that westerners put a toilet inside their house. The Maasai system works well in their environment, and I personally prefer it to the stinking pit loos that are used in other rural areas.

Another aspect of life in a mud hut was learning how to behave with different members of the tribe. Greetings at first seemed very complex. Women and children are expected to greet older men with a bowed head. The rule of thumb is that if the man is old enough to be your father, then you initiate the greeting with a bowed head. The elder then places his hand gently on your head and greets you with words such as '*Enkerai ai*' (my child) or '*Pasanai, supa*' (my dear). This is a beautiful gesture, bestowing protection and blessing on the younger person and showing respect to the elder.

If you meet a particularly sweet old man, he may even gently spit on your head, hands or feet. This is a special blessing, and I learned quickly to overcome my initial horror. Younger men may be greeted with a handshake. The Maasai do not traditionally grip hands, but just touch palms lightly. Small children greet their elders, male and female, with a bowed head. The Maasai also kiss when greeting, but strictly between women and women, women and children, and brothers and sisters. The latter is a delicate kiss on the cheek, the brother bending his head a little and the sister reaching to greet the brother.

Like many other parts of Africa, it is not at all unusual to see men walking together hand in hand. Close friends will greet each other with delight, and then, unwilling to lose the touch of each other's hand, walk off hand in hand as they 'eat the news'. Such public displays of affection are rarely demonstrated between boyfriends and girlfriends and never between husbands and wives. This is not to say that the Maasai are not affectionate; it is just that they show it in different ways. They are not romantic in a western sense, but are very loving with their children, extended family and friends.

Once the initial greeting is over, then commences the long process of inquiring as to your health, that of your family, your cattle and goats. Then it is repeated from the other person's perspective. Only when this is settled does any other conversation commence, if indeed there is any. To rush straight to the point is considered impolite. I loved to listen to this gentle rhythm of question and answer. Each reply or statement (I am well, my children are well, my cattle are well, etc.) is greeted by a response of 'Oh' or 'Eh' from the listener. In the musical language of the Maasai, it sounds very beautiful. It is also easy to fudge a conversation just by adding in an 'Oh' or 'Eh' at the right place. Direct eye contact is not necessary; often two people will talk to each other but look at the ground, or down at their hands.

An important event occurred around this time. It happened very gradually, so I cannot pinpoint exactly when or how. All I know is that three-year-old Mesianto (who has the family nickname of Ndoondo – pronounced Don-doe) officially became part of my family. We had formed a special friendship during my last visit. When the older children tired of my novelty value, Mesianto stuck around. When I moved into my new house, Ndoondo moved right on in with me. Daniel recognised what was going on one day when he said, 'You and this baby love each other, so this must be your child'. This was fine by me, because she had already charmed me completely: it was fine by Robert who declared, 'I am happy because I love this baby'; and it was fine by Ndoondo, who enjoyed all the extra attention from her *mzungu* mother.

Her real mother, Narygunkishon, also encouraged the relationship. She comes from a progressive family who were able to educate some of their children. Her sister is a school teacher and one brother is a district commissioner, so Narygunkishon has an appreciation of how useful education can be. She often comments to me that Ndoondo is an exceptionally bright and clever child. Daniel and Narygunkishon could never hope to send all their six children to school. Their oldest boy, who is a keen pupil, will be lucky if his father agrees to sell enough cattle to send him to high school. So on one hand, Narygunkishon sees this as an opportunity for one of her children to get an education. On the other hand, she is also typically Maasai – generous and loving with children and willing to share them around her extended family.

The Maasai measure wealth in terms of both cattle and children, but if they could only choose one form of wealth, they would choose children. It is considered a tragedy for a couple to remain childless, and here was I, a grown woman and without a child. I would never admit that my childless state had been carefully preserved by modern contraceptive means, for this would be incomprehensible to many Maasai women. A childless couple will often be given a child by another member of their immediate family who has many. The child learns very early that he or she has two sets of parents, but within the closeknit Maasai community, this seems to be naturally accepted by all concerned. Ilampala and his wife Nosotua have been given two children in this way. When only a few days old, a friend of mine was given to a childless relative of her 'real' mother. Her adoptive mother even produced milk and breastfed her new baby. Children are also fostered out to wealthier relatives so that they may benefit from plenty of food and other opportunities their own parents may not be able to offer them. As a mother, I could now be addressed by the polite term *Ngoto* Ndoondo which means mother of Ndoondo and my Maasai family took great delight in acknowledging me thus.

Of the dozen children who lived in our *enkang*, three went to school. Leseamon, a nine-year-old boy, and Sitaiyo, an eight-year-old girl, were two of Daniel and Narygunkishon's six children. The other schoolboy was Momposhe. He was one of eight children who belonged to a beautiful woman named Nolmemeri. These three in particular helped to keep me company and teach me their language. They would gather in my house at night, sing songs and then test my knowledge by pointing to things or body parts until I named them correctly. Thus I learnt that *enkutuk* meant mouth and *lorika* meant chair and so on.

When I first met them, these three children were all attending the local government primary school, a walk of around two kilometres from our *enkang*. Like everywhere else in the world, some schools are better than others and, like most schools in Maasailand, Entasekera Primary suffered from lack of resources. Lack of education is a vicious cycle; to be a teacher, you obviously must be educated to a tertiary level.

Very few Maasai can reach this level of education; therefore most teachers who come to work in Maasailand are non-Maasai. Most would consider a position in a Maasai school to be a hardship posting. And for non-Maasai, in many ways it is. The teachers have huge classes of sometimes more than forty pupils and virtually no resources, drastically inadequate housing, non-existent social lives, no public transport to connect them with their families easily or to bring them back on time after long holidays. Most would be used to supermarkets, piped water and electricity – none of these is available in this part of Maasailand. So they become demoralised and lack commitment, they arrive late from holidays and take too many sick days. Many bribe the education authorities not to send them here in the first place, and some leave for holidays, never to be seen the next term.

There has never been a full complement of teachers at Entasekera Primary School while I've been living there. The headmaster is dedicated but has only two Maasai teachers. The answer is to have more Maasai teachers. Not only would the children have teachers, but they would (hopefully) benefit from a more understanding and positive reinforcement of their own cultural values.

I'll never forget the day Leseamon announced to me that he didn't want to be a *morani* because they were dirty and smelt. I asked him who had told him that *moran* were dirty. My teacher, he replied. His teacher no doubt thought he was doing the right thing in dragging these 'primitives' into the twentieth century. I would like to think (though I couldn't be sure) that a Maasai teacher would encourage his or her students to be proud of their Maasai heritage, while making them aware of other options now available to those

who have the desire and resources to pursue their education seriously. Maasai history should be taught in all its glory to Maasai children, not all of whom will get it at home. Only in this way will
Maasai youth be empowered to be free and equal citizens of
modern Kenya.

The curriculum at present is geared to children from non-
pastoral backgrounds. It aims to enable young people to go on to
high school and then enter the modern economy. This may not be a
realistic or desirable goal for many Maasai children and their families. If the curriculum could be flexible enough to include subjects
relevant to these children, it would have greater relevance to, and a
more positive impact on, the majority of young Maasai.

In our *enkang*, there were another nine children. Some of these,
like Ndoondo, were too young to attend school. Others were needed
at home to help their mothers with the younger children and other
livestock chores. Maasai children have a lot of freedom to play.
There are games like jacks, trees to climb, baby animals to cuddle,
clucking grandmothers to run to and always toddlers to mother.
There are also certain chores expected of them. Chasing baby goats
around at dusk soon develops into an ability to herd and handle
young animals. Boys and girls both learn how to milk goats and
cows and will help their mothers with this task. By the time they are
eight years old, most children are capable of taking the goats out to
graze during the day. In our *enkang*, twelve-year-old Nataiya takes a
mixed herd of more than sixty cows to graze and water every day.
This is no mean feat, as the cattle have to cover quite a distance
to feed well, they are susceptible to attacks from predators, and
bulls often fight one another. Mothers rely on their older children to
help with the younger ones, and all little girls become quite broody
about their siblings. Children are also used as part of the intra-
village courier system. Women are often tied to their fire cooking or
occupied with babies, so children carry messages and return
borrowed items between the houses. In our *enkang*, I have the best
vegetable knife and Narygunkishon has the sole cast iron skillet
used to fry bread. These items in particular are constantly passed
back and forth, with children doing all the leg work.

I began to develop relationships with other members of Robert's
family. Narygunkishon was especially helpful, not the least because

she knew English. Robert's father was almost entirely bedridden by this time. Every day I would visit him in his dark house, where his third wife, Kokoo, cared for him. Papa would usually be sitting up, and the light from the fire would be reflected in his eyes. To greet him, I would lean over the bed and he would place his hand on my head, *'Oh, enkerai ai, supa'*. Unless Robert or one of his brothers was present, we couldn't talk about very much apart from exchanging pleasantries. One day Papa asked if I had bought him some buffalo. I had no idea what an old man would want with a buffalo, and I told him that I didn't have any. Later that day I repeated this to Robert, who cracked up with laughter. Apparently his father had been asking me for *bofflo*, a common name for white bread which is his favourite food.

My visit lasted only two weeks this time, as I wanted to return to Nairobi to apply for a work permit, my key to remaining in Kenya. Before I left, Papa conducted a small ceremony for me in his house. Present were Kokoo and another three ancient men. Daniel took me into his father's house, where a heated discussion was going on. They were deciding upon my new name. They chose Nentasekera. The Maasai often name their children after wealthy and successful people – apparently Nentasekera was a rich woman who had lived in this place generations ago. Entasekera was also named after her. Imbued in the name was a wish that I would return to this place and become part of it. The old people then started to pray, one man leading and the rest repeating the name of God after every phrase. For the next part of the ceremony, Daniel passed a handful of green grass to Papa who then called me to him. He stuffed a handful of grass into the side of my shoes and then gently spat on each foot. Daniel explained that this was a powerful blessing to ensure a safe journey and a sure return. Grass is a potent symbol of peace and prosperity for the Maasai. It is often used during blessings, as part of ceremonies and as a peace sign between fighting warriors. Finally, Papa gave me one of his cows.
I returned to Nairobi and began the long process of applying for a work permit. There is high unemployment in Kenya and high under-employment among tertiary graduates. Kenya is not predisposed to letting in foreigners without a good reason, so I knew this was not going to be easy. There are many categories of work permits,

some for church workers, some for aid workers, some for individuals under contract to a particular Kenyan company and so on.

The one I was after was known as an 'H' permit, for individuals who wished to start their own business. My qualifications and experience were all in the entertainment industry. Even though my heart was no longer in it, it seemed that entertainment was my best bet for a work permit. Once I actually had the permit, I could always try to branch out into other areas, such as conservation or development where my real interests lay. A fledgling entertainment industry had grown up in Nairobi. Down south there were a number of successful playwrights and theatre companies based in Johannesburg, such as the Market Theatre. With the imminent reintroduction of South African Airways' Australian service, I thought there might be a chance to get a touring circuit going between Johannesburg, Nairobi and Australia where good African theatre and dance was in demand by the major arts festivals.

I was also confident that, once I had a work permit, I could scratch up freelance work as a publicist, production assistant for films and commercials, and artists' management. My permit application stated the case for allowing me to work in Kenya as a freelance arts consultant and outlined some of my ideas for projects, including the touring circuit. I also did the rounds of advertising agencies and production houses, who all said that some work was available but not unless I had a work permit. Some individuals and organisations even kindly wrote letters of support for my application.

Sally Perry, an Australian woman who ran her own design house, let me use her typewriter and make calls from her office. This was a lot easier than the Nairobi phone boxes which were much in demand. For every horror story I heard about a work permit being denied, there was another about miraculous success. The success stories kept me going. What I needed, every ex-pat assured me, was tenacity, persistence and patience. Well, I certainly had the first two. Besides, they said, just tell them that you are going to marry a Kenyan, you'll get it!

After the application was complete, including letters from Robert and his family, only one detail remained – money. In addition to paying a hefty fee, to qualify for an 'H' permit you needed to show you had a big, fat bank account. If you are seeking to establish a business in Kenya, this is a fair stipulation. However, I didn't have a cent in my account – just a big, fat debt. I hoped to show that, as a freelance consultant, I didn't require the same amount of capital as a more conventional business. Arts management is about information and organisation; the necessary equipment was my phone book and brain. I could work out of a cupboard as long as I had a phone, fax and computer. But some investment capital would obviously be to my benefit.

To my rescue came my ex-employers, two Melbourne entrepreneurs I had worked for prior to the Melody Lords. They deposited five thousand dollars in my bank account and sent me a bank statement as evidence of my 'instant' wealth. Once I had submitted my application, I would send them a cheque for the same amount so they could retrieve the 'loan'.

Armed with the correct forms, support documents and bank statement I went for my first interview at Nyayo House. I was prepared to be charming, patient, respectful and firm. I had also decided that I didn't want to pay a bribe. Bribery is part of daily life in Kenya. If you want anything official, you must be prepared to pay a little extra for it. Salaries are low, and everyone from policemen to postmasters earn their little bit of 'chai'. However, bribery is also a bit of an art. It doesn't do to be too up front about it. Better to wait for some hint about 'times being tough' before offering to 'help a little'. It was an art I was no good at. I had heard stories about *wazungus* who had offered a little something and then been officially accused of bribery, or blackmailed for more with the threat of it. Apart from not being sure how to handle the actual niceties of bribing a public official, I also had an aversion to it and felt it was one of the most damaging aspects of Kenyan bureaucracy.

After waiting a while in a shabby, depressing reception area, I went to meet my allotted public servant. His equally depressing office was bare except for his desk, telephone and small mountains of files on the floor. He gave my application a cursory glance and asked me to outline why I needed a work permit. He found my relationship with a Maasai most amusing. Why not marry a Kikuyu? he wanted to know. His shiny nameplate sitting squarely on his desk plainly marked him as a member of Kenya's most powerful tribe.

Why do you need to earn money, he went on, you can just be a housewife and look after your husband, he will give you everything. My tenacity and patience was no match for his patronising attitude. He released me after twenty minutes and told me to come back in three weeks.

Robert had long had an ambition to earn his driving licence. Like young men the world over he dreamed of his own car. Our plan was for him to meet me in Nairobi and stay for six weeks in order to complete a course at a driving school, which he was prepared to sell two cows to pay for. I had been staying with Kenyan friends, but it is another matter entirely when your hulking great Maasai boyfriend arrives. Not only because of the room, but also because a lot of urban Kenyans do not understand the Maasai. They envisage a smelly warrior with red ochre and scant clothes pogo-ing around their loungeroom. Staying in a hotel for six weeks was out of the question financially, so I cast around for alternative accommodation.

My friends Susan and Martin told me that a room had become available in their compound. They made all the arrangements for us to move in. Their compound was in Dandora, a Nairobi 'estate' about forty minutes' bus ride from the city. On one side it dips down into the Mathare Valley, site of the city's worst slums. Despite the burning piles of garbage on the streets and the numerous goats and chickens, Dandora just escapes slum status by virtue of the water system and unreliable sewerage pipes that service it. Dandora has many nicknames including Beirut, Kuwait or more kindly just 'D'. Phase Four, where I was staying, was the worst.

I moved in before Robert arrived to set everything up. Martin's family and my friend Richard Nzomo had loaned me a bed and essential furniture. (Richard is an energetic young jewellery dealer whom I had met earlier in Nairobi. He let me use his post office box, bought me lunch occasionally and helped me out when I was in need.)

I lived in a typical compound, divided into twelve cement rooms known as 'cubes'. Access to the compound was through a heavy metal door which was bolted at night. Four of the twelve cubes were assigned to a man who operated a posho mill out of one of them (a posho mill grinds dried corn into maize meal). He didn't use the other three cubes, but the noise of the posho mill rendered them unlivable for anyone except the rats who survived on the maize chaff. The families who lived in the other eight cubes shared two cold water taps, a cold shower and a flushing loo. There was no ceiling, just a corrugated tin roof that made the rooms terribly hot. There was electricity. A naked bulb socket hung from the centre of each cube. It was simple enough to attach a series of wires and adaptors from this and run other appliances. Most families had a lamp and a cassette radio player. Everyone had to turn their music up loud to hear it over their next door neighbour's. But as most people seemed to favour Dolly Parton and Kenny Rogers tapes, it didn't make much difference. I had expected to learn many things in Dandora, but the entire words to 'Coward of the County' was not one of them.

I was the only white person, not only in our compound, but in the whole of Dandora. The women in our compound were initially reserved, but they became friendly when they saw that I did the same housework as they did and was not 'proud', as they put it. I hardly ever saw their husbands as they left very early in the morning for work, often before dawn. The children were interested in me, except for one little boy who screamed every time he saw me. He adored Robert and finally reached a compromise whereby he would come into our cube to climb over him, all the time covering his eyes with his hands so that he didn't have to see me. I must have looked like a real monster to him.

Outside our compound the garbage festered; the drains were permanently blocked and a strong smell of urine wafted from our shared loo. Nobody had much money. But Dandora, for all its faults, was not a depressing place to live. For one, the friendship and help from Susan and Martin sustained us. Martin's mother and siblings lived in their very own compound at the end of our street and we would often visit them to watch television. Everybody's favourite show was 'Music Time' which was broadcast on a Sunday night on the Kenya Broadcasting Service. This was the 'Countdown' of Kenya. An eclectic mix of Kanda Bongo Man, Yvonne Chaka Chaka, Janet Jackson and Dolly Parton.

The average cube housed a parent or parents, an average of three children, furniture, clothes, a kerosene ring for cooking, and a housegirl. The bed was usually curtained off along one side of the room and into the remaining space a sofa set, folding cot, coffee table, cooking utensils and knicknacks were strategically placed. The housegirls slept on the sofa or a mattress on the floor. Rent was around 600 shillings per month or around $7.50 per week. When you consider that many Kenyans make less than 2000 shillings per month (around $100), Dandora is more expensive than you might think.

Robert arrived in Nairobi and was amazed as we made the forty-minute bus journey to Dandora. 'Where did you find such a place?' he asked. Coming from the immense beauty and open space of the Loita Hills, Dandora's overcrowded squalor really shocked him. It is ironic that urban Kenyans are proud of their so-called progress and consider the Maasai to be the backward ones. Give me the open, unspoilt beauty of the hills any day.

Robert adjusted very quickly to urban living and started at the disturbingly named Glory Driving School. He was the first Maasai to have studied there. He was also the first Maasai that many of our fellow Dandora dwellers had met. They were soon impressed by his quiet, polite manner and some of the women confided to me that 'If he didn't have his ear stretched, you would never even know he was a Maasai!' Exactly what they expected a Maasai to do I wasn't sure.

I went into town each day to continue meeting and greeting potential employers. Sometimes to read in the MacMillan Library which is a large public library. Downstairs is pretty boring, but upstairs is a huge room with polished wooden floors scattered with lion-skin rugs. A huge oak table sits in the centre of the room. The shelves contain an excellent selection of Africana books, including first editions of explorers' accounts. It was here that I loved to read. Of course I pored over everything and anything about the Maasai.

In the evenings, Susan and I cooked together, usually rice with stew, or sometimes we roasted goat meat on our doorstep on the coal jiko cooker. Susan was a very good cook, and a very fierce one if necessary. The day I moved in, she prepared a special welcome feast of chicken stew with chapattis and rice. She had bought the chicken from her mother-in-law, Mathey, down the road and had slaughtered it herself. It was delicious, and I'm glad that she told me the story of the slaughter after I had eaten and not before.

Apparently it had been a very energetic chicken, and even after having its legs tied together, continued to flap and bounce around, evading Susan's axe. Her solution was to break its back by stepping on it, before she delivered the *coup de grâce* and chopped off its head. The macabre vision of Susan, in her high heels, wielding an axe and nonchalantly breaking a chicken's back will stay with me forever.

While I was in Nairobi at this time, I contacted a friend of a friend named Mary. We had dinner and the following week we saw a movie together. Mary, who was British, worked in Nairobi for the International Conservation Union (IUCN). She was whippet thin, very stylish and had what I wanted very badly – a work permit and a fulfilling job working for sustainable development in East Africa. She was proof positive that it was achievable. While Robert and I were living in Dandora, Mary went back to the UK for a three-week holiday and asked if I would like to mind her house situated in an enormous garden in Karen. Would I? I jumped at the opportunity.

Karen and neighbouring Langata are two suburbs about 20 minutes drive from the city. Together they make up one of the green, leafy enclaves of Kenya's most bizarre tribe: the whites. There are about 40 000 whites (*wazungu* in Swahili) living in Kenya today. The majority live a most amazing existence made possible by a small army of household staff. Mary's house came complete with a live-in gardener and a cleaning woman who also did all the laundry by hand. While there was no live-in cook, there was of course a night guard or *askari* whose function was to sit on the verandah all night to protect home and inhabitants. In a city where the gulf between the few who have plenty and the majority with very little is enormous, the security firms benefit most of all.

It is by no means the exclusive domain of whites to employ household staff. It is usual for Kenyan families to employ a 'housegirl'. All women work in Kenya. Those in Nairobi have to travel hours from the outlying residential estates into the city via a skeletal public transport system that shudders along appalling roads. From seven to nine in the morning and from four to seven in the evening are known as the 'crush hour'. City workers beat the rush by leaving home at 6 am and cooling their heels until office hours start at nine. Housegirls fill an essential role by caring for other people's children, working impossibly long hours for meagre wages. Many housegirls sleep on the floor in a one-room cubicle they share with the entire family and all their possessions. The saying goes that a good housegirl is hard to find. I might also add that so is a good employer. I have heard some shocking stories about the exploitation of these girls.

Mary's house was a picturesque stone cottage, set in a rather formal but beautiful garden tucked away behind a hedge about two metres high. Magenta bougainvillea and scented jasmine climbed the walls. Mature rose bushes, strelitzias and other exotic flowers bloomed. Robert only had eyes for the view; Mary's house looked straight onto the Ngong Hills. For Robert, this was almost as good as being back in the Loitas. The Ngong Hills have long occupied a special place in Maasai cosmology and history. The Maasai say that the distinctive appearance of the hills was caused by the imprint left by the knuckles of a giant. Kidongoi, the first oloiboni was discovered in the Ngong Hills. Robert's own father was born there at the turn of the century when Ngong, Karen, Langata and surrounds were still part of Maasailand. The Maasai name for the Ngong Hills is *Oloolaiser*, which means Mountain of the Laiser clan. I was glad to be out of Dandora for a while, but it was Robert who really needed this respite from the city life, and there was nowhere better than the birthplace of his father and the Nkidongi clan.

For the next three weeks we had a real holiday together. During the day, while Robert was at driving school, I read in the garden, listened to music, and cooked in Mary's excellent kitchen. In the evening, after dinner, we would watch one of the videos that I had borrowed. We watched everything from *Star Wars* to *Out of Africa*. The ones that had the greatest impact on Robert were those that had black actors and dealt with black issues, such as the civil war story *Glory* and *Cry Freedom*, about Steven Biko and apartheid. Robert was horrified at apartheid, which he had never heard of before. There is a scene of the Soweto massacre in the movie, where schoolchildren are gunned down by white South African police. Robert watched it and turned to ask me a question I could not answer, 'Why did they shoot the children?'

I felt almost guilty because I had shown him many evils that he did not know existed before. Another video which made a big impression on Robert was the mini-series *Roots*. He also had not known about the African slave trade. Upon watching it through twice, he declared that his first son would be named Kunte Kinte in honour of the West African who was abducted and forced into a life of slavery, because 'he was a brave warrior'. Watching these videos with Robert was like seeing them clearly for the first time. His discovery was also mine.

The gardener, Richard, did not take too kindly to a Maasai living in his mistress' house. Mary had broken the news to him gently, that her friend Catherine would be staying there with her boyfriend. Who was African. 'You mean a black African?' Richard exclaimed. Yes, I mean a black African. He is a Maasai. Richard was doubly horrified.

We were very sad to leave Mary's house. We had been truly spoilt by the experience, and especially the view of the Ngong Hills. But the ex-pat ghetto was not for me, so it was back to Dandora and back to Nyayo House. I received a letter notifying me that my application for a work permit had been refused. I knew I had the right to appeal twice, so I returned to see the public servant, this time with Robert. The public servant was amused to meet Robert in the flesh and asked many polite questions about cattle. He pointed out that my five thousand dollar bank statement was not enough, and that if I had more like fifty thousand dollars, then my work permit would be issued. Flying to the moon would have been easier. He accepted my appeal and warned that it would take time.

Meanwhile Robert had undertaken, and failed, his first driving test. The theoretical exam was no problem. Because of the poor literacy rate, the road rules are taught using a large board marked out as a town with toy cars. The test is administered using the same board. When it came time for the practical test, Robert was well prepared with a reasonable bribe. The Maasai do not practise bribery among themselves, but everyone had told us that you will never pass your test unless you pay a bribe, so when in Rome … The instructor got into the car next to Robert, who promptly handed over the 'lunch money'. Halfway through the test, the examiner got out and a second one got in. Robert had used all his money on the first one and so he failed the exam. The second time he sat for the exam, he was far more savvy. He kept his money in his pocket until the very end, ensuring that the one examiner stayed with him, then handed over the 'lunch money' and passed with flying colours.

In Kenya, you live and die with pieces of official paper. Robert was delighted with his new one, but my own piece of paper, my work permit, seemed further away than ever. I had applied for two jobs, one in the communications department with the International Conservation Union and one as press officer with the World Wide Fund for Nature. I didn't even score an interview with either. I had been around to several aid agencies, and applied for a position as an LES (locally engaged staff) with the Australian High Commission. There was no interest there. My hopes of permanently settling in Kenya were slipping through my fingers. Meanwhile, I kept hearing of other foreigners who waltzed in, loved the climate and found jobs straight away. Despondency and doubt set in. It was time to head for the hills, so back to Maasailand I went.

Robert and I faced another perilous *matatu* journey back to the Loita Hills. I filled my pack with plenty of flour and rice as I planned to stay for around six weeks. This was the longest I had ever stayed in Maasailand in one stretch. It would be a real test.

After settling back into my little house, I was reminded of the problems very quickly. First of all, my back ached constantly from the strain of bending and carrying water. In Australia, you mostly clean when standing up and work at waist height; here everything was on the floor and required constant bending. I needed to prove to myself that I was as capable as a Maasai woman at all this work, which of course I was not. I threw myself into carrying water, scrubbing pots, cooking, sweeping the floor and washing children and clothes. Except for chopping firewood, I did all my own work.

Ndoondo was with me all the time, helping me with the language and trying to help with my work. She was only three and a half years old and desperately wanted to do all the work she saw her older sisters do. One day I left her unattended for a few minutes in the house to put some hand-washing on my clothesline. It was a big mistake. When I returned, I saw Ndoondo had decided to wash her clothes too, managing to tip over my two buckets of precious water in the process. I could have cried. Filling buckets and carrying water is such backbreaking work. I had already made an extra journey in order to have enough water to bathe with. Now I faced yet another trip down to the creek and up again carrying two full jerrycans!

However, Ndoondo was a source of joy in my life. I was discovering how precious a relationship with a child could be. I flatter myself when I say Ndoondo reminded me of myself when I was small, but in some ways she did. After the episode with the water, she got three hard smacks on her bum with my hand. She was shocked, but stubbornly refused to cry. Instead she stayed just outside the doorway, refusing my entreaties for a cuddle, her silent protest a terrible reproach to me. I always refused to cry too when I was smacked by my mother – which I should point out was not very often. My mother tells me that one time, after she had smacked me, I turned dry-eyed and inquired, 'Did you enjoy that?' It has long remained a point of pride with me that she broke a wooden spoon on my bum without a tear from me.

Ndoondo enjoyed the attention of being an 'only child'. It is always a bit tough on the second youngest child in a Maasai family. For the first two years or so, they enjoy the closest possible relationship with their mother. They are fed in her arms, carried on her back and sleep by her side every night. Such a richly stimulating relationship is evident in the brilliant smiles and bright minds of all the Maasai toddlers I met. Ndoondo must have initially felt a sharp sense of loss when her baby brother, Melubo, appeared on the scene. But as a walking, talking baby doll, she would have been immediately smothered with 'mother love' from all her sisters and cousins. A Maasai family is a loving place to be, and no one feels lost or alone for long. But obviously she wanted some extra attention, which is why she gravitated towards me.

Her relationship with Robert was a delight to watch. All the children called Robert 'Papatee', which means 'my little father', Clinging to Robert's knees, both their brown faces shining in the firelight, Ndoondo would tell him all the stories she could not tell me. When Maasai children grow older, around five years of age, they start to learn respect for their elders, and spontaneous displays of affection are replaced by formal greetings. Little girls then stay with their mothers, and little boys with their fathers as their education into the ways of their clan begin.

My problems with a sore back paled into insignificance compared with my longing for food, real food, any food but rice and chapattis. What a fool I was to think that I could survive quite happily on boiled rice and the occasional chapatti. I know millions do, but after a few weeks of the same diet, I found that some days I could not face another bowl of rice. On these days, I would just sip water and spend most of the day resting, weak from lack of food. I would then be really hungry the next day and be able to eat again. Except for some beans, and meat only twice, I ate very little protein during those six weeks. My main diet was rice, and sometimes potatoes fried in fat, plus one cup of milk tea every day. In the last two weeks of my six-week stay, I spent a lot of time resting and dreaming of food. Most of all I wanted a processed cheddar cheese sandwich made with fresh white bread and butter, cut into little squares – not triangles. When I was small, we used to patronise a particular cake shop in an arcade in the Sydney suburb of Epping. On the window was the frosted silhouette of a baker in a fluffy white hat carrying a tray of freshly baked cakes. It occupied a corner position opposite the Italian greengrocer, and displayed spotless glass shelves full of good old-fashioned Aussie cakes. Most of all, I loved the jam tarts. They made small ones in four flavours and large ones with pastry latticed across the top that sat on crisp white paper doilies. At certain moments, lying in my mud hut, I would have gladly given a year of my life for one of those large raspberry jam tarts, preferably with runny cream. One of my life's ambitions is to return to that cake shop and spend a small fortune.

Lack of privacy could be added to the list of daily irritants. Each day there would be a steady stream of visitors to my house. I would be lucky to have an uninterrupted twenty minutes. It would start with the men coming to drink tea and talk to Robert first thing in the morning. It then continued throughout the day with people who wanted to greet me, who needed minor medical attention, who wanted a headache tablet, soap, water, cordial, sugar, tea leaves, cooking fat or who just simply wanted to have a stickybeak at my house. Then there were also the *Ilkishili moran*, men from Robert's age group. Custom demanded that I offer hospitality to them. This meant stirring up the embers and making them a cup of milk tea and enduring a stilted conversation in Maasai. I am prone to moodiness and have always found it hard to utter polite nothings. To be polite when I was tired and dirty was perhaps the hardest challenge of all. The Maasai themselves enjoy a certain amount of privacy. They do not live communally within the *enkangs*, though there is considerable co-operation between families. Women tend to perform their chores, such as washing and collecting firewood, individually or they may do them with a close friend. Cooking and eating are always performed within the privacy of each house.

Another persistent problem during this time was lack of money. There was food to buy in the *dukas*, such as potatoes and beans, but I couldn't afford it. I had used all my own money paying for Robert's driving school and bribes. He was planning to sell two of his cows to repay me. The selling of cattle, even if they are your own, is a very complex matter in Maasailand, especially if you are the youngest son in the family. For one reason or another, through no fault of his own, the sale never eventuated and I was left with less than $13 to last six weeks.

Attitudes to money are so different between cultures. Traditionally, the Maasai never used money, but traded their valuable milk and livestock for commodities they needed such as cooking pots, knives, cloth or vegetables. Now with some families earning money through the occasional spot of safari work, and others finding work outside of Maasailand as *askaris* and National Park staff, a sort of monied middle class has emerged. Only some people have access to cash, and everyone needs it. The Maasai's traditional diet has changed. The last frontier against twentieth century consumerism has been passed, and now the Maasai must buy maize meal from the *dukas*. The government and aid agencies tell them to grow crops, so they must buy seeds, tools and inputs, but, because they are pastoralists and do not know this work, they must also hire labourers to till the soil. Only wealthy families can afford to do this. Poor families must scrape by, sustained by the crumbs of the collective wealth of their extended family.

Children are encouraged to go to school, which means fees, uniforms, books and pens. The women are told to keep their children clean, therefore they need to buy soap and the ubiquitous Omo washing powder. Cattle must be dipped, so all Maasai men desire dip, salt and antibiotics for their cattle. Everyone wants torches, therefore batteries, as well as headache tablets and Coca Cola. (I have often wished that we could harness the distribution powers of Omo and Coke to inform Kenyans about AIDS prevention, for it seems that even in the furthest corners of this country, these two products are to be found.)

Saddest of all to me, is seeing how power and wealth has fallen into the hands of only a few educated Maasai, often connected by clan. Instead of using their positions to benefit all Maasai, they tend to concentrate on fulfilling their own political ambitions and furthering the position of their clan to the exclusion of others. I look forward to the day when a greater number of young Maasai start to work in the professions and become advocates for their people.

My personal lack of money was a real lesson for me. I could certainly exist without it, and I was in no danger of going hungry. But at times I craved the taste of potatoes or orange cordial, which were sold at the *duka*. The safari operator, Tony Church, paid a visit to the Loitas. When I finally got up the courage to ask him to lend me 200 shillings (about $10), he refused. I guess he saw my request for a loan as just another person asking for money. I also perceived an air of disapproval of my relationship with Robert coming from him. Nonetheless, I was shocked that he declined to lend me such a small amount of money. Two days later, Robert got a job as a guide with an overnight safari. The group was from the National Museum and wished to see a local waterfall that is some distance inside the forest. He returned with money and two packets of spaghetti left over from the safari. I had a tin of tomatoes and one garlic. It was the best meal I had ever tasted in my life.

Every couple of days, I would set my aching back to the task of cooking chapattis. My friend Susan had shown me in Nairobi how to mix the dough, and then roll out each chapatti twice. I improvised in the bush with a plank of wood and an empty Coke bottle (what else!). Each flat circle of dough was then cooked slowly on a cast iron skillet over a slow fire using plenty of fat. These chapattis I then took to Robert's father. It wasn't *bofflo*, but he nevertheless enjoyed his fried bread.

I witnessed my first Maasai wedding around this time. I knew the groom, for he was Robert's best friend, Seketo ole Sumpati. He was always great fun to be with as he had an infectious sense of humour and an almost girlish giggle. He had been to school for eight years and his English was excellent, though he was shy about using it in front of many people. Once I got to know Seketo, I felt I had a friend for life. Like Robert, he was a *morani* of the highest integrity. I was delighted when he invited me, not only to attend his wedding day, but also to accompany the wedding party on the last stage of their journey to Morijo, where his *enkang* was.

The whole business of a Maasai wedding is totally different to that of a western wedding. It is really the groom's big day, and the bride features very little in the celebrations. All marriages in the Loitas are still arranged by the parents and relatives. Marriages may be made for reasons of friendship between families, or politics or economics – the same motivations that have inspired marriages for centuries the world over. The wedding day is not a happy one for the bride. She is leaving her family and friends to start life as the new bride on the block in a strange *enkang* which might be days' or weeks' walk from her family. She may have seen her husband from a distance during the 'bride price' negotiations, but she would almost certainly never have spoken to him.

Seketo's wedding day was held up by his mother-in-law. The mother of the bride must be present to officially give her daughter to the groom. However, Seketo's mother-in-law had run away with grief at the thought of losing her daughter. Seketo and his best man, Leyan, stayed there for two days hoping she would return. Eventually, the girl's aunt arrived and gave her niece away on behalf of her sister. All the while, back at Seketo's home *enkang*, the women were on standby to cook food, and the prepared home brew was slowly being drunk by the guests who assembled each day waiting for Seketo and his bride to arrive.

On the morning of the wedding, the bridal party arrived at my *enkang* where they stopped for tea. Seketo and Leyan were dressed in bright cloth with red ochre in their hair and carried fly whisks made from wildebeest tail – the exclusive accoutrements of elders. Leyan was wearing a black theatrical cloak with bright green lining, which gave the group a slightly bizarre edge. The bride was about fourteen years old. She was colourfully and elaborately dressed; orange, white and blue cloth was draped softly around her and topped off with a red patterned *kanga* worn as a cape over her shoulders. Around her neck hung the exquisite beaded wedding necklace, *entende*, the long strands of beads hanging to below her knees. Her arms were dripping with beaded bracelets, while her ankles and lower calves were coiled thickly with silver wire, known as *lipurukat*. Upon her head sat a tall, beaded crown. She looked very beautiful, very shy and very, very sad. When we set off, she walked slowly, taking tiny, dainty steps and kept her eyes downcast. She held a corner of her cape over her mouth.

The day was beautiful as we crossed the stream and walked up over the ridge that marked the boundary of Entasekera sublocation and dipped down into Kisokon sublocation. I tried to say 'Hi' to the girl, but she would not answer me. Seketo told me not to worry, explaining that all young brides were stupid and that they 'come to be good' after a while. I wanted to tell her not to worry because she had a good husband. Seketo was a good-looking young *morani* who was hard working, gentle and funny. She could have easily been married to an old man four times her age with a bad temper and foul breath. Or else a younger man who had fallen out with traditional life, squandered his parent's cows on blue jeans and a ghetto blaster, and turned to drink in disillusionment. She would have a happy and prosperous life with Seketo.

During the wedding walk, it is considered bad luck for the bride to look back towards her parents' home, or to stumble on her journey, so the pace is very slow. If any obstacles lie in her path, or there is a difficult stream to cross, then it is the duty of the best man to help the bride across. The only time the young girl laughed was when she heard me speak about Robert. Only she heard me call him by his real name, Oloimooja. She was amused to hear me break the Maasai taboo against speaking the real name of your husband. (Even though we were not married, everyone referred to me as Robert's wife.) The Maasai believe that your teeth will all fall out if you speak the true name of your spouse. Instead they say '*Olpayian lai*' (my husband), or '*Enkitok ai*' (my wife) rather than use their names. As Robert was only a school name, it was permissible for me to use it. However, I loved to use his real name, pronounced

Ol-lee-moj-jah. It was the name of a famous Oloiboni who lived in Tanzania, where the first Iloibonok settled, many generations ago.

Leyan carried a small tin suitcase, which contained all the worldly possessions of the bride. Upon her back, she carried a calabash of milk. At one point during our journey, Leyan told her to drink some milk and she made a show of refusing. According to custom, the bride must refuse to drink this milk unless the best man promises to give her a calf. Eventually Leyan made this promise and the girl knelt down to drink. She was very careful not to accidentally look behind her as she knelt and rose. When we were about five kilometres from Seketo's home, we began to pass neighbouring *enkangs*. Groups of women emerged from an *enkang* and ran towards us. I thought they were coming to greet the happy couple. Instead they hurled abuse at the young bride, pulling and pushing and calling her names. 'She has the head of a goat.' 'Look, she is pregnant!' 'What sort of bad girl have you brought us?' These are typical of the comments. An old woman snatched the walking stick I was holding and made as if to beat the girl with it. Only at this point did the best man intervene on the bride's behalf. This scene was repeated as we passed each *enkang*. Throughout the entire ordeal, the bride stood solemnly, looking at the ground still holding the corner of her cape over her mouth.

When we finally arrived at Seketo's *enkang*, I was relieved to see that the greeting was warmer. He and Leyan had gone on ahead; I had too, with a group of brightly dressed women attending the celebration. In the *enkang*, *moran* sang and danced. Old women sat in groups, sunning themselves, outside the cattle enclosure. When the bride arrived, Seketo's mother went to greet her and then led her into the house. Everyone craned to see the girl, what she was wearing, how pretty she was but no one abused her as I had feared they might. That was the last I saw of the bride that day. Her duty was to sit inside her new mother-in-law's house, while outside the *moran* danced, and the guests feasted on roast goat, chapattis, rice, soda and honey beer until the sun was low and the cows came home for milking.

There is no actual exchange of vows during a Maasai wedding. It is less of a betrothal between man and woman and more of a financial transaction between the groom and his in-laws. If there are any vows, then they are part of the complex discussions that precede any marriage arrangement, including the payment of the appropriate amounts of honey (for brewing beer) and livestock to the parents-in-law. The groom may take years to finally pay off his bride debt. The usual amount paid for a bride is around ten to fifteen cows, plus honey, blankets, *kangas* and *shukas*. As few as five cows and as many as twenty may be paid depending on the circumstances between the families. If there are long and honorable ties between them, including other marriages, then the price will be less. Romantic love as we know it in the West does not figure largely in Maasai culture. There are some songs and stories of romantic love so it is not entirely unknown. Papa's fourth wife ran away from her first husband because she loved Papa so much, but such an occurrence is very rare.

I once asked Nolmemeri if a wife and husband often grow to love each other. She replied that it is not so much a matter of love, but if the husband is good and provides for his family then the wife will respect him. Mutual respect is the basis of a good Maasai marriage. If the marriage is not a happy one, there is no divorce in Maasailand. The Maasai find it impossible to repay livestock. Small differences between a husband and wife are usually worked out within the extended family. Large disputes, such as accusations that the woman is being beaten or her children's basic needs are not being met, can be settled by a council of elders.

In the midst of all this, my relationship with Robert developed and we grew closer. At some point the idea of marriage came up. I don't have a romantic proposal story. I honestly cannot remember when Robert and I first talked about marriage, though he says he raised the subject first. In truth, I think it was his friends and family who raised the subject with their continual questions about when we would be married. In Australia, I would never have considered marriage. I would have just lived with a bloke. Marriage had never featured in my plans at all. But, like everything else, it was different here in Maasailand. Everyone got married. It seemed the most honourable way to formalise my commitment to Robert. At some point I think I realised that I was in too deep to get out now. I knew there would be problems to face, but I didn't want to give up

Robert. The issue of marriage just slipped into our daily conversation and our separate futures began to entwine.

Of course the main problem for me was the issue of a second wife. It took a good six months' discussion to help me get my head around this one. Robert's main concern was this: as the youngest son, he had the ultimate responsibility of caring for his aging mother. (The eldest must care for the father.) He also had more than sixty cows and one hundred goats that needed full-time care. He was often away on safari, or with me, and he could no longer impose on his brothers to look after his livestock. Did I want to do this work? No way in the world was I planning on spending the rest of my life looking after Robert's mother, goats and cows. No way. My very western response was to suggest we employed a woman to do all this. According to Robert, all Maasai women get married, so the only way to get someone on a permanent, full-time basis was to marry her.

Part of me found the idea of polygamy repellent. Part of me probably always will. But marriage is different in Maasailand. Robert wasn't asking if he could have a romantic relationship with another woman. He didn't want companionship, affection or friendship. He needed someone to help him fulfil his work and cultural obligations. I knew that I had no right to force Robert to abandon this aspect of his culture. His father had four wives and wished all his sons to be settled with at least two each. It was I who had entered Robert's world and I had a paramount responsibility not to destroy the natural balance of his life. I had chosen to stay, so therefore it was up to me to bend – hopefully without breaking. I agreed to Robert marrying one other wife, on the condition that he did the deed when I was in Australia. If I am painfully honest with myself, I must admit that I also saw this as my safety net. If, in two, five, ten or twenty years, I decided I no longer liked life in a mud hut, then it was going to be simpler for me to leave if I was not the sole wife.

Six weeks came to an end and it was coming time for me to return to Australia. The prepayments on my loan would run out in August. It was now July and I had to return and look for work. The appeal for my work permit had been refused. No wonderful jobs had magically appeared in Nairobi. If Kenya was trying to teach me patience and perseverance, then I was ready to listen. All these problems seemed far away in the Loita Hills. On my last day in Narotian, the sun was baking hot and a cool breeze blew softly. The normal activities of the *enkang* went on around me; Narygunkishon and one of her daughters had gone for firewood, while Sintiman watched over the maize crop for baboon raiders. Other women and children sat nearby in the hot sun, chatting or doing bead work. As usual, the men were all off talking. Ndoondo had been sticking close by me for the last few days. She knew I would be going tomorrow and wanted to come too. I sat in the sun feeling very content. Despite the difficulties, life was enormously stimulating among the Maasai. My life was enriched from living and learning with Robert and his family. Under their deeply humanising influence, I was starting to learn about patience, grace, compassion, respect and the true meaning of community. To step beyond materialism and taste life in its simplest, purest form with the Maasai was a gift I had been offered and accepted happily.

There were no safaris at this time to give me a lift to Nairobi or Narok. Instead Robert and I decided that we would walk to Morijo, where I was more likely to find a lift with one of the trucks that supply the *dukas* every few weeks. One of Robert's age group was getting married in two days in Morijo and Robert had been asked to help out at the wedding with the slaughtering and cooking of meat in the forest. It was hard for me to say goodbye to Ndoondo. She would be almost five years old by the time I returned and very grown up. Even harder was saying goodbye to Robert's father. I was only too aware that it might be for the last time.

We set off early the next morning for Morijo. When I say we, I don't mean Robert and me, but one of his friends and me. In this instance the very tall Marefu. Robert refuses to walk with me because I am so slow. He says I make him feel tired. So he cons a friend into walking with me and then meets us at the other end. Marefu valiantly shouldered my very heavy pack and set off with me in tow.

For the next few days I stayed with Marefu's mother and sister, Naserian. Robert's mother's *enkang* was less than a kilometre up the hill. I didn't stay there because her *enkang* was very old and dirty and the flies were atrocious. Naserian and her mother spoilt me in a Maasai kind of way. Naserian cooked me rice and potatoes every day – luxury food for the Maasai. They brought water for me to bathe in and made me sweet cocoa to drink. Despite all this excellent attention, I was miserable. I missed having my own space and privacy. It was difficult to go back to being a guest in someone else's house, living out of my backpack and not being able to participate in any sort of work. Worst of all, I was not able to spend any time alone with Robert. He would visit me in the morning and sit in the house at night for an hour or so. It was unseemly to spend more time with your wife, even if she was a *mzungu*. I was also painfully aware that I would soon be saying goodbye to Robert, and for a long time too. I knew I would need a good ten months to save up enough to return again, as well as continuing to pay off my loan. I had heard from friends that things were tough in Australia, and I didn't expect to find work as easily as before. Ten months was a long time to be away from someone you plan to marry. It was enough to make anyone cranky and miserable.

The *enkang* where the wedding was to be held was practically next door to Naserian's. On the day, I washed and dressed up in all my Maasai jewellery. I walked over with Naserian and her neighbour, Nasha. Nasha was a classificatory mother to all of Robert's age group. She was tall and regal looking with the cheekbones that the Maasai are famous for and almond shaped eyes. Whenever I visited, she insisted on cooking a meal for me and gave me a necklace or other piece of jewellery. She had also given me a black sheep during another visit, so I called her *Pakuo*. We arrived in time to see the bride arrive, dressed in all her finery, looking sad as usual. Everything was as it had been for Seketo's wedding. The *moran* singing, the women cooking inside the houses and the old men drinking honey beer outside. The bride disappeared inside her mother-in-law's house and the celebration continued.

Robert was busy in the forest, slaughtering goats and organising food for the men, but he remembered to send Marefu with a choice cut of roast meat for my lunch. We left the main group so I could eat my meat and chapatti in private. I preferred roast meat, while most Maasai women would rather fry theirs with fat. I was surprised to see two *wazungu* arrive at the wedding. When I saw them, I immediately ducked for cover. I had become very *wazungu*-shy, and avoided all contact with other whites when I could. I just couldn't stand all their stupid questions. What are you doing here? Oh, I'm just hanging around and planning to marry a Maasai warrior, you know. Never a good basis for meaningful conversation. Robert had seen them too and was soon talking to them about giving us a lift. They planned to leave the day after tomorrow and agreed to take us as far as Narok.

The day we were to leave, Robert and I arrived where the *wazungu* were camping. Actually, she was a white Kenyan and had no doubt seen stranger things in the bush than me, so I was spared the dumb questions. He was an English friend. They had both been to the Loitas before on an organised safari, but this time they were just wandering around Kenya in their own vehicle. They had stumbled back into the Loitas almost by chance and met up with an old acquaintance from their safari, a Maasai elder named Soly. Their Landrover was packed tightly with all their camping gear and they were willing to take just three passengers – Robert, me and Leyan, the best man from Seketo's wedding. Leyan was going to Nairobi to meet up with some of his cattle that were being driven to market across the Great Rift Valley. At the last minute, Soly declared that he was coming too. He had some 'business' to attend to in Ewaso Ngiro, a shanty town outside of Narok. This meant that Robert couldn't come with me in the car. Soly took precedence because he was their host; Leyan came next because he had asked first; I was included because I was white.

It was totally unfair and I felt angry and frustrated with the whole patriarchal system of the Maasai. Just because an elder wanted to feel important riding into town in a car, Robert could not go. That was the way things worked with the Maasai. The older men got preference in everything – women, cattle, grazing rights, political power. No recourse, no compromise. This was the last straw for me. I had four days left with Robert before my flight and I wanted him with me — not stuck in the Loita Hills. Didn't everyone understand? Hadn't they ever heard of love? No, of course they hadn't.

Robert insisted I take the lift. With my bottom lip trembling, I said I would stay with him and walk. The discussion ended with me telling him loudly, in front of the *wazungu*, that Soly was stupid, the Maasai were stupid and he was stupid. Robert's expression was set as a rock as he quietly called me over to his side. He spoke very softly: 'That is very bad talking. If I hear you talk like that again I will not come to Nairobi at all. Now go with the car and I will meet you at the Spear Hotel early tomorrow morning.' It was not so much what he said, but how he said it. I got in the car and we left.

Later that afternoon, showered and sitting in front of a plate of grilled chicken, I was glad I had taken that lift. Robert caught up with me as promised the next morning. He had walked twenty kilometres to Narosura and caught a lift into Narok with a *matatu*. Later that day we were on the bus, Marura again, to Nairobi. In a kind of daze we made our goodbye plans. Robert promised to try and write more regularly. If he was in Nairobi, maybe we could talk on the phone. Before I left, we decided that we would be married in a traditional Maasai ceremony upon my return to Kenya next year. I really hadn't thought that I would be returning to Australia this time. I had really believed that a job and work permit would come through, but they hadn't.

I took a taxi to the airport, checked my luggage and in a daze eventually made my way onto the plane. The whole time I felt as though I was doing the wrong thing. With my heart kicking and screaming the whole way, the plane dragged me back to Australia.

---

[1] To Leeyio, like Maasinta, was sent to earth by *Naiteru kop* (another name for God). Both names appear in different myths, so they may be the same man known by different names. Leeyio and Maasinta are both patriarchal figures in Maasai myths of origin.

CHAPTER NINE
DIRECTIONS
August 1991 to May 1992

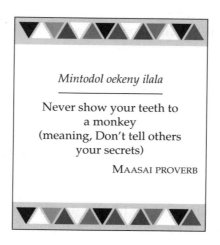

Mintodol oekeny ilala

Never show your teeth to
a monkey
(meaning, Don't tell others
your secrets)

MAASAI PROVERB

BACK IN AUSTRALIA, MY DISAPPOINTMENT AT NOT GETTING A WORK permit slowly faded. I began to realise that I had actually been saved from a horrible fate: working in the entertainment business in Nairobi would be virtually the same as working in Melbourne. What I really wanted to do was to live in the Loita Hills. OK, so there was no employment there. I would just have to find another way of earning money. I began to try to loosen up my thinking. Do what you really want to do, and the money will follow I kept telling myself. This period marked a real shift in thinking for me. Instead of just working madly at anything to save, I started looking for projects that would connect me to Kenya. I was helping with promotions for a small club, so we started to plan an African night. It never eventuated, but it was fun to talk about it and the ideas nudged me in the right direction. I was also working on raising sponsorship for the Next Wave Youth Arts Festival. The director was keen to make contact with youth theatre groups in East Africa and asked me to check it out for him. Another connection.

The idea of putting together a special safari kept floating around in my head. Robert and his brothers had asked me many times if I could bring over Australians for a safari. I kept on telling them that I didn't know anyone who had the money for a safari or who even wanted to come to Africa. Now I started asking myself, 'Why not?' I figured there must be other people who were interested in seeing a side of Kenya that few tourists get to see. A combination of wildlife, wilderness and a genuine experience of Maasai culture. I also wanted to help provide opportunities for Robert and his community to earn more money from small scale tourism. But not as glorified spear carriers. Why not take the skills development opportunities that the National Outdoor Leadership School gave Robert and a few others and build them into our own safari. Allow the Maasai to take centre stage, to be the guides and teachers. And not just the men; I wanted to involve the women too. A special trust fund could be created to channel part of the proceeds back into the community, so that all Loita Maasai — and not just my immediate family — could begin to benefit from culturally sensitive tourism. The Maasai Culture & Wildlife Safari was born. My plan was to promote and co-lead one special three-week safari each year, starting in July next year. July was my favourite time of year in Loita. The long rains were finished, leaving the land alive and green. The cattle grew fat, the milk flowed and the Maasai had time to enjoy any visitors.

Now the idea had taken shape, it just left the hard, but exciting, work of planning and promoting the safari. The first thing I had to do was find a safari operator to subcontract the physical side of things — the vehicles, tents, staff and food. I faxed every operator I could think of, asking for their expressions of interest and quotes. When the dust settled, one operator stood head and shoulders above the rest — Tropical Ice. The owner of the company was Iain Allan, a white Kenyan with a particular passion for mountain climbing and trekking. I had first met Iain in December 1989. He was leading a walking safari in the Loita Hills, and I had run into his group at a Maasai ceremony. I hadn't seen him since then, but I knew he was one of three commercial operators the Maasai allow to trek in the Loita Hills. The other two operators were both horse-riding safari outfits. Tropical Ice was the sole walking safari operator. I knew the Maasai had a lot of respect for Allan, as they called him.

Less than a handful of elite safari operators had been bringing their clients into the Loita Hills for more than ten years. They lease camping sites from the Maasai and employed some of the men as guides and night watchmen. They conducted their activities with respect for the environment and people, most of the time. Occasionally they were helpful with lifts to hospital and into Narok. Robert's family had been the main contact point for these operators since the beginning. Daniel was known and respected by them all and he had introduced his younger brothers into safari work. First Ilampala, who earned himself the nickname 'Le Safari', and later Robert. Not everyone in the Loita Hills was happy with the close relationship Daniel and his brothers had with the operators. Some people were jealous of the small amount of money that was earned. A particular point of conflict was the camping fees — less than $4 per client per night.

Years ago the camping fees for the Narotian camping site had been given to the local school fund. However, all this meant was that the school committee allegedly had a good time with the money. Now Daniel and his neighbours responsible for the camping site decided that if anyone was going to 'eat' the money, then it might as well be them. After all, they were the ones that liaised with the safari groups and put up with the noise from the camp sites at night. They were the ones who invited the visitors into their homes and kept their cattle away from the camp site.

I hoped that the trust fund I wanted to establish along with our Maasai culture safari might be a solution to this problem. As I saw the situation, at this time the Maasai were fighting over a very small amount of money. Compared to, say, the fees payable in the Maasai Mara Game Reserve, the safari operators paid very little per client to come into the Loitas — and it was this region that was usually the highlight of the itinerary. My proposal was for each operator to pay $70 per client which would go into the trust fund. After a few years building up capital, the trust would be a useful source of funds for the benefit of the Loita Maasai. The trust should not be proactive, but simply another source of funds that the community could draw on.

Already there were structures in place within the community that could take on the annual disbursement of such a trust, and the Maasai have a long tradition of *noblesse oblige*. For example, Robert was part of the Loita Youth Committee and every year all the members donated 400 shillings ($20) each. This money was then used to pay school and medical expenses for poor families. Perhaps an offshoot of the youth committee, with a representative from the safari operators, could make the decision about how to spend income from the trust fund each year. Such a committee could include a representative from each sublocation and should reflect a healthy balance of clans and age groups. No single committee member could serve for more than three years. The committee should also include some Maasai women. Through the establishment of such a trust fund, the entire community could benefit from small scale, sustainable tourism activities on Maasai land.

I developed an itinerary for a three-week trip based on the premise that it was more satisfying to get to know one or two areas well when travelling rather than pay quick visits to twenty different places. I was not at all interested in becoming part of the zebra-striped mini-bus brigade that drove from game park to game park, ticking animals off the list as they saw them and eating endless lodge buffets. These companies are to tourism what fast food chains are to the restaurant industry, and I wanted no part of it.

With the itinerary and budget in place, I turned my thoughts to how to promote our safari. I fired off press releases to all the media, and *Woman's Day* responded instantly. They had picked up on my relationship with Robert, and wanted to do a story on the Aussie girl and her Maasai warrior. In November I met the Melbourne editor, Bunty Avieson, over lunch at Chinois Restaurant in South Yarra. Stuck in Australia, I enjoyed nothing more than talking about Kenya and the Maasai, and I blabbed away happily. Of course Bunty was more interested in my relationship with Robert than our safari, but I made her promise to write about our safari too; after all, that was my purpose in doing the interview.

Six weeks later Bunty's story titled 'Love in a Mud Hut' hit the news stands. There was a tiny mention of our safari at the end of the story. People often think that you earn astounding amounts of money by talking to *Woman's Day* and *New Idea*. Ninety-nine per cent of the people who talk to the media do so because they have something to sell — an organisation, a political campaign, a book, a product. I was selling our safari, and never received any money from *Woman's Day*.

DIRECTIONS

The *Woman's Day* story was the start of an avalanche of interest from other media. I was totally unprepared for this. After Bunty's story broke in early January, I was contacted by producers and current affairs programmes from all over Australia and the UK wanting to do a story about Robert and me. My first (and best) instinct was to shy away from all the attention. However, I also knew that here was a golden opportunity to promote our fledgling safari business and, as everyone kept on telling me, make some money. I still needed money desperately to get back to Kenya, as well as to keep paying off my loan. In the middle of all the media interest, a friend in London sent me a postcard which read 'Contact Janet Eastman at "60 Minutes" to do a story for big bucks'. As provocative a message as I will no doubt ever receive by post. What else could I do but call? When I did so, the '60 Minutes' office explained that Janet was now freelance and based in Europe, but that they would pass on a message when she came to Australia next. That was the end of that I thought.

A few days later I was astounded to receive a call from Janet Eastman. She was back in the country and had got my message. My London friend had given her my letters to read and she was very interested in the Maasai. Could we meet to talk? I was due to go to Sydney for work in February, so we made a plan to have dinner then.

I had a good feeling about this. I liked the way this connection had unfolded into my life. I instinctively trusted the little quirks of fate that deposited the right people to you at exactly the right time. February came and I went up to Sydney. At my meeting with Janet I found her to be charming, funny and warm. She seemed to be a woman of integrity and high ideals. She had worked for Channel 9 for many years, but was now freelance and was very keen to produce a one-hour documentary about the Loita Maasai, using my relationship with Robert as the initial angle. Obviously the best time to film would be during the week of our wedding, with the ceremony day itself the climax. Robert and I had tentatively set the date for July, after our safari had ended. Over the next few weeks, Janet began to develop a plan.

There were several ways such a documentary could be financed. Janet spoke to the Australian Film Commission, as well as all the television stations. At Channel Nine, '60 Minutes' were very keen to cover the story and their interest seemed to offer a means to an end. Janet and I were both interested in what we were calling the 'British style' one-hour documentary. If '60 Minutes' covered the story for Australian television, they would let Janet transfer the film onto video. After they had aired their version of the story, Janet would be free to edit her own documentary to sell in other parts of the world. We were both aware of the '60 Minutes' tabloid style. However, on the plus side, they were known for excellent crews, they shot on film rather than video so the whole thing would look fantastic, and they had no qualms about the budget. Janet had no illusions about '60 Minutes'. She knew them warts and all, which as far as I was concerned was perfect. With Janet producing, I was confident that the story wouldn't turn out to be just another segment used to fill the gaps between commercials on a Sunday night.

First I had to get permission from Robert's family to film. I sent a telegram to Robert asking him to come to Nairobi. I enlisted the help of Tropical Ice to arrange money and a telephone call. I spoke to Robert in January. It was the strangest thing to hear his voice on the phone. We had never done this before. I explained what was going on as best I could over the long distance line. Robert had spent time with a small film crew once before when one of the safari companies had shot a promotional video for the US market, so he knew something about the process of filming. I explained that I would be paid some money, there would be a bit of money for Robert and his family, plus they would fly both my brother and me to Kenya for the wedding. Robert thought it would be OK, but promised to call again in three weeks once he had discussed the plan with his brothers. I also told him that we had three people signed up for our first safari — this was the most exciting news of all.

True to his word, Robert got himself back to Nairobi in three weeks and we had another weird, stilted conversation. His family had given permission to film the wedding ceremony. We agreed on a date, 5 July, which was chosen to coincide with my brother's holidays. I said goodbye to Robert, feeling slightly ill at ease. I put it down to pre-wedding jitters.

At the end of February a letter arrived from Robert. He wrote that his father had died. What a magnificent life that man had led and now, nearly a century on, it had ended peacefully. I felt sad that I would never see Papa again, and even sadder for Robert who I knew must be grieving.

The final details of my agreement with Janet were settled. One of the points in the contract stated that I agreed to talk frankly about my relationship with Robert — as openly as I had in some of my letters. Photocopies of these were attached to the contract. Now it is one thing to write about a romantic relationship in a letter to girl-friends and another thing entirely to be interviewed on television about it, but I agreed to do it.

I had been away from the Maasai for too long, and my judgment was poor. I should have known that relationships were never discussed openly. It was my first big mistake. The other area that Janet was especially interested in was female circumcision. I was less willing to talk about this, for I knew there was no western reporter or producer on earth that could look at this issue in a balanced manner. Everything would be judged from the western viewpoint. But Janet was insistent that this was a crucial aspect of the story. I should have listened to the warning bells that had started ringing, but like a stupid fool I didn't. I allowed myself to get swept along, and it wasn't until much later that I finally realised that I was well and truly out of my depth.

Filming started almost immediately, while I was still in Sydney, as Janet was returning to Europe and wanted to film some sequences with me and my family before she left. Being filmed is worse than having your teeth pulled. There is no way that a reporter, producer, cameraman and sound recordist can set up in your home and anything like natural life continue. Every scene, every sentence spoken is set up around the camera. The first thing we had to do was go for a walk along the beach. My mother, brother and I have never walked along the beach together. But that hardly matters when it means you can get in a nice shot of the ocean. We walked up and down the same stretch of sand, repeating the same conver-sation and the same gestures, about a dozen times. Next was the lunch sequence. Food has never tasted so bad as when eaten while being filmed. The reporter asked questions and tried to get the conversation going. Mum looked frozen to the spot, like a rabbit in a searchlight. My brother squirmed uncomfortably and said nothing. So it was up to me to blab on and try to be animated. And blab on I did, my words oiled with a mixture of nerves and stupidity, giving away secrets that were not mine to give.

All the time I answered questions, Janet was gesturing to me in the background. This was incredibly distracting. Afterwards Janet explained the gestures. She was trying to guide my answers, but didn't want the reporter to know that she was doing so. I had sort of blown it by asking her outright why she was waving at me. What we want here, she instructed me, is just short answers. Don't get so long-winded and detailed. Above all it's important that you come across as charming. The story won't work unless people like you. Don't be too serious. Keep your answers brief, and humour is great. Think charming. Also, when you answer, try to use the question in your answer if you can. This will make it easier when it comes to editing. I was learning that this documentary business is not as straight as it looks.

Think charming. I might be many things, but naturally charming is not one of them. I don't think anyone has ever described me as 'charming'. Honest, direct, rude, insensitive, overbearing, pushy … but never 'charming'. Why, oh why was I doing this again? Oh yes, that's right. It was for the money. I was being paid five thousand dollars which would easily cover the costs of an enormous Maasai-style wedding ceremony and leave me a little to live on. Robert's family would also benefit. Plus my brother and I were both given return economy airfares to Kenya. It would be great to have my brother at the wedding. The ultimate carrot was the promise that, if the story was good, '60 Minutes' might want to film a follow-up story in Australia the following year. This would mean that they would fly Robert out to Australia. It was a dream of ours for Robert to see my country and meet my family, but neither of us had the money to make it happen. I guess I could learn to be charming.

CHAPTER TEN

THE WEDDING FROM HELL

June to July 1992

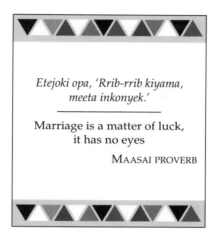

*Etejoki opa, 'Rrib-rrib kiyama,
meeta inkonyek.'*

Marriage is a matter of luck,
it has no eyes

MAASAI PROVERB

I HIT THE GROUND RUNNING IN NAIROBI, ALL FIRED UP WITH FINAL PLANS for the safari. Our group of eleven Australians was due in Nairobi the next week. In the meantime, I had time to smooth out every detail before they arrived. Robert met up with me the next day. We had not seen each other for ten months, so it felt a little weird to be with him again. That feeling disappeared within a few hours and we were a team again. It suddenly struck me that I was going to marry this man in less than four weeks. A sobering thought. I never expected to be married. I had not grown up thinking of marriage as my inevitable adult state.

In my early twenties, I had pictured myself older and alone except for scores of dogs and horses. Alone but not lonely. I didn't want anyone to interfere with my independence. I had no desire to see my personality and dreams tangled in the web of modern marriage. But here I was, getting set to marry a Maasai *morani*, a man of the East African plains, a wanderer, a nomadic herdsman and one very conservative guy to boot. Robert is so straight that if he was an Australian, he would wear cardigans, long socks and vote for the National Party. Fortunately he is a Maasai, so instead he wears a short red toga, heaps of beads and runs around making noises like a lion. This helped me keep things in perspective. As for feeling nervous about my impending wedding, the only solution for that was to take a deep breath and forget all about it. We had a safari to lead first.

The image that most people bring to mind when they hear the word 'safari', is of Great White Hunters in pith helmets, African porters bearing 25 kilogram loads on their heads, and imperious memsahibs dressed in pyjamas, downing gin and tonics. The pith helmets and porters are the stuff of legend, though some of the romance of a safari in the African bush remains today — if you travel with the right operator that is. There are as many different ways to travel in Kenya as there are budgets to be spent and adventures to be sought. You can relax in five-star tented camps complete with your own *en suite*, or wander the northern deserts astride a noble camel with Samburu herders, sleeping under the stars at night in a 'fly camp' — a stretcher bed enclosed in mosquito netting. There are luxury flying safaris, fishing safaris, golf safaris, balloon rides over game reserves that end in a champagne breakfast, and homestays with old colonial families. There are Swahili fishing dhows, simple beach bungalows and discreet island hideaways on the coast, in addition to the multitude of beach resorts that cater to those who have no wish to know that they are in Africa.

Many Australians opt for budget camping safaris, such as the famous Turkana Truck run by Safari Camp Services or make their own way around with a backpack on the *matatu* shuttle between major (and minor) towns. Unfortunately all too many end up joining the zebra-striped mini-bus brigade, where they spend most of the day driving from one national park to another, eating the dust of other mini-buses and chasing around after the 'Big Five': lions, leopards, rhinos, elephants and buffaloes. Their main contact with the people of Kenya is the waiter who serves them a drink, and perhaps the ubiquitous visit to a fake Maasai *manyatta*. Otherwise it is a quick stop at the border town of Namanga where Maasai women thrust handfuls of bracelets through mini-bus windows and shrilly urge the *wazungu* to buy, buy, buy.

Despite the fact that the traditional culture of the pastoral Maasai is generally despised and oppressed, individuals and corporations use symbols of Maasai culture and art for commercial purposes. Images of the Maasai are found throughout the tourism industry in Kenya: on the letterheads and logos of the operators, in the foyers of hotels and on t-shirts. Wakamba carvers produce statuettes of Maasai *moran*, the curio shops sell Maasai beadwork, fake swords and spears. Even Maasai men, dressed in imitation red woollen wigs and red *shukas* serve *'Karibu'* cocktails to guests at the coastal resorts and some lodges in the Maasai Mara. Thus those who are still proud of their culture become objects through which others benefit at the expense of the actual creators of the culture. The intellectual property rights of the Maasai are clearly being infringed, and they have a right to earn royalties from non-Maasai who employ their images for commercial gain. It is an ethical problem that deserves to be tackled. Despite their status as the unofficial symbol of the Kenyan travel industry, the Maasai have benefited little from tourism. They have lost much of their land to game reserves and national parks — where some of the most exclusive lodges operate — with no compensation. Areas such as the Maasai Mara Game Reserve and Amboseli National Park were traditional dry season grazing areas. There is no provision in the tourist lodges for the Maasai community to share in the profits, and no 'positive discrimination' policy of training and employing Maasai, though some of the smaller camps and homestays appear to be doing much better in this regard than the big lodges.

In terms of the quality of the experience, environmental sensitivity and low impact on local communities, the best way to see Kenya is with the family owned 'boutique' safari operators who, like good wineries, seem to know that small is beautiful. This is camping with flair. Here the romance of an old-fashioned safari can still be found. Accommodation is mainly in walk-in canvas tents that sleep two people. Beds are made up with sheets, doonas and, on the more adventurous itineraries, sleeping bags. Hot showers in a special canvas shower tent are prepared each day. A spade flush loo tent completes the set up. This is a wonderful mixture of comfort and adventure. You camp in private areas, usually leased from the local community, surrounded by the sights, sounds and smells of Africa. There is no hint of the modern world, except for the 4WD vehicles that brought you here and will take you to the next camp in a day or so.

When you depart, there will be no sign that you have ever been there, except for some freshly earthed-in holes where the loos have stood. These operators will take you on foot, on camel, on horse-back and in 4WD vehicles to some of the most remote places in Kenya. And let me assure you that there are many of those left.

Kenya, being the birthplace of the safari holiday, has suffered in recent years from the reputation of being a bit 'done'. So popular is it that the truly intrepid traveller finds it hard to imagine that there is any place left that could be described as off the beaten track. But some of the wildest places on earth can be found in Kenya; vast riverine bushland, pristine forests and the mesmerising arid expanse of the Northern Frontier District. The people who know this area consider it to be the most beautiful, mysterious and chal-lenging part of Kenya to travel in.

Our own Maasai Culture & Wildlife Safari aimed to give travellers a genuine experience of Africa — a mixture of wilderness, wildlife and people. Eleven intrepid Australians arrived safely on the regu-lar Air Zimbabwe flight. Our first day in Nairobi was very busy. We saw the Great Rift Valley from the misty top of the Ngong Hills, visited the Langata Giraffe Centre and walked around some of the city before taking in the first Maasai language session. We left early the next morning from the Fairview Hotel in 4WD vehicles on the long journey to the Loitas. Robert had travelled back to Narotian a few days before to ensure that everyone and everything was ready. When we finally arrived at our camp site, it was awash with red blankets. Robert had brought all the men in our family to welcome the visitors to Loita. After the introductions, we made our way to the spacious, walk-in tents which had already been set up by the camp staff. The stretcher beds were made, and there was hot water in the individual canvas wash basins. It was very satisfying to see our plans come together like this. When everyone had gathered for a drink in the open-sided dining tent, I dashed off up the hill to greet my Maasai family, whom I hadn't seen for ten months. I was especially anxious to see Ndoondo and, after a few minutes of feeling shy, she was in my arms again.

The head of our safari team was Clive Ward, a professional photographer and expert mountain climber. Clive has the heart and soul of an African, but he is English. However he has managed to get over that by spending most of his adult life in Africa. He even looks a little lionine, with his lean, athletic build and mop of long, greying hair. The first way our safari differed from others was that we stayed in the same place for the first five nights. This meant the group could get to know the Maasai of our *enkang* as individuals, rather than just as members of a tribe. This is what true cultural tourism is all about. And of course it is the real exchanges with people from other cultures and countries that are the most precious moments of our travels. They represent the 'Ah ha' moments, when we suddenly understand that the world really is a small place. Despite the differences in appearance, dress, accommodation and language, when you sit down to share a cup of tea with a Maasai woman, who has prepared it slowly over a small fire, surrounded by the bright faces of her children, you begin to realise that her concerns and your concerns are not all that different. A doorway is opened; a connection made. A moment that could never be 'captured' by a photograph but held forever in the heart and the mind.

We set camp at Narotian in the same idyllic glade that I first visited in 1989. Over the next week we combined half-day hikes with guided interaction with the Maasai. A team of six *moran* and elders, including Robert, led us on the daily walks. They taught us about their environment, the medicinal uses for plants, how to find wild honey, how to spot animal signs, and how to read the sounds of the bush. The Maasai have a medicinal use for almost every plant. It was fascinating to learn that a cure for gonorrhea was to be had by boiling a concoction from a certain root. We also had a chance to chew a twig from the toothbrush tree, which has an aniseed flavour. The wildlife that lives in the Loita Hills is abundant, but very shy. Monkeys are the easiest to spot, while impala, dik-dik and other smaller gazelle take off as soon as they see you. The larger game, like wildebeest and zebra, graze the Morijo Plains where they can be easily seen, as long as you keep a respectful distance.

The oldest of our Maasai guides was Ol Aranka. He was a

Ndorobo, hence his nickname of Ol Dorobo. If Shakespeare had been an African, Ol Dorobo would have been his Puck. At a glance you can see that he is different from the other Maasai. He is small in frame, with sinewy muscles on his arms and legs, whereas the other Maasai are tall and nicely rounded with flesh. His face has a different shape too, elfin-like, with a more prominent chin. He spoke no English, but is the best communicator I have ever met. I would not be at all surprised to discover that he is really a forest spirit, for he knows its secrets and can make all the sounds of the animals. Once I asked him if he went flying in the forest at night, and he solemnly replied that he did. I know that he can spend an entire night in the forest, sitting quietly at the foot of an ancient tree, listening to the sounds around him. It is his way of checking the forest's pulse.

The other thing which distinguishes Ol Dorobo from all other Maasai men is that he is ever industrious. A master craftsman, at any given moment of the day you will find him carving arrows, walking sticks, *orinkas* and cylindrical leather arrow cases. Around his waist he wears a black leather traveller's pouch, and over his red *shukas* he wears a black woollen coat, which he never takes off, no matter how hot it gets. In the pouch and the jacket pockets are his work tools and fire sticks. With a truly impish grin, he loves to demonstrate his fire-making abilities and his prowess with the bow and arrow. When our group moved from Narotian to Morijo, we said goodbye to Ol Dorobo, but not for long. The same night he arrived in Morijo to say hello; we found we had missed his puckish presence so much, that I immediately put him back on the payroll.

The Maasai can be very sensitive about having themselves or their livestock photographed. Many visitors to Kenya and Tanzania wonder why. Some Maasai believe that if you photograph their cattle, it will make them sick. This has frustrated many tourists, who insist that they were taking a photo of the landscape and not the cattle. Other Maasai are simply sick and tired of being treated like just another species of wildlife. I know I wouldn't be too impressed if someone I had never met before pulled up in front of my house and started taking photographs. Some Maasai have a policy of being paid for posing — many men and women in the West make a handsome living out of doing the same thing.

When I travelled in Tanzania in 1989, our tour guide stopped by the road, where a group of Maasai *moran* and children were standing. He selected the best looking and best dressed of the group, negotiated a price and then invited us all to take photos. The tour guide lined up the Maasai so that we didn't even have to get out of the bus to 'shoot' them. Out of frame, the uglier faces, and bodies dressed in scant rags stood patiently.

I have always found that if you sit down and spend time with someone, get to know their name, and perhaps show some photos of your own family, they will usually be happy to have their photograph taken. Because we were visiting the Loita Maasai as invited guests, I made it a rule that no cameras were permitted in the family settlements for the first few days. Our own camp and out hiking in the bush was not a problem, but when it came time to visit the *enkang* the cameras were left behind. Most of my group understood the reasons for this, as it had been explained in the predeparture notes. However, one of our group expressed concern that he might 'miss something'. I asked him to trust me and assured him that his photographs would be so much better for waiting a few days. At the end of the safari, he thanked me for making him wait. He was now sensitive to how the Maasai felt about photography and as a result he admitted that he had taken fewer photos. Those he took, however, were very good. His patience and respect were rewarded with genuine smiles. He and his wife sent copies of their photos to Robert and me to distribute, and they are treasured by our family.

Through my own experience of gradually learning about the Maasai way of life, I knew that food played a very important part in breaking down barriers between different cultures. I had thought that there were two things which separated people: language and food. I now know that language can be overcome, but unless you can sit down and share a simple meal or a cup of tea, you will never truly know the other person. With this in mind, I set up a number of activities with the Maasai that were based around food. Westerners often travel with a lot of fear about food in Third World countries. I believe that it is exactly this fear that can make them sick. I told our group that if they were fearful, it was better to politely refuse. But if they ate with appreciation and respect, then they would live to tell the tale.

For the first meeting with the Maasai, our group broke down into three smaller ones, and each small group of three or four visited a different house in our *enkang*. I gave one person from each group some sugar and tea to give to the mother of the house, who promptly made them sweet, milky tea. An English-speaking *morani* or I stayed with each group throughout to interpret and explain. The gentle ritual of making tea is a lovely introduction to Maasai life. The house is soft and warm in the firelight and the sense of loving community shines through. It is almost enough to make you forget the smoke stinging your eyes and the flies. With experience, you quickly learn to sit down low to avoid the smoke, and to ignore the flies. We returned each day for the next few days to visit the same houses so we could gradually develop a connection with each family and a genuine understanding about how they lived.

One afternoon, the *moran* and the elders took us into the forest to slaughter and roast a goat. Two other women and myself chose not to watch the actual slaughtering and butchering, but the rest of the group watched the whole process. We joined them in the cool of the forest when the pieces of meat were roasting on upright sticks over the fire. We all ate the meat, as well as roasted cobs of fresh maize. The Maasai men made a pot of medicinal soup, using offal and forest bark and herbs. Almost everyone took a swig of peppery, bitter soup.

Another day we walked to the Entasekera trading *dukas*, and past the Catholic clinic to the home of Baba and Mama Hannah. When they moved from our *enkang* two years ago, they settled near the Mission by a small stream. Baba and Mama Hannah were Kisii people from western Kenya. They kept no livestock, except for a few hens, and concentrated on agriculture. Baba Hannah was the local *fundi* or handyman, and Mama Hannah knitted exquisite cabled jumpers and sewed clothes to make extra money. Their house was square, with three rooms, and windows with wooden shutters smiled at us from all sides. We all sat on benches around their large wooden table, which dominated the light and airy centre room. The window behind the table looked out onto a plot of green maize, which rustled softly in the breeze. Mama Hannah served us all with a cup of milk tea and a large, soft chapatti each. Over this deliciously simple meal, Baba Hannah told us about his life and work. It was a glimpse into the lives of a typical rural African family which was very different to the Maasai, and it provided another insight into how people live in Kenya.

The highlight of our ten days in Maasailand was Murrianga's *Olkine lorrbenig* ceremony. Murrianga was a junior elder who had married one of Robert's cousins. He had walked with us for the first week as a guide before going to prepare for his ceremony in Morijo. We hiked to Morijo a day or so later. It was fortunate that our group had had the opportunity to get to know Murrianga. This made our attendance at his ceremony far more meaningful. *Olkine lorrbenig* is the same type of ceremony as *Olkiteng lorrbaa*; it is a purification ceremony, but a goat is slaughtered instead of a bullock. Each Maasai man must carry out his own ceremony in the same manner as his father.

The day before the ceremony, we visited Murrianga at his home to meet his family and observe the preparations. It was important for our group to be a little bit familar with the *enkang*, and to know what to expect so that they could enjoy the day, rather than feeling on the outer.

The next day we all walked to Murrianga's *enkang* which was less than two kilometres from our camp. We were permitted to visit the site of the *olpul* in the forest, where Murrianga sat with his father and other venerable elders. All had red ochre painted on their heads and faces. Murrianga himself was radiant with pride. I had never noticed his looks before, but today, resplendent in red ochre, beaded earrings, a calf-skin cloak and a ceremonial fly whisk, he was incredibly handsome.

When the roast goat was ready, Murrianga was blessed by the elders and offered a bite from the heart. Next it was offered to his father and the other venerable elders. Then other men shared in the meat.

Back at the *enkang*, I found Clive and another member of our safari group holed up in a calf-pen drinking honey beer with Maasai friends. The *moran* sang and danced inside the thorn-fenced enclosure and the honey beer flowed. Amidst the madness, I noticed members of our safari group absorbed in different activities. One woman was dancing with the *moran* and senior women, while another was almost invisible under a mound of playful children. It is always a strange thing to attend a Maasai ceremony for the first time. The Maasai party hard, and their energy can be overwhelming. At the end of the afternoon, we were all exhausted.

Although we had one more day scheduled in the Loitas, I decided it was better to leave on a high note. There was absolutely nothing the Maasai, Clive or I could show our group that would top Murrianga's ceremony. Clive agreed, and we decided to leave the next day for the Maasai Mara.

The Maasai Mara Game Reserve extends from the edge of the Loita Hills in the east to the Soit Oloololo escarpment in the west. The reserve's southern border is contiguous with Tanzania's Serengeti National Park and the northern border cuts across the Loita Plains. The Mara, which covers around 1550 square kilometres in total, is divided into two sections.

The inner reserve, an area of about 500 square kilometres known as the Mara Triangle, is run along the lines of a national park. This means that the Maasai may not use any part of the land. The area is set apart solely for the protection of wildlife and tourism activities including lodges, camping sites and roads. The outer area is largely undeveloped. In 1961, when the reserve was created, the Maasai were permitted to remain with their cattle. Surrounding the park are a number of group ranches originally owned by small collectives of Maasai men. Many of these have since been sold to agriculturalists. The activities of the Maasai are in harmony with wildlife. Those of the agriculturalists are not. It is very sad to see the once beautiful Loita Plains covered in wheat fields. Wheat farming has interfered with the game corridor between the Loita Hills and the Maasai Mara, and has condemned many Maasai families to landlessness — a lamentable state for any Maasai.

The traditional owners of the Maasai Mara were the Loitai Maasai. Today the region is shared by three sections of the Maasai, the Siria, the Purko and the Loitai. The word Mara in the Maasai language means spotted, which refers to the mottled mosaic of bushes, trees and cloud shadows on the grassy plains. It is a beautiful area, rich in game and bird life.

Our private camp was set up in a small glade on part of the Koyake Group Ranch. Even though it was mid-July, the long rains had been late and on our first night in camp it rained steadily. Over the next three days, the pace of the safari wound down. We really had been very busy with the Loita Maasai. There had always been something to see or do or someone to meet. In the Mara, the long grass made it inadvisable to go walking far from camp, and we all felt constrained and restless by the end of the second day.

We started each morning with an early breakfast and then went off on game drives in the 4WD vehicles. By around 11 am all the predators usually had retreated into the shade and we returned to camp. In the cool of the late afternoon, we ventured out again. As always in the Mara, the game viewing was excellent. We saw several lions and also two exciting episodes with cheetahs.

First, we saw a cheetah teaching its cub the arts of hunting gazelle. We were lucky to be in the right spot at the right time. For a while we watched silently as the cub played cat and mouse with a baby Thomson's gazelle while the gazelle's mother stood horrified, rooted to the spot a few yards away. The baby gazelle was permitted to bound away, apparently unhurt. Its mother still stood transfixed and in a second the adult cheetah had caught her by the neck and dragged her into the long grass not far from our vehicle. There she and her cub ate their fill. When they seemed to be finished, we started our engines and drove off. Cheetahs are diurnal hunters, and vehicles can often interfere with their hunting. I was glad to see that our presence had not seemed to disturb them.

The next day we saw a group of four cheetahs who had decided to take advantage of a vehicle, which they nimbly climbed onto, in order to scan the plains. They lay on the bonnet and roof, much like a house cat likes to sit on a warm car. Inside the vehicle sat two researchers whom the cheetahs knew. The cheetahs' playfulness afforded us an excellent opportunity for photographs.

On our last night in the Mara, we had a wonderful roast turkey dinner and sat quietly around the camp fire. Everyone was sad that the safari had come to an end.

I knew that somewhere else on the ranch, the '60 Minutes' crew had arrived with my brother Mark and were set up in their own camp. The next morning, when everyone else started on the long drive back to Nairobi, Robert and I joined the '60 Minutes' camp for a few hours' filming. They wanted a sequence with Robert and me walking amongst the wildlife. We found this very funny, because we had never gone off walking 'amongst the wildlife' before. But, like the sequence when I walked along the beach with my family, it made for pretty pictures. A family of giraffes and some zebras were very co-operative, and Robert and I strolled in front of them repeating our pretend conversation. 'What's that, Robert?' 'That's a zebra.' 'Oh, and what's that, Robert?' 'That one is a topi.'

A few hours later, Mark and I drove back to Nairobi to meet up with our safari group, while Robert stayed with '60 Minutes'. Two nights later, I said farewell to everyone at a very convivial dinner. The next morning, my hangover and I were dressed and ready to leave for Loita by 5.30 am. The '60 Minutes' people had arrived at Narotian the previous night, and today was scheduled as a non-filming day. Janet thought this would be a good idea so that the Maasai could 'sniff them' as she put it. I thought it was an even better idea because it would give both her and the reporter a day to chill out and hopefully start to tune in to what the Maasai were all about. Nothing is hurried in Maasailand, and to start filming within the first twenty-four hours would be in poor taste. When I finally arrived at the camp site in Narotian later that afternoon, I was dismayed to learn that Janet had already started filming that morning.

Janet was soon to learn that what the Maasai say and what they mean are not always the same thing. I don't mean they lie, or even that they bend the truth. It is a matter of different perceptions. I had learnt the hard way that in order to get a clear and detailed answer from a Maasai, I had to really think about my questions first. It was me, the asker, rather than the answerer, who had to be on guard to 'get it right'.

An example of this was an interview with Mumai, who is Robert's father's first wife. Janet was under the impression that this had been an interview with Robert's mother. Just as my mum had been interviewed, so Robert's mother was to give her opinion. Now Mumai is one of Robert's mothers, so I guess it is a case of Maasai semantics. I mean, how would a westerner know that instead of asking to meet your 'mother' (which could lead you to any one of many women), it is necessary to ask to meet the 'mother whose stomach you came from?' I love Mumai, and she said some lovely things about Robert and me, so there was no problem with her being interviewed. I did hope though that these 'different perceptions' would not continue to crop up each day.

The five days leading up to the wedding were spent filming. Even when I was not being filmed directly, there always seemed to be a question to answer or something to be sorted out. For example, '60 Minutes' wanted to film the Maasai collecting honey in the forest. Ol Dorobo was the elder who was best at finding honey, but he had only been employed as a watchman for their safari camp. To organise the honey collecting meant several long conversations through a translator to determine that he would be paid an extra 200 shillings ($10) for his scouting efforts. I was determined that the Maasai directly involved with filming would not be ripped off financially. Consequently I was involved in every negotiation and got very tired and ratty towards the end.

Ndoondo was staying with us in the safari camp and fortunately Mark was able to help me look after her. They soon became firm friends and he taught her all kinds of silly things in English. After her head was shaved for the wedding ceremony, Mark christened her 'Kojak'.

The Maasai were wonderful with the whole task of filming and turned out to be natural actors. One scene had me moving into my new house, accompanied by six women all carrying various pieces of furniture or cooking pots. We all had to troop past the camera in single file chatting and laughing. The women did eight takes in exactly the same way. Another time, the producer requested a scene with the Maasai women and me washing our clothes by the river. The fact that we never washed together like this in real life had nothing to do with filming a documentary. Another example of this was when they set up a scene which had me going off with the warriors to collect wild honey in the forest. I never do this; it is work for men only. In fact, except for the actual ceremony day, nothing in the '60 Minutes' story bore much resemblance to my real life.

The logistics of the wedding were enormous. More than half of my fee from '60 Minutes' had gone into buying a huge amount of food for the celebration. Lou Allan (Iain's wife) at Tropical Ice had managed to find 300 kilograms of sugar in the middle of one of

Kenya's regular sugar shortages. The sugar was needed mainly for the traditional honey beer which was brewed in a variety of gourds, waxed bags and plastic containers. We had 100 kilograms each of flour, rice and potatoes, plus stacks of cooking oil, salt and onions. Enormous quantities of milk tea would be served on the day, plus we had ordered 700 bottles of soda from the *duka* at Narosura.

The day before the wedding, the sodas still hadn't arrived. They were supposed to be delivered to a trading centre about 10 kilometres away in Olngarua. One of the Tropical Ice drivers took Robert to try and track them down and ended up continuing on another 30 kilometres to Narosura to find them. He arrived back triumphantly with 700 bottles of soda rattling away, just in time to film his master interview.

Meanwhile in the *enkang*, teams of women were busy sorting through the rice, cooking hundreds of chapattis and peeling mounds of potatoes. All the women in our family had been recruited into this task and it was lucky that Robert, Ndoondo and I had a tent to sleep in as the *enkang* was bursting with visitors and tipsy old men who had started 'tasting' the honey beer a few days earlier.

The day before the wedding I had been feeling sick with a mixture of nerves and a reaction to Bactrim tablets which I had taken for a throat infection. While I was feeling lousy, Janet left me alone to sleep. It was the only time I got to rest during the entire six days. That night our friends Susan and Martin arrived. Susan slept with Ndoondo and me in my tent. Martin shared with Davis, the representative from the Ministry of Culture who was accompanying '60 Minutes'.

Over the course of the previous few days, '60 Minutes' had turned from being co-operative and considerate to a disturbing presence. The two man crew, Ben and Paul, remained terrific to work with throughout and were keenly interested in the Maasai. However, as time went by, Janet grew more and more intense. The Maasai naturally reacted to this and withdrew from her. This was a source of frustration to Janet who did not understand what was going on. In all fairness, she was under pressure to 'do her job' and was unaware of the effect she was having on people. Instead of building relationships and putting in extra time talking with the Maasai, Janet went into a huddle with reporter Jennifer Byrne at the end of each day. It seemed that around the camp fire at night there were the two of them, and then the rest of us.

No one is permitted to sit in on a '60 Minutes' interview. This is supposed to make things as easy as possible on the interviewee in such a strange and unnatural situation. So I was not present for any of the interviews with the Maasai. Robert's master interview went well enough, except for when Jennifer asked him directly about our sex life. Even though I had warned him that he might be asked about this sort of thing, he was still shocked that a woman he barely knew could ask him such intimate questions so brazenly. The '60 Minutes' people were aware that the Maasai are a sexually conservative society and do not discuss physical relationships. Robert declined to answer the question.

Another scene also proved to be particularly difficult to film. Janet wanted a sequence where Robert and I walked into our hut and shut the door. She would really have preferred us to walk into the sunset together hand in hand, but of course that was impossible. When the scene was explained to Robert he refused to co-operate. I hadn't realised that it was not acceptable for a man to be in a house with any woman (but especially his wife) during the day with the door shut. This may sound amazing after I'd spent so much time with the Maasai, but actually the door to a house is never shut during the day so the situation had never arisen. I now learnt it was the height of bad manners. Robert and Janet were at an impasse until he suggested a solution: have three old men sitting in the house and then we wouldn't be alone. The men were invited inside, and Robert and I performed the scene. We had to walk in through our gate; outside the door Robert planted his spear; we walked inside and he shut the door. We repeated it about eight times, which made Robert very embarrassed, but I thought it was fairly innocuous. Unfortunately, when the story was edited, this sequence was used to imply that Robert was claiming his woman by planting his spear and shutting the door. Robert could not understand why the narration hadn't explained that there were three old men acting the part of chaperones inside.

To make matters worse, this scene was preceded by a piece to camera by Jennifer Byrne alleging that all a Maasai man had to do if he wished to sleep with a wife of one of his age mates was to plant his spear thus (she demonstrated) in front of her house, and the woman was his for the night.

This piece of fantasy has become one of the great legends about the Maasai; unfortunately this inaccuracy has been perpetuated in some books. The truth is less titillating to the western mind. Within the strict society of the Loita Maasai, a man's spear is customarily placed out the front of the house he is visiting in order to act as a signal to children to keep away and to his friends to join him. It is forbidden for children to see any man eating. Any Maasai would be deeply offended by this part of the '60 Minutes' story. However, the *Iloibonok* would be even more offended. Because the power of prophecy is passed down through the male line, blood purity is very important for the Nkidongi family. A man must be certain that his child is really his. To put it simply, they don't fool around. For '60 Minutes' to have implied that they did was a grave insult.

The day before the wedding, the reporter and photographer, Bunty Avieson and Neil Holbrook, from *Woman's Day* arrived too. A stills camera is positively enjoyable compared to a film camera. The great thing about a press interview is that you have an opportunity to really express yourself fully. Good interviews are genuine conversations where you have time to think and experiment with ideas. It may have been the (bad) actress in me, but I felt a terrible pressure to perform in front of the camera. Janet kept urging me to be 'light' and above all 'charming'. As a result a lot of ill-considered rubbish spewed out of my mouth during the '60 Minutes' interview.

I really began to resent the intrusion of the television people the night before the wedding. The only time a Maasai wedding comes close to exchanging vows is when the groom talks with the bride's family. In my case, this happened with Robert, my brother and I inside Mumai's house the night before the wedding. Maasai law decrees that no one can marry within the same clan. Robert's clan is Ilaiser, so Mark and I were both adopted into the Ilmolelian clan. An elder and good friend of Daniel, Samwell ole Nkwo was appointed as our clan father. He would guide Mark through the ceremony the next day. The small house was packed with elders. I was asked if I wanted to marry Robert. I replied that I did. Only the woman is asked as the groom's consent is implied. Then my brother was required to say a few words to Robert, specifically telling him to treat me well, not to beat me and stuff like that. He also asked Robert for a number of gifts including a cow, a spear and a rungu.

Unfortunately an important and serious discussion was turned into a sideshow. This was a difficult sequence to film, not the least because we were really trying to get some serious business completed. Mumai's small hut was very smoky, and that combined with the cramped space made for trying working conditions for Ben and Paul, who had tears running down their faces from the smoke. Jennifer Byrne directed and interjected constantly. For a woman to interrupt a Maasai elder is very rude. However, it becomes positively outrageous when it is done under bright lights with a mike in your face. The special atmosphere was quickly ruined. Once the crew had got what they wanted and left, we all quietly dispersed feeling ill at ease.

I took a long time to fall asleep in my tent that night. I wasn't worried about actually marrying Robert, but I was feeling apprehensive about the exact nature of the ceremony. In particular I was worried that I might cry if the women harrassed me. Crying is not acceptable to the Maasai, except for little children. And of course knowing my every action would be filmed didn't make me feel any better. Robert had gone off by vehicle to commandeer some extra cooking pots. One of a million details he had to attend to.

I was up at 6.30 the next morning and took advantage of the canvas bush shower. My clothes and jewellery were ready to put on. First there was a long silky, blue skirt made by a girlfriend in Melbourne. Long rectangles of cloth, one orange and the other white, were tied across my shoulders and it was all pulled together in a beaded belt. One of my Maasai mums, Interekei, and her daughter had made my traditional jewellery. Usually Maasai women wear four beaded collars, but I had decided to wear only three. The most magnificent of all was the wedding necklace, or *Entende* which had long strands of coloured beads falling down to my knees. Around my shoulders was another cloth or *kanga* in a riot of white, green and deep orange. This was only my second time 'dressed up' as a Maasai woman and I had expected to feel a little strange in all the gear, but I felt very comfortable and certainly very exotic in my wedding outfit. No white satin and bouquet for me!

Not long after I was dressed, Narygunkishon and Nolmemeri

came to escort me back to Mumai's house where I was to wait for Robert and his best man Seketo. We had arranged for Noronkula, a Maasai friend who speaks fluent English to be my helper and cultural interpreter today. All the women immediately fussed around me, retying my belt and stitching my shoulder ties so they would not fall down mid-ceremony. My hair posed a problem. The beautiful head-dress I was given was too small, so I gave that to Ndoondo to wear and instead put on a plain circlet. I tried lots of hairstyles, but in the end I decided to leave my hair in a simple ponytail. I probably would have looked better bald, like the Maasai women, but it seemed a bit of a radical move.

Mark commented that I looked like an old hippie. When we arrived in Nairobi the following night and were finally alone, Robert said that I had looked beautiful. I had to wait until then to hear that as the groom never talks to the bride on the wedding day.

Ndoondo and I did some mugging for the cameras and the women had to pretend to dress me all over again. Ndoondo looked beautiful in a matching blue skirt and red *kanga*. She wore even more beaded jewellery than I did and was obviously feeling terribly important.

When enough wedding preparation business had been filmed, I was allowed to go back inside the house to await Robert. I had huge butterflies in my stomach. I was given a glass of milk to drink, which I normally dislike, but this tasted sweet and fresh. The buzz outside was growing, and by around 11 am I could tell that a considerable crowd had gathered. Inside the house, I sat quietly while the never-ending stream of chapattis continued to be cooked over the fire. Seketo put his head around the corner. 'Are you sad?' he asked. 'Maasai girls are always sad on their wedding day, so you had better pretend to be unhappy.'

Robert came in next, but it was too dark to really see what he looked like, besides I was doing my best to look miserable and kept my eyes to the ground. Seketo and Robert both drank milk, then left the house. Outside, excited voices and singing could be heard clearly. A gourd of milk was placed on my back against my skin. This was the milk that a bride carries from her old home to her new one. There is a way of positioning the gourd against your back but above your belt that makes it pretty secure.

To me, it sounded as though a thousand people were standing outside waiting to see me. Then I was led to the doorway of the house and instructed to stand still on the threshhold for the blessing. Samwell ole Nkwo, as my clan father, first put a small handful of grass in the right shoe, wedging it alongside my foot, and then in the other. Next he took a swig of milk and another of honey beer from a small gourd and sprayed the mixture gently over both my feet. Then it was my brother's turn to spit on me. He showed none of Samwell's finesse and instead his whole mouthful of milk and beer was gobbed all over my shoes. Our laughter broke the tension.

I then stepped outside into the morning sunshine. Robert stood a little way off with Seketo, both splendid in new blue capes with bright red ochre on their heads. Robert also had ochre patterns all over his legs. I wanted to speak with Robert, but this was impossible. As usual he was looking very serious while Seketo was all smiles. We were in a sheltered position away from the crowd, which by mid-morning numbered about five hundred.

In addition to Robert and Seketo, I was also accompanied on the 'wedding walk' by four women: Nolmemeri, my favourite Maasai 'mother' and Robert's sister-in-law; Nolmunai, a half-sister of Robert's; Meiyoki, another sister-in-law; and a grandmother from a neighbouring *enkang*, Nolkisortoo. Nolmemeri had shaved her head in honour of the ceremony for 'her child', which is what she calls me. They were all dressed in their best *kangas* and beads.

Normally, a Maasai bride lives far from her new husband's home and the journey may take days or at least several hours. However, as Robert and I already lived in the same house together, we had to symbolise this journey by going away from one house in the *enkang*, through the safari camp at the base of the hill behind a section of forest and up a different track on the hill back to another house on the opposite side of the *enkang*. We all set off in a line, with me at the end walking very slowly and carefully. A Maasai bride must not look back or stumble for that would be considered an ill-omen for the marriage. If there are any obstacles in her path on the journey, the best man must clear them and even carry her over streams. Luckily for Seketo, we were on a well-worn path and no hernia-inducing heroics were demanded of him. I kept my eyes to the ground and took one tiny step at a time. As we arrived at the safari camp, members of the media contingent made a few jokey comments which I ignored. While it might have been their 'story', it was my wedding day and I was very serious about it. I was also enjoying myself.

We stopped for a while at the safari camp so that Neil, the photographer from *Woman's Day*, could take some shots. In the background, discreet as ever, our friend Clive Ward was snapping rolls of black and white film. In the end, his artist's eye and respect for Maasai culture produced the best record of the day. Neil had trouble getting Robert to stand next to me for portrait shots. Maasai men rarely stand close to their wives and Robert was obviously annoyed at being asked to do this. He kept stepping out of shot or shuffling away from me with gritted teeth. Of course any romantic shots of us touching were completely out of the question.

We were finally released from the photo call and could set off again up the hill to the waiting crowd. Seketo told me to drink some of the milk from the gourd on my back. I knew from Seketo's own wedding walk that I must refuse until he promised me a calf. After a few moments, I took a swig and Seketo was one calf poorer. We continued on our slow shuffle.

The singing grew louder as we neared the *enkang*. The whole area was a sea of bright colours, but it was predominantly red. The part I was dreading was coming nearer. I had seen the bride insulted and harassed by groups of women at the other weddings I had attended, and the whole idea of it scared me. We were almost there when I saw a group of women from Morijo come forward. Paul, Clive and Neil danced about me filming and clicking. All of a sudden I understood that the women were singing in Swahili *Karibuni* meaning welcome. My friend Nasha from Morijo placed a beautiful necklace over my head and said one word, '*Maendeleo*'. I knew she meant that the Morijo Maendeleo (or Progress) group had made this for me as a gift. I was completely overwhelmed with such a loving welcome when I had been expecting abuse. The gesture was so unexpected, so large and generous that I did end up forcing back a tear after all!

It was a magnificent sight — hundreds of Maasai women and children decked out in their vibrant best on the top of the hill against a blue, blue sky. I lifted my head and, through the beads that fell over my eyes from the circlet, drank in the energy and colour that surrounded me. I smiled to show the cameras that I was happy and went back to my mock solemn pose. Once I had walked through the crowd to Daniel's house, which represented my new home, I knew that I must refuse to enter. Now was the time for Robert's family and friends to declare their wedding gifts to me. The crowd pushed against me as friends and strangers craned to see the white girl dressed as a Maasai bride.

Robert's eldest sister walked past me and into the house as she sang out, 'I give you a goat.' Narygunkishon did the same, calling, 'I give you a cow'. Next was Ilampala who gave me a cow and eight goats. One by one, each family member stepped past me calling out their gift. Daniel said, 'I give you a cow and a child.' Now was not the time to point out that he had already given me those gifts two years ago. Noronkula stood beside me, furiously writing down each offer in a notebook. Those inside called for me to come inside, but I was not satisfied with my gifts yet. I did a quick mental check to see who had not pledged a gift yet.

'*Koree Asae?*' (Where is Asae?) I called.

The crowd took up the call, '*Koree Asae?*'

Asae soon stepped forward to pledge a goat.

'*Koree Julius?*' His mother stepped forward to say that Julius would give me anything I wanted. I asked for a donkey. I called a few more names and then remembered Moses, a wealthy cousin to Robert. He came forward, took the paper from Noronkula and ostentatiously wrote (rather than called) four sheep. Moses was a half-educated Maasai and liked to remind everybody of that fact. Ilampala took a quick look at the list and said '*Paashe*, I think you can go inside now,' I had pledges of more than forty sheep, goats, cattle and one donkey.

I was led inside and instructed to sit on the cowhide bed where Mama was waiting for me. She gave me a big wet kiss on the cheek and promptly promised me one cow. The rule is that the bride may not drink from her gourd of milk inside the house until her mother-in-law has promised her a cow. I now took a swig to seal the bargain. My last ceremonial task of the day completed, I was free to relax inside the house.

The fun continued outside for everybody else. I'm told that my

wedding day was magnificent — the biggest and best ever celebrated in Loita — but I only saw part of it. I knew that in the forest
two bullocks and ten goats had been slaughtered and roasted this
morning. My wedding was famous for being a 'two-cow feast';
normally only one cow would be slaughtered. Noronkula brought
me a Coke and I listened to the deep bass sound of the *moran*
singing and leaping outside. In the flurry of feeding guests and
making tea, I was forgotten. I closed my eyes and dozed on the
cowhide bed.

At around 2 pm, Noronkula led me outside and away from the
enkang for a pee. Then I stayed outside for the next couple of hours
co-ordinating the photographs for *Woman's Day*. I had too many
relatives to fit in one shot, so we did several big family portraits.
Scores of young *moran* had come out of the forest to attend the
wedding. They all looked so young and fierce with long, ochred
plaits in the hair and skimpy togas. The uncircumcised girls,
Ndoondo among them, clustered around them singing and dancing, like so many bright flowers. Older men were flaked out on the
grass or sitting in groups drinking honey beer. Inside the houses the
women cooked and served. A bit like an Australian wedding really.

Robert's age group, *Ilkishili*, were there in force too. Several
groups of senior *moran* sang and leapt high in the air. Finally I spied
my brother. He was completely drunk, even his red eyes seemed to
be spinning. Mark explained that Samwell had insisted that his role
today was to sit in a hut and drink honey beer, which they had both
obviously done. Mark's face was spotted with flecks of dried cow
blood. Earlier in the day Mark had gone to the slaughtering place in
the forest where the bullocks had come to a sticky end. Upon being
invited to taste blood straight from the dewlap of a freshly slaughtered bullock, he took up the challenge and on bended knees had a
big drink. The problem was, he told me later, that most of the blood
had already been drunk, so he had to put his entire face deep into
the dewlap which acted as a natural bowl. He said it tested like
salty steak soup.

Meanwhile back at the wedding, the afternoon wore on. Exhausted,
I slipped away with Noronkula, back to the safari camp to have a
drink and to sort out the wages for the Maasai employed by '60

Minutes'. I still hadn't eaten all day. It felt wonderful to take off my heavy necklaces. My ear lobes were red and swollen from two sets of earrings.

At 7 pm, I was taken back to Daniel's house to be given my new name. Mark, being totally off his face, was excused from attending. The house was packed with Maasai elders, but I managed to push my way through to the woman's bed. It sounded like an argument was in process with a lot of drunken men shouting. I noticed that Robert was sitting on the opposite side of the fire, and then I couldn't see anything at all from behind the woven screen in front of the bed. A voice shouted out 'Nasha, Nasha'. Noronkula whispered, 'You are now Nasha.' Then the blessings started. One at a time, the senior elders present called my new name four times and I had to respond with 'Eeo'.

'Nasha!' 'Eeo.' 'Nasha!' 'Eeo.' 'Nasha!' 'Eeo.' 'Nasha!' 'Eeo.'

This was followed by a series of prayers asking *Enkai* to bless me with cattle, children, health, good fortune and other such things. I was delighted with my new name. Not only could I pronounce it and spell it, but best of all it meant rain — a priceless blessing from *Enkai* in Maasailand.

After that, feeling extremely tired but very pleased with myself for getting through such an emotion-packed day, I made my way back to camp for dinner. It was a dark night and a fire blazed in camp. I still had not spoken to Robert all day and longed to know how he was feeling, and if he was happy with how the day had turned out. The cook had prepared a beautiful roast turkey with golden roast potatoes, green beans and gravy. I heaped a large serving of white meat on my plate and sat down by the fire to eat, but I never had a chance to taste it because Janet started in on me.

Previously Ilampala had promised Janet that they would be secretly allowed to film a male circumcision ceremony the next day at dawn. Filming of sacred ceremonies such as circumcision is not permitted, though I understand that a couple of cameras have managed to get past this elsewhere in Maasailand. Ilampala was really going out on a limb here and I had a sinking feeling that it was all through misguided loyalty to me. I did not want '60 Minutes' to film a circumcision — after all it is a sacred ceremony. Also, if the Kenyan Government found out, there could have been repercussions for the community and myself. All negotiations regarding the filming of the circumcision had been conducted between Janet and Ilampala out of earshot of Davis from the Ministry of Culture.

By tonight it was all a bit academic anyway because the circumcisor had not arrived in Narotian. Unfortunately Ilampala exhibited classic Maasai male behaviour when dealing with a problem. He ran away. Instead of fronting up to Janet and saying he'd changed his mind, he simply ignored the problem.

I was at my most drained at the end of an emotional day when Janet decided to question me about why Ilampala had disappeared, why the circumcision didn't appear to be going ahead and what was I going to do about it. I inwardly groaned; this was all I needed.

In the middle of our discussion inside the dining tent, Jennifer Byrne walked in and quickly assessed the situation. She had told her executive producer that they would be filming the ceremony and she wasn't all that keen to go home without it. Jennifer turned to me and accused me of 'not wanting to know about it' (the problem of the circumcision, that is).

At this point, Janet could have stepped in and prevented any conflict between Jennifer and me. To sort out the problem was the producer's responsibility. Janet could have gone off searching for Ilampala herself rather than pressure me. Clive was available to assist; there were vehicles to be used. Instead, she simply stood back and let Jennifer accuse me. Totally counterproductive and unnecessary. I realised much later that probably Janet had not felt the need to protect me because filming was completed. Pushed into a corner about a problem that was not mine, I felt my hackles rise, totally lost control and launched a counterattack.

'What do you mean, I don't want to know about it!' I screamed. 'I have been nothing if not totally co-operative with this entire project. I know it is your fucking *story*, but it also happens to be my fucking *life*!'

I grabbed Noronkula, who had stood by quietly during all this, and stormed over to the vehicle where Clive was waiting to drop Noronkula home. If Davis had not picked up on the clandestine circumcision negotiations during the week, he sure knew about it now. We all climbed into the car, including Daniel and Robert who had arrived in camp. I took a deep breath and burst into tears. While my reaction was perfectly understandable from a western point of view, Daniel and Robert were deeply shocked to see me cry. Daniel's reaction was, typically, to run away. Robert stayed put, feeling a mixture of anger and confusion. I tried to explain to him why I was crying, but how could he possibly understand what it felt like to go through your wedding day and then be verbally savaged.

While sobbing in the car, feeling the wreck of my glorious wedding day lying around me, Jennifer Byrne came to apologise. She admitted that her job had hardened her, and that she tended to go for the icing on the cake. I had given her a wonderful story already and she was wrong to keep pushing for more. It was an honest and sincere apology that I accepted. Now, when I look back at my wedding night, my strongest feelings are of being harassed to the point of tears, upsetting my new husband, and never getting to take a bite of that beautiful golden turkey, cooked with such special care out in the middle of the African bush.

There is no 'wedding night' in Maasai tradition. The groom does not usually consummate the marriage until four nights after the ceremony, and none of that applied to us anyway. Besides which, I didn't think that Robert would even be talking to me after my tears in the car. So instead, still feeling miserable, I curled up to sleep in my tent with Ndoondo and Susan.

The next day we were up early to return to Nairobi. The '60 Minutes' people were flying back from an airstrip a few hours drive away, but I preferred an eight-hour drive over bumpy roads to spending any more time with them. Robert was also very angry, and I could see he was reaching the end of his patience. I knew we both needed space away from our interrogators, so I made my excuses and set forth in our vehicle. We arrived in Nairobi that night and checked into the Norfolk Hotel, where we enjoyed a honeymoon courtesy of Kerry Packer. I wasn't exactly sure why '60 Minutes' had wanted us to come to Nairobi with them, because it was soon clear that we weren't required for anything in particular. I would have much rather stayed in the Loitas for our honeymoon, but we made good use of our time in Nairobi and got married again at the registry office.

In the aftermath of the television show, the five thousand dollar question I have asked myself countless times is, why did I do it? Why, when I was learning about a simpler life, did I roll out the red carpet for one of the most insidious instruments of western culture? Five thousand dollars seemed small compensation for the amount of intrusion and grief caused. It is scant excuse to say that at the time, I needed the money. The truth is that I was a short-sighted fool of the worst kind. As time progressed, I came to realise the enormity of my stupidity. I had torn a hole in my universe that could never be fully repaired.

ENKIYAMA *(Marriage)*

A u g u s t   t o   D e c e m b e r   1 9 9 2

Mimun enkashe olekipa

Don't pinch the heifer's vagina
(meaning never argue with
a new bride)

MAASAI PROVERB

MARK WAS TO 'STAND UP' AS A WITNESS FOR ROBERT, AND BUNTY AVIESON
had kindly agreed to be my 'bridesmaid' at the registry office.
Along with Neil, the photographer, we drove to the marriage
registry office in Sheria House on Haile Selassie Avenue. We went in
a maroon taxi driven by Jimmy, my favourite driver at the Fairview
Hotel. Jimmy now refers to his cab as the 'bridal car'. We decided to
do this extra ceremony so as to avoid any future visa problems. As a
foreigner officially married to a Kenyan I would be allowed to live
in the country as a dependent spouse, though it remained illegal for
me to work. Most *wazungu* and urban Kenyans found it hard to
believe that Robert and I were really married, so the 'piece of paper'
would serve as proof of our relationship. I was amazed (though
friends tell me that I shouldn't be) that some people actually
thought the whole wedding was a publicity stunt.

After a celebratory lunch at the Norfolk Hotel, Robert went to
catch the bus to Narok. He would be working for the next month in

the Maasai Mara and Loita forests with the National Outdoor Leadership School. In the meantime I was going to show my brother around Kenya. That afternoon we boarded the train for Mombasa. Much has been written about this famous train journey along a track built by 31 983 imported Indian labourers between 1896 and 1901. The Mombasa to Uganda railway was largely responsible for abolishing the slave trade that had flourished up and down the East African coast. It opened up the region to the rest of the world, and changed forever the lives of the people who lived there.

The Maasai were greatly affected — they lost more land than any other tribe as a result of the railway and the changes it heralded. The revered Oloiboni, Mbatiany ole Supet, foretold the coming of the railway, which he described as a black rhino with strange pink men riding on it. He also accurately pictured the disaster the 'rhino' would bring to the Maasai, saying, 'I see the end for my children and the land.' He was right, but he died in 1881 long before it came to pass.

Sipping soda and watching the urban squalor of Nairobi whistle past from the comfort of our first class berth, we rattled along. After we had been travelling for less than an hour, our train stopped just outside of Athi River with a mechanical problem. There we remained for the rest of the night until around 3 am when the train lurched and shuddered into action again. This meant that we could enjoy a stationary dinner and a good night's sleep and, best of all, still be travelling through Tsavo National Park during the daylight hours.

We arrived at Mombasa mid-afternoon and then drove to Shimba Hills National Park. This is a small jewel of a park just inland from the coast. Emerald hills that afford glimpses of the distant Indian Ocean make this one of Kenya's most beautiful areas. The park management were just building up the wildlife, and a recent addition was four giraffes. Other game in the park included elephants, warthogs, buffaloes, impalas and the rare sable antelopes. During our drives around the park, we came upon an excellent camp site on a hilltop with thatched roof huts complete with beds and, best of all, ocean views. This would be the ideal place to stay in Shimba if you could come with your own vehicle, food and bedding. As we had none of this gear, Mark and I stayed in the Shimba Lodge.

ENKIYAMA (MARRIAGE)

The lodge has been built around a floodlit waterhole, the idea being that animals will come down to drink at night to the delight of the tourists. Elephants are sighted at the waterhole most days, but not while we were there. The design of the whole place is wonderful, like a giant kids' treehouse with connecting walkways to viewing platforms high in the trees. Rooms 23 and 16 have even been built around a living tree and offer excellent views over the waterhole.

After two days spent reading and recovering from the '60 Minutes' ordeal, we returned to Nairobi and rented a serviced apartment at Heron Court just on the edges of Nairobi city. After Narok, Heron Court has to be the most bizarre place in Kenya. The downstairs restaurant and bar, Buffalo Bill's, is a microcosm of the seamier side of Nairobi nightlife — plenty of exotic bar girls and middle-aged *wazungu* busy making fools of themselves. We lived on the top floor which we shared with the Judo Gym and Ricardo's Latin Dance School. In the early evening we could hear the salsas and rumbas punctuated by the sound of bodies being thrown onto crash mats. Our apartment was labelled 'The Penthouse', for no obvious reason, except perhaps that all the carpet tiles were present.

Mark and I used Heron Court as our home base to explore Nairobi and further afield. We went to Lake Naivasha in the Great Rift Valley and stayed at the delightful La Belle Inn. This is a classic country inn with the added bonus of serving great French food. The croissants were the best I have ever tasted.

Another time we travelled all the way up north to Isiolo at the edge of the Northern Frontier District and embarked upon a four-day camel safari. The town itself is a mix of tribes including the Samburu, with a heavy concentration of Somali traders. We met up with our camel safari operator, Malcolm Destro, and the others who had booked on the same trip: an Australian girl and a young English couple. From there we headed north-west into Samburu land. The country around the Ewaso Ngiro river was parched. There had been no rain for more than two years, and the Samburu herders were in danger of losing their herds of cattle and goats. We passed a ramshackle assortment of empty stock pens and tin rondavels. This, Malcolm explained, was an aid project aimed at converting the cattle-loving Laikipia Maasai into camel herders.

Given the perennial lack of rain here and the hardiness of camels, this is a very practical idea if you can ignore the almost mystical connection the Maasai have with their cattle. I hoped that while waiting for this great conversion to occur, the aid administrators would see fit to spend some of their dollars on supplementary feeding for the cattle so that Kenya doesn't end up with another group of destitute pastoralists.

Malcolm's base camp safari operation is along the banks of the Ewaso Ngiro River. This area is home to three hundred or so remnants of the Laikipia Maasai. Some of the men now work for Malcolm as camp staff and camel handlers. They were amazed and then quickly delighted to discover that I spoke a little Maasai.

Camels are perfectly designed for living in this fragile environment and are ideal as a means of transport. They are browsers and do not tear the roots out like cattle do. Their soft feet cause no damage, whereas 4WDs would tear up the topsoil. Over four days our small group walked and rode camels. I had never before experienced the mystic beauty of the desert — peaceful, very alive and a little eerie. We were not in true desert, but rather a semi-arid zone. The wildlife was different to what I saw down south. For the first time I saw the reticulated giraffe, the paler northern Grant's gazelle, long-necked gerenuk and Grevy's zebra.

On the second afternoon, we rode into camp on the banks of a dry river bed. Along the bed, groups of Samburu herdsmen and their families were digging deep watering holes for their livestock. When enough water had pooled in the hole, the families would herd their animals to the water, females with young first, then subadults and finally the adults. These Samburu also had some camels in addition to the more numerous goats and cattle. I watched a young girl no older than ten hold back a group of thirsty camels with nothing but a stick and the experience that comes from growing up a herder.

This was my first encounter with the Samburu. The Samburu have many names; they call themselves *Iloikop*; the tourist brochures often describe them as the 'butterflies of the desert' but the Maasai refer to their Maa-speaking cousins as Loibor Kineji (people of the white goats) and Isampur, after a distinctive leather bag that they used.

ENKIYAMA (MARRIAGE)

The Samburu are closely related to the Maasai. In fact it would not be wrong to describe them as a separate *olosho* of the pastoral Maasai. It appears that as the main body of the Maasai migrated southwards from the Nile Valley in the 1600s, the Samburu broke off and headed east to occupy the arid region to the north of Mount Kenya. They speak the same language with a few local variations and share most of the customs of the other pastoral Maasai *iloshon*.

After four days in the desert we drove back to Nairobi. My brother returned to Australia and Robert arrived in Nairobi to escort me back home. We had been apart for more than a month. During this time I had missed him and become heartily sick of Nairobi. I was, as my friend Iain Allan put it, 'longing to get back into the real world' — Maasailand. We had arranged to hire a vehicle to take us back to the Loitas. This meant that I could buy dry foodstuffs in bulk to last me several months.

I had a great time shopping at the Hurlingham Centre buying great quantities of rice, sugar, eggs, UHT milk (it was the dry season by now and fresh milk would be scarce), tinned tomatoes and fruit, oil, cordial, potatoes, onions, dry biscuits, soap, shampoo, insect repellent, writing materials and candles. I also bought a small water filter, blankets, cloth, and wool for knitting. (I am no great knitter, but I had decided that this would give me something to do when I sat with the women as they did their beadwork. Though I would have loved to learn how to do this, every time I tried one of the women kept taking my thread and beads away to help me do it more quickly, so my 'relaxing' pastime turned out to be a bit stressful. Knitting would be better.)

Two nights before we left, a friend of Robert's visited us at Heron Court for dinner, Patrick Mores ole Loolpapit. He was the first Maasai from Loita to study medicine and was in his third year at Nairobi Hospital. I had discovered his whereabouts through the Nomadic Health Unit, where he had been helping with research into the incidence of AIDS among the Maasai in Kajiado district.

It had occurred to me that the Loita Maasai might want to know more about AIDS and how to protect themselves from the disease. My idea was to employ two Maasai or Maasai-speaking health workers (rare birds, I admit) to work on a residential programme that took them to every *enkang* to talk about AIDS prevention to male leaders in each age group. Two years would be a minimum time frame to achieve this. Very low key, very low tech. Just doing what the Maasai do so well — talk. I wanted to talk to Patrick about this, and he thought the idea could work. To the best of our knowledge, AIDS has not reached the Loita Maasai yet. Like most isolated rural areas in Kenya, it has been protected so far.

It was refreshing to listen to Patrick, with his passion and commitment to his people. Most medical students in Kenya would see a career as a doctor as a one-way ticket to join the urban elite. In a city where a shiny new Mercedes stands for more than good works, there is very little idealism. The last thing a young doctor wants to do is practise in some remote backwater. Luckily for the Loita Maasai, Patrick Loolpapit is made of different stuff. Like his father before him, he wants to return to help his own people. Major Raphael Loolpapit served as Mzee Jomo Kenyatta's ADC in the 1960s. Upon his retirement, he returned to his traditional home in the Loita Hills, where his education, leadership skills and of course his thriving trading store have benefited the community greatly.

Most health workers throw up their hands when you mention the Maasai and AIDS awareness. Too stubborn, they exclaim. Unwilling to change. However I knew from Robert that his generation were more open to new ideas than their elders. It seemed that we should at least be trying to reach them and give them the option. I don't believe that the Maasai are particularly stubborn about anything at all; they just have a remarkable ability to detect bullshit. Bring a genuinely good idea to their attention and they can be very quick to act.

One example of this occurred when I suggested that we set up bank accounts to hold the camping fee money paid by tour operators. This money goes to the families who live near the camp site, who put up with the travellers and maintain the camp sites. What usually happens is that the most senior and powerful man in the family gets the money and spends it on buying honey beer.

I suggested that the money could go into a bank account and then be divided at the end of each year between all the families entitled to a share. This way the amount of money would be larger and hopefully this would encourage the men to do something more significant with it, like buying a goat. The idea was discussed and agreed upon very quickly and as a result, we now have two bank accounts and fewer disagreements about this money.

Another time I got hold of 16 000 condoms through an American aid project. It sounds like rather a lot, but they come off the boat packed in cartons of 8000, so I took two. The older men don't want to know about them but the younger men are becoming interested in family planning and protecting the health of themselves and their families. Ironically for someone used to the west, the concept of STD protection is much easier than the issue of birth control for the Maasai to deal with. A woman who openly expresses a desire to practise family planning is accused of 'not loving children' and ridiculed.

At one time a Maasai woman came to me in desperation. Still in her thirties, she had seven children, and had had two miscarriages and suffered ill health for the last two years. An educated friend had given her a supply of oral contraceptives, but they were now finished. The district nurse had warned that another pregnancy would be very risky. 'I just need a rest for another year,' the woman said. Her youngest child, a girl, was not yet three and she was generally concerned about how she would feed and educate her family. When she broached the subject with her husband, he refused to discuss it and declared he wanted still more children. In the end, I smuggled six months supply of oral contraceptives to her, disguised in a sack of potatoes. Her husband would have been furious if he found out.

Fortunately the young men are more receptive to new ideas. Many of them express the wish to have only one wife and two or three children, so that they can afford to send them to school. The government clinic here has no contraceptive stocks, so I gave them one carton of condoms. The other carton we shared with various members of Robert's age group to distribute among their peers. They were given some picture booklets explaining how to use them properly, and Robert was often embarrassed by my graphic descriptions. One of the supply points was the 'bachelor house' behind mine. Late at night I would hear young men arrive, then there would be murmured discussion and then they would leave with a supply.

Sunday morning two days later we were ready to drive home. Our hired Landrover was loaded up with my luggage and supplies. Robert, as usual, travelled light and only had to pack two spears which he had bought for age group comrades. We drove off very early in order to reach our *enkang* by late afternoon. Patrick had decided to catch a lift. I was delighted to be going back to see Ndoondo, and to move into my new house. Of course I had not seen anyone since the wedding. As that had been such a busy time with the safari and then '60 Minutes', I was dying to see my family and do some serious 'nesting' with my new husband.

Two hours later we were winding down the Kijabe road into the Great Rift Valley when the brakes failed going around a sharp corner. The vehicle sped off to the right, across the road and into a ditch. The speed was such that we went up the other side of the ditch, miraculously missing the scattered trees and through a fence into an empty schoolyard.

It had been immediately obvious that the car was out of control and I had only had a second to decide that I did not want to watch my worst nightmare come true. Sitting in the middle of the back seat next to Robert, I folded my arms across my body and turned my face into his shoulder — an instinctive response that saved me from serious injury. As we hit the ditch I felt my knees take the weight of impact and I thought, 'Not my legs'. A second later the boxes of supplies and bags came crashing down onto my neck and back. Please not my neck. When the vehicle finally stopped in the schoolyard, we sat there for a few seconds, stunned.

I asked if everyone was OK and received three replies. So we were all alive but that was all I knew. Next I suggested we should try and get out of the car. I looked at Robert. We were both trapped under the load on our backs. Patrick and the driver came to our assistance and half-carried us out of the crushed interior and onto the grass. We were all in shock. I had attended first aid courses in Australia and Patrick was a third year medical student but all we could do was breathe and stare at each other.

Then Robert announced that he thought he had a broken arm. There was blood on his trousers, and I tried to remember what I had learnt. By this time fifty or more people had run to our assistance from nearby homes.

ENKIYAMA (MARRIAGE)

A nurse on her way to work had seen the accident happen and had run to get help. A couple of vehicles quickly arrived.

'Check Robert's legs for bleeding,' I called out.

'No,' said Patrick. 'The blood is from his arm.'

Great, a compound fracture. It was then I saw the puncture wound on Robert's left arm. People were lifting Robert to put him into a vehicle. 'Don't move his arm,' I cried, but too late. I saw the pain in his face as he was carried away and then it was my turn. I could half-walk, so I knew my kneecaps were not broken. Thank God we were close to Kijabe Hospital. The hospital was run by American Seventh Day Adventists. Their general surgeon soon took charge.

X-rays confirmed that I had nothing broken, just bad bruising to my legs. However, walking hurt, so I was put in a wheelchair. Patrick had a simple fracture of the ankle and was soon plastered up. Robert had two compound fractures to the left arm. The ends of the bones had been shattered. The American surgeon said that he could operate, but he advised me to take Robert to a specialist in Nairobi Hospital.

Kijabe is only two hours out of Nairobi but it felt a million miles away from help that day. The phone lines were down, so it was impossible to call my friends or the hire car company to rescue us. There was no such thing as an ambulance service. The American stepped in again and found a colleague, Veronica, who was willing to drive us to Nairobi. (Bless you, Veronica, wherever you are.)

The accident occurred at 8 am. By 4 that afternoon, a whole eight hours later, I had Robert admitted to Nairobi Hospital, where he was taken straight into the operating theatre. Nairobi Hospital is a private hospital and payment is required up front before they will admit anyone. Fortunately they accepted my credit card as I had no cash. The whole day taught me a lot about how the Maasai handled pain. Robert never complained once during the entire process. Not an ouch or a cry. The only way that I could gauge the extent of the pain he was experiencing was seeing him break out into a cold sweat a few times.

Pain is something all Maasai, but particularly the men, learn to handle from an early age. To a Maasai, pain is something like cold, they don't expect to avoid it. I, on the other hand, am naturally cautious and have dedicated my entire life to avoiding pain and discomfort, starting as a toddler when I would slowly inch down our staircase on my bum, rather than risk a fall.

During a two-hour operation, the surgeon Mr Sheikh, put two metal plates inside Robert's arm. Mr Sheikh was pleased with the operation ('I've done a good job'). He told me that there was no major nerve damage. The metal plates would help the damaged ends of the bones knit together. Robert was still very out of it when he was wheeled into his room. He managed to ask me, 'Are you OK, *siangiki?*' before falling into an unconscious sleep. I went back to the Fairview Hotel, ordered a spaghetti bolognaise and half a bottle of white wine. Still in shock myself, I watched CNN for a while, had a good cry and then I too fell asleep.

Robert was in Nairobi Hospital for a week. During the whole time he was remarkably gentle with himself. I had feared that he might try and rush things a bit, but he obviously knew his limits and rested completely. The nurses asked us lots of questions about Maasai culture, for it wasn't often that they had a Maasai in their hospital.

We both rested for another week at the Fairview Hotel. Here Robert indulged his passion for TV. Like many young men in his age group, he is a news junkie, and always listens to every broadcast on the national radio as well as the BBC African service. It was sheer heaven for him to be able to watch the local news twice each night on television; the Swahili news at 8 pm and the English version at 9.30 pm.

His plaster cast was very heavy, and the deep cuts along his arm were still tender. He continued to impress me with his patience and calm acceptance of the situation. I had seen warriors with dreadful cuts who refused medical treatment because they were too proud. I also remembered the time Robert took himself into the forest when he had a swelling in his side.

Finally we were able to return to the Loita Hills. This time I made sure that Tropical Ice supplied the vehicle and driver, so I knew we were in good hands. Even still, I closed my eyes and prayed when we went downhill. We stopped first at the *enkang* in Morijo. A woman started screaming and crying as soon as she saw

Robert's plaster cast. We tried to tell her that it was only temporary, but she thought her cousin would have a thick plaster arm forever. She caused a terrible scene and wept like Robert had died. The Christian wife of another cousin led the assembled group in a prayer, and then we continued on to Narotian.

I was pleased to see that everyone was a lot more reasonable at our *enkang*. Our family members came to greet us and there was much raising of the eyes heavenwards and praising *Enkai* for bringing us back safely. But no more hysterics. Mama started to hyperventilate and went all woozy for a second, until her co-wife Kokoo tapped her on the shoulder and told her to stop it.

At the time of our wedding, I had been presented with my new house. Now, for the first time, I could begin to unpack and settle into my home for the next four months. In fact it wasn't a new house, but the old children's house where Robert's older sister used to sleep. She was now staying in Morijo, so Robert arranged for some major renovations. The exterior was pretty much as it had been, and the cow dung was faded and cracked. However, all the women of the *enkang* had helped remake the interior which looked beautiful. They had woven new partitions in front of both sleeping areas and had rebuilt the interior wall.

The house was much bigger than my first one. It consisted of a main room, with fireplace dug in the centre of the floor and two semi-enclosed sleeping platforms, and a second room at the front of the house. I used the second room for storage space. The door was positioned for maximum light and the roof was made of thatch. A frontyard enclosure had also been built. A fence made of upright branches and thornbush ran in a circle from the back right-hand corner of the house to the front left-hand one. There was no gate at the entrance, so the children and my personal *bête noire*, the goats, still wandered in and out at will, but it offered a certain amount of privacy. At the end of the thorn fence was a clothesline made out of three posts with a wire strung between them.

I commissioned Baba Hannah to build some furniture. The first item to arrive was a western style double bed frame. Now I know some people will accuse me of selling out by sleeping in a bed with a mattress, pillows and sheets. I have slept on a Maasai style bed,

MY SECOND HOUSE

(Given to me after our wedding)

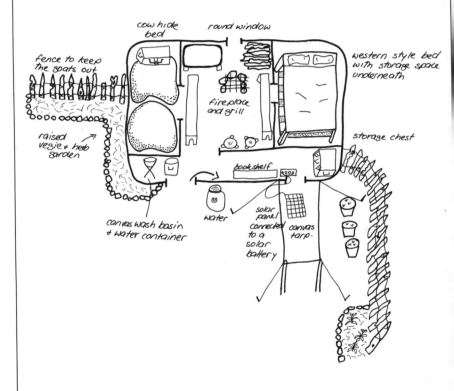

cow hide bed

round window

western style bed with storage space underneath

fence to keep the goats out

fireplace and grill

storage chest

raised vegie & herb garden

canvas wash basin & water container

water

bookshelf

solar panel connected to a solar battery

canvas tarp.

and no doubt will again, but my back finds a solid frame and thick mattress more comfortable. The bed was very tall and a shelf had been built underneath so I could store my suitcase and *sandukus*. These are rickety tin boxes of varying sizes that all Maasai use for storing their clothes and other personal belongings. They are nick-named 'Maasai suitcases', because you will see Maasai walking along with a small tin box, carrying it by the handle. When a bride leaves home for her husband's *enkang*, she usually carries all her worldly possessions in a new *sanduku*. Between us, Robert and I had about six *sandukus*. They kept the dust out and were fairly light to handle. Under our bed, they served the purpose of a wardrobe, chest of drawers and treasure box. The traditional Maasai style bed across from the fireplace was where Ndoondo slept. I tried for a few nights to teach her to sleep on her own, but she would always wake up and crawl into bed with us. Maasai children never sleep alone, so we invited her sister, Gunisai, to sleep in our house every night.

Next a small table arrived from Baba Hannah and two long, low benches. The benches ran along in front of either side of the fire. The table also had a bench underneath for storing plates, pots and other utensils. A very large, black *sanduku*, measuring about 1.5 metres wide and 60 centimetres deep, contained all my food stocks, which included rice, flour, pasta, longlife milk, cocoa, coffee, tinned tomatoes, butter, cream, condensed milk and golden syrup (these last for making golden steamed puddings). I also had a good supply of soap, tissues, shampoo, washing powder and a ten litre jerrycan full of paraffin to fuel my new lantern.

Ndoondo had started nursery school at the beginning of the year. For me this meant waking at 6.30 am every morning and getting her off to school by 7.00 am. The school was two kilometres away and class commenced at 8 am. Ndoondo would walk with her brother, Leseamon, Momposhe and his two sisters, the twins Hannah and Napalell, who had also started nursery at the same time, though they were a year older than Ndoondo. There were forty children in nursery, so the teacher divided them into two groups, and each child was expected to stay in nursery for two years before being able to pass into Standard One.

Ndoondo seemed to enjoy school and by the time I arrived back in her life after the accident, she was firmly entrenched in the school routine. This meant that there was now a distinguishable weekend – the days no longer blended into one another. Every now and then, Ndoondo would ask me for an empty bottle. I discovered eventually the reason behind this request; all the school rooms have dirt floors which harbour fleas and jiggers, which burrow into the largely shoeless feet of the children. To lessen the dust and jiggers, each morning the children walked down to the nearby stream and filled their bottle with water, which was then used to sluice the floor.

As I settled back down into life in the *enkang*, a new friend came into our lives. He was a strapping senior warrior from Tanzania whom I promptly nicknamed *Morani Sapuk*, meaning Big Warrior. He was the same age group as my husband, *Ilkishili*. Because he was one of the oldest in the age group he was usually addressed respectfully as Olngetiai, or sometimes by the old women as Ol Salei as that was his home area in Tanzania. He showed me his 'real' name once on his ID card, but I cannot remember it as Morani Sapuk suited him so well.

We had first met a year earlier at a wedding ceremony in Morijo. Like many Tanzanian *moran*, he had kept his long warrior braids which were plastered in red ochre. He and a brother both wore scanty robes which only covered one side of their body and carried splendid spears. The Morijo warriors had all shaven their locks off, and the younger warriors known as *Ilmarjeshi* were not present at the wedding so the Tanzanian visitors were by far the most glamorous guests. I remember how proud and arrogant they were, standing to one side like two peacocks who find themselves in a chicken yard. I was carrying Robert's camera, which he had used to take photos of the groom and bride. Now I couldn't resist asking the 'peacocks' for a photograph. They granted me permission to do so, obligingly turning around so I could get a shot of their long, red braids which came together in a cone of soft leather halfway down their backs.

This time Morani Sapuk became part of our lives and helped Robert after the car accident. When a *morani* is injured or ill, he stays away from the family *enkang* and builds temporary accommodation in the forest. There he remains with a select few of his age group comrades, living off freshly killed livestock and brewing medicinal soups. The sick warrior is thus assured of a good supply of nourishing food and plenty of rest. He is also returning to the place of his greatest spiritual strength – the forest. Robert had some goats and sheep in another *enkang* far away near Narosura. Robert wanted to take these particular animals into the forest with him but it was impossible for him to fetch them with his arm in a cast. Morani Sapuk kindly took on the task.

While Robert was away in the forest, Morani Sapuk stayed in our *enkang* and gravitated to my house for meals. I did not mind this in the least as he was excellent company, even though he spoke no English. I soon thought of him as part of our family and looked forward to his visits. He was much better than Robert around the house, not the least because he had two good arms. He would play with Ndoondo and her sister Gunisai, teasing them about which one he would marry. They both shrieked in delicious horror and refused to sit on the same bench with him. I think we all fell in love with him a little bit that spring. I couldn't have done without his help, which included walking the four kilometre return journey to the trading *dukas* every two days to bring back food and essentials.

He also helped chop my firewood into manageable pieces and even carried jerrycans of water from the river for me on several occasions. Some days I felt too tired to cook a midday meal. Then Morani Sapuk would ask for flour and fat to cook chapattis. He would cook and eat his meal in the bachelor house behind mine and would cook extra for Ndoondo and me which we ate in our own house. Later, I discovered that he could make *mandazi*, a type of sweet donut. He made big batches for me, including some on my birthday in November. The children and I were in heaven, shovelling in the neat triangles of sweet fried dough. Ndoondo would go from house to house with a bowl full of *mandazi* offering them to the other women.

My alarm clock each morning was the throaty croak of the colobus monkeys that lived in the trees at the bottom of our hill. They would start calling to each other at 6.30 for half an hour and then they were largely silent for the rest of the day. I could see their dramatic black and white plumes from my house, for they liked to sit at the very top of the trees and survey their domain. Black-faced vervet monkeys also lived there. In the golden afternoon sun, I would often catch them searching for food on the ground close to the stream.

The other animals who liked our stream were the buffaloes, but fortunately they came only at night. In the day they grazed on the edges of and inside the forest. Olive baboons liked to raid the maize *shambas*, and so young children would be stationed to shoo them away. I always knew if a leopard was on the prowl, for the baboons would scream and hoot out the warning.

Papa's dog, who was called Simba like 99 per cent of the dogs in Kenya, used to fight with the male baboons. He had many scars as mementoes of these battles. Simba was an old dog; most of his teeth had worn away, so he found it hard to get enough food. In good times, he survived on excess milk, the scrapings from the pot and sometimes a meal of *ugali*. In lean times he suffered along with everyone else. He looked like a dingo. His body was small and compact, with a deep chest and a long labrador-like tail. He was golden yellow all over, with light brown eyes. His ears would prick up straight when he was listening. When he was wiggling his body in supplication, he would lay them back flat against his head and grin shyly. His forehead was perhaps a little too broad at the skull for a dingo and his chin a little heavy. He was our *askari*, and it fell to Simba to guard the cattle from hyenas and lions at night. If the hyenas started to 'whoop whoop' a little too closely, then gallant Simba would bark his head off until someone came out to check. He was extremely shy and gentle with people. If a murderous robber arrived, Simba would not stir, but never let it be said that he let a hyena get within twenty metres of the *enkang* without a fight.

Apart from around sixty goats and eighty head of cattle, the other working animal was Mumai's cat. She was a pale grey mouser with round lemon eyes, prematurely aged from too little food and too many kittens. She had no time for people, probably because they had no time for her. Small rodents and insects were plentiful, and with the odd drink of milk she survived.

I had rats in my house. I would hear them running under my bed at night and occasionally saw them dart across from the wood-pile to beneath the table. I really hate rats and having them in my house gave me the heebiejeebies. Mumai suggested that her cat come to catch them. However the mouser didn't like hanging around unfamiliar territory. Mumai's solution was to bring her small kitten and tie him with a string around his neck to a pole in my house. It works with cattle, but not cats. The mouser would have none of it and abandoned her kitten to a slow death by choking so I had to untie him. Over the next few days, I noticed that the kitten was starving. His mother was not producing any milk and he was still too small to manage to catch much of anything.

One day I found him lying under a bush next to my house, only just breathing. I took him inside and tried to give him water and milk, which he wouldn't take. He slept on a chair for the next twelve hours. Every now and then I would prod him gently to check whether he was still alive. The next day he drank some milk. I slowly fed him up and even bought meat for him. The Maasai thought this was outrageous. He was a terror with the meat. Morani Sapuk would have to hold him down while I cut it up. If he managed to escape, he would pounce on the meat and could drag double his bodyweight off the table. The Maasai name for a domestic cat is *Embuss* (rhymes with puss), so that is what I called him. He became so tame and gentle that all the children loved to play with him. At night he slept at the foot of Ndoondo's bed. His presence in my house was enough to clear out the rats. He grew into a sleek grey tom, and we now call him Bwana Buss.

At night, when all the work of cooking is over, there are few places on earth as cosy and comforting as the interior of a Maasai house. After the girls had fallen asleep, I would sit up knitting or reading by the warm light of the fire and Morani Sapuk would play with the radio. We both liked African music and he would search through the short wave frequencies until he found some good music. We would sit together in companionable silence, each with our own thoughts, Embuss asleep upon one of our knees. Sometimes he would teach me some Maasai and I would teach him some English. He loved to look through my books, which was how I learnt that he could read and write Swahili and Maasai very well. His handwriting was the best I had seen. He set himself a task of copying English words and Maasai meanings from my dictionary into a small notebook.

On other evenings, Loldudula (whom I now had to call *Paashe* because he had given me a calf) would join us, and because he could speak English we got into some hilarious three-way conversations. Morani Sapuk insisted he was a Christian, but in the same breath he would say that his wife must be a circumcised girl (a practice the missionaries are against). Both he and Loldudula were fascinated by my descriptions of western courtship and marriage rituals. One day they both escorted me to a mission church service. After the service (which was of course conducted in Maasai), I asked them what they had thought. Loldudula thoughtfully replied that the lessons were good, but he didn't agree with what the missionary said about having only one girlfriend. He considered this to be a mistake in the lesson.

I considered Morani Sapuk a fine man and a hardworking warrior. Unfortunately he was not held in such high regard by others. I was puzzled by this, as to my western way of thinking he seemed far more industrious and helpful than any of the other men. He did not drink honey beer and his only vice seemed to be the odd snort of snuff. Daniel ordered him around a lot, and especially bothered him when he was drunk. I discovered that he was looked down upon because he was a poor man. The Maasai are terrible snobs when it comes to cattle and apparently Morani Sapuk didn't have many. As a poor Tanzanian, he had crossed the border in search of work, either for cash or livestock. Robert arranged for him to dig a large garden for maize and paid him in goats. One night I asked Nolmemeri why she didn't marry one of her daughters to Morani Sapuk. She laughed and explained that you must never marry your daughter to a poor man!

By this time Nolmemeri (Memi) was my other special friend in our *enkang*. I came to think of her as my 'Maasai Mum'. I know she loves me fiercely and thinks of me as her own child. She is a remarkable woman in many ways, but it would be impossible not to mention just how beautiful she is. Now in her early forties, Nolmemerie is a knockout. And it is not just her wonderful eyes, teeth, skin and cheekbones. I adore just watching Memi because her inner strength, her pride and her gentleness pour from her like golden sunshine.

Memi came into our family as a young bride married to one of Robert's half-brothers in the early 1960s, the same year that Robert was born. Her husband was the only son of Kokoo, the favourite wife of Robert's father. Early on in Memi's marriage, after her first three children had been born, tragedy struck. Her husband was killed by a spear that was meant for a charging rhinoceros. Robert was a small boy when this happened. I know about this accident only from what he has told me privately, for, in cases where a young person tragically dies, it is forbidden to talk about the dead or even mention their name. Robert explained all this to me when I was trying to write down his family tree and cautioned me not to write the name or ever to speak of it to his family.

When it comes to older people, the Maasai have a very natural, accepting attitude towards death, for they understand that it is part of life. Robert explained to me that when an old man or old woman dies, nobody cries for it is not really a sad thing. Traditionally, the Maasai did not bury their dead but left them out in the bush. The body was positioned towards the setting sun and eaten by hyenas. Very important old men, like major Iloibonok, were the exception to this rule. They would be buried in a shallow grave marked with a pile of rocks. Nowadays the Loita Maasai bury all their dead including babies.

Robert told me later that he had been away in Morijo at his mother's house when his father died earlier in the year. He went immediately to his father's home in Narotian. A week before Papa died, he called all his seven sons and put his affairs in order. First he told them that he would die within the week. When an old man dies, a bullock is slaughtered, but instead of waiting until he had died, Papa instructed his sons to slaughter an ox now, so they could enjoy eating the meat. He didn't want anyone to be sad when he died.

Custom demands that the bullock may not be white; it should have generous horns and must be owned by the oldest son. Ol Morijoi, the oldest, did not own a suitable beast, so he bought one from another of his brothers. Papa also wisely divided his cattle between his sons. Ol Morijoi, the eldest son, who was also blind, was given four cattle. The other six brothers were all given two each. Robert, because he was his father's favourite, was given the two best cattle: one black and white cow and one red cow. When they give birth to their next calves, they will be given a new name. Robert will not use their old names, given to them by his father, for fear of making them sad. The Maasai believe that cattle grieve for their owners when they die.

One week later Papa died peacefully in his sleep early in the evening. Daniel and Ilampala sat with Papa's body throughout the night, pouring milk into his mouth at intervals. The preparation of the body for burial was the sole responsibility of the sons. Grandsons, nephews, wives and daughters stayed in their own houses. This was not their work. In the morning, when all the sons had arrived, Papa's body was smeared in fat reserved from the slaughtered ox. Each son helped smear the fat, standing in a line from the oldest to youngest. Meanwhile, friends of the family gathered to help dig a grave just behind his house. The grave was first lined with leaves from an *olmisigiyoi* tree.

Papa's body was dressed in a brand new blanket, and then wrapped in the soft ox skin. Finally the body was placed in the grave and covered with soil. Up until this point, everything had been done by the sons. Now they could call the other men who had been waiting inside the houses, who then came and stood with the brothers by the left side of the grave. For the Maasai, there is no prayer or blessing and there are no special rules about clothing. Jewellery is worn as usual. No special formalities are observed when passing the grave after that. Women have no formal part in male burial. When a woman dies, her female relatives perform the rituals and it is the men who keep away.

Two days after the burial, elders arrived for another ceremony. First they drank the honey beer which had been prepared for them. Next all of Papa's wives swept out the house where their husband had died. When it was very clean, the elders blessed it. This small ceremony is known as *Iatoropil enkaji*, which means 'They sweep the house'. From the time Papa died, there was a taboo against drinking pure water. This applied to everyone in the family, even children. When they wanted to drink water, the family had to add a few drops of milk so the water was cloudy. This continued for a few weeks until another ceremony called *Aook enkare*, which means 'They drink water'. For this ceremony, a black ox was slaughtered in the forest. The ox can be of any solid colour except brown. The second son has to provide this ox — in this case, Daniel.

The seven sons were the first to eat the meat, once again going from the oldest to the youngest. Then all the assembled men started eating. When the meat was finished, the men returned to the *enkang*. Then everyone – men, women and children – was given fresh water to drink, once again starting with the seven sons, who took turns drinking from a special gourd. The elders then drank the honey beer. Some of them remained in the *enkang* overnight. Very early the next morning, before the cattle went out for grazing, the elders and the seven brothers assembled to divide up their father's belongings between them. Maasai custom decrees that the oldest son gets the *enkidong*, stool, tobacco container and walking stick. The other sons then divide the rest between them. Each son has the right to state if a particular item is a favourite memento. Robert chose a silver bracelet. This business is known as *Apika ilkatari* or 'Putting on the bracelets'.

This blessing and the distribution of mementoes concludes the official business that accompanies the death of all important old men. However, one last task remains. The death of the head of the family means that all the sons must move their homes, even if it is only 45 metres to the left. As I saw it, this doesn't seem to happen within a set time limit. This signifies a fresh start and an end to the sorrow of the family and their cattle. As a mark of respect for these grieving cattle, Robert's family would not sell or give away any of the cattle until they have moved. All the sons must move at around the same time.

The Maasai do not believe in an afterlife, but they do say that sometimes very important men will come back to this world disguised as a snake. Robert doesn't believe that, but he cannot offer any suggestion as to what happens when you die. If pressed, he will say that when you die, there is nothing more. However, sometimes we say that Papa is watching us, or that Papa knows what is happening, so this is an acknowledgment that the spirit continues.

Because of the tradition of never speaking the name of a young man who has died tragically, I was always very careful when questioning people about their family background in case a young person had died. I learnt that if you see a woman without a husband, it is best not to ask where he is. If you gently ask a third party as to his whereabouts, they will simply tell you *'eshomo'*, he has gone away – one of the most delicate euphemisms for death I know of. Robert's family must have discovered quickly that my father had died when still a young man, the greatest tragedy imaginable for the Maasai, for no one ever asked me about him.

Robert was away healing his body and soul in the forest for a little more than a month. He says he finished that work quickly because of me. Robert and I are a classic case of 'opposites attract'. Where I was quick to act or to anger, Robert was thoughtful and patient. I acted from the heart, while he used his head. We had much to teach each other, but it didn't mean that getting used to being married was any easier. We had one serious fight during this time, the sort of battle that ended with Robert storming out of the house. Would you believe that it was over crying? I had been feeling tired and unhappy during the day and as a result was a bit weepy. Instead of offering comfort, Robert was shocked and disgusted that I would cry 'like a child'. He refused to see my point of view, which only made me cry harder, and he left to sleep in another house with Morani Sapuk.

I felt as though I had lost my best friend. I mean, if Robert couldn't comfort me when I was feeling low, who could? My tears stopped and I prepared to go to bed alone, all the while playing with the thought that I had made a terrible mistake and our relationship would never work. Not long afterwards Robert walked back in, having thought about it in his typical methodical fashion, and having decided that I must be crying 'because of my culture'. Yes! That was it, I was crying because my culture permitted it.

This was to become the standard by which we could negotiate all our differences. It was our catchcry for agreeing to disagree. I was not Maasai, and did not want to be Maasai. You can only be what you are, and we both accepted that about each other.

I was used to not being able to show any affection to Robert during the day, but it didn't mean I always liked it. Even when we were alone, he was never comfortable touching me during the day in case 'someone walked in'. Slowly I adjusted my expectations. I invented a game which made me feel better. If we were alone during the day I would ask Robert if he wanted to kiss me. He would laugh shyly and softly reply, 'I wish'. I was reassured and he maintained his own standards. It was a good compromise.

ENKIYAMA (MARRIAGE)

Initially being unable to touch or even be with Robert in public had been very hard. It went against all I knew about romantic love and how to express it. To be a couple, I thought, meant being together – in public and private – most of the time. Or if you couldn't be together, then you should at least want to. I now realise that gradually I had grown used to the Maasai way, and in fact even preferred it. I didn't miss having my hand held in public, hello and goodbye kisses.

I also got used to not sharing all my meals with Robert. Food and food rituals were no longer part of my romantic conventions. I liked eating early with Ndoondo and the other children. Organising and sharing food with other women and children felt different, more challenging, more nourishing. It was to do with me and not with 'feeding my man'. Sometimes I would cook for Robert later at night, but often I would give him and Morani Sapuk the ingredients and they would go and cook for themselves. I cherished the independence and freedom I had in my relationship with Robert. I liked the space to be with other women and children. I liked the extra privacy and respect that Robert gave me. Once it had seemed too formal and stiff, but now I valued it enormously. Without the suffocating closeness of romantic intimacy, I was free to be my own person, and from my own space I began to redefine my ideas of how I could be within a relationship.

Even though our wedding ceremony was held in July 1992, I had in fact been acknowledged as Robert's wife by the Loita community since 1990. Robert's second wife was a young Maasai girl named Enoolomala from Kajiado district. As we had agreed, he had married her quietly back in March before I returned to Kenya. The first time I met her was very anti-climactic. One day she arrived in Narotian from Morijo, where she lived with Robert's mother, to help with the preparations for our wedding. Robert pointed her out to me and I suggested that we should be introduced. Like all young girls, she was shy and didn't reveal very much about herself. She was very pretty.

The second time we met was two months afterwards when she came to help me with housework for a few days when Robert went into the forest after the car accident. He was worried I would get sick from doing too much, so he arranged for Enoolomala to come over. This was incredibly weird. Here was this fifteen-year-old girl, very quiet, very sweet. She worked hard and stayed with me for five days. But she was married to my husband and one day (though I tried not to dwell on it) I could expect her to have his children. This was a very challenging time for me. A Maasai woman in my place would have welcomed this girl as her own child. Well, as I've said before, I'm not Maasai, so I had to force myself to rise above the immediate, immature response and to muster all my understanding and compassion. I managed to do it by going into a sort of autopilot mode where I refused to give in to jealousy by concentrating on respecting her as a young woman who was now part of my family.

Of course Robert was and still is completely baffled by my ambivalent feelings on the subject. He desperately wants Enoolomala and I to be friends, as is usually the case with co-wives. He doesn't understand why I don't see her as being just like any other Maasai woman. Enoolomala also constantly asks when she can visit me, only to hear excuses invented by Robert. He could never explain that I felt anything less than total love for her as it would reflect badly on him as well as me. To fully understand how the Maasai approach marriage, you have to put aside all notions of western style romance and love. This is a business proposition.

Enoolomala was chosen by Robert's third oldest brother, Langisa. Robert, like most respectful Maasai men, would have left the choice and arrangements entirely in the hands of his older brother. Her family were once wealthy and managed a large herd of cattle so her skills in this area are highly prized. Maasai men like to feel that their precious herds are in good hands if they have to go away. The negotiation of the bride price between two families is the most serious part of the marriage process, in fact you could equate it to the saying of Christian vows.

Bride price is one of the major ways that cattle wealth is redis-tributed among the pastoral Maasai. The negotiations involve the fathers or uncles and senior brothers or the intended couple, but rarely the groom himself. Cattle are paid to the bride's family to compensate them for the loss of a working daughter and also serve to bind the girl to her in-laws. For example, if a Maasai girl feels trapped within an unhappy marriage, she will hesitate to return to her parents because they have already accepted cattle payment for her. To return five, ten or fifteen cattle is unthinkable, and so the unhappy girl will be inclined to stay with her husband and sort things out rather than compromise her parents.

The Maasai say that if a daughter is especially loved, they will only ask for one cow for her. If 'she gets a problem' sometime in the future, it will be relatively simple to exchange the single cow for the girl. Robert says that this is what he plans for Ndoondo. (I suspect that Ndoondo may hatch plans of her own ...) New brides are often chosen in order to build a stronger association between the senior men of the two families. Marriage cements a friendship and a potential, new grazing alliance. The days of one man having many wives are almost over, even in the conservative Nkidongi family. At the turn of the century, a wealthy man might have a dozen wives, especially the Iloibonok. Robert's father had four wives; his own sons will have two and their children will probably limit themselves to one each. This has as much to do with economics as it does with influences from the West and Christian missionaries.

During this time two other people became part of my life. Once a week, Kikuyan came to wash our clothes. (Kikuyan was the first woman I had met when I came to Narotian.) She also brought me a load of firewood from time to time. It had taken quite a bit of talking to convince Robert that I should pay for these services. He believed that the women of his family should help me as a matter of course and that payment could introduce other problems. In the end, he agreed and I paid Kikuyan for her work. She was a widow, the youngest wife of a very old man who was an uncle of Robert's. She had at least eight children and only a few scrawny cattle. She wanted to start up a small business selling snuff and so she needed the shillings for capital. The other new influence was Regina. She came to help me with my Maasai language studies for two hours every second day. She was an educated Maasai girl who taught Ndoondo's nursery class. Her English was very good and we would work on vocabulary and simple phrases. In this way, I added slowly to my knowledge and use of the language, though I was still very much a beginner.

After a wedding, it is customary for the bride to go around visiting various relatives and collecting livestock gifts. I followed the custom and went to stay in Empurpitia for a week at Ilampala's *enkang*. Empurpitia is at the edge of a great forest known by the Maasai as Naimina Enkiyio. The story goes, that a long time ago a small girl was lost in the forest, so it is called *naimina*, which means lost, and *enkiyio*, which is the name the Maasai give to a dead child. Only a living child is *enkerai*. The Naimina Enkiyio Forest is one of the last pristine forests left in Kenya. It covers hundreds of kilometres of ancient, undisturbed trees and is rich in animal and bird life. The forest harbours almost all species found in southern Kenya, including elephants. In addition to the animals and birds, the plant life represents a veritable medicine chest for the Maasai. Honey is harvested, berries are collected and the forest obviously plays an important role as a catchment area for the entire region.

The Loita Maasai revere the forest as a holy place. The Nkidongi clan are the stewards of this special forest, which has been passed down from the time of Mbatiany, through to Senteu, Simel, and now to the great Oloiboni Makompo ole Simel. He is the chief custodian of the forest.

The area is dotted with sacred ritual sites, such as the Loitokitok River, where the spiritual leader of each age group must bathe before walking home to be circumcised.

Standing on a small rise looking over the edge of Naimina Enkiyio forest is Ilampala's *enkang*. He lives here with his beautiful wife Nosotua and their two children. At dusk you can hear the elephants rumble to each other from inside the protective green walls of the forest. Ilampala has built an *enkang* different from any other I had seen in Loita. The most striking difference is the trees, for he has built right at the edge of the forest and kept trees and grass around his three small houses. One house has been built especially for goats and the other two are for people. Another striking difference is the flies, or rather the lack of them. The cattle are kept in an enclosure about ten metres from the houses and that makes all the difference. The materials used in building the enclosure are not the traditional thorn fence, but cedar poles over four metres tall. The result is a stronger fence and one that requires less maintenance. There are two small vegetable gardens, one for the dry season which is closer to the river and one for the wet season next to the house. Purists would say that Ilampala has sold out, and has become 'Kikuyu-fied'. I say he has built a comfortable home and the basis of a solid and secure future for his family.

One day during my visit in November 1992, I witnessed a small ceremony that I had never seen before. Known as the *Eokutu kule*, which means 'milk-drinking ceremony', it marks a boy's transition from an initiate, *olaibartani*, into a junior *morani*, or *olbarnoti* ('the shaved one'). Risee had been circumcised in July 1992. He was an orphan from a poor family across the border in Tanzania. Ilampala had taken over the task of organising and paying for his circumcision ceremony in return for Risee helping care for our family's cattle. Initiates may only wear black or other dark-coloured cloth. During this period of their life they are not permitted to wash their body or cut their hair. They wear no adornment except for the traditional stuffed bird headdress or a chain circlet worn around the head with extra chains hanging over the eyes.

Risee, like all the men in our family, wore only a simple circlet made of silver chain and blue beads. All initiates go through a symbolic cleansing the evening before the ceremony day. Their heads are shaved and all adornments are discarded.

Risee, Nosotua, Mama and I all gathered by the side of Nosotua's house. The cattle had been brought into the *enkang*. Risee sat on a cow skin – the same skin that he had been circumcised on five months earlier. Nosotua wet his thatch of long hair with a handful of milk and then deftly shaved his head clean, section by section with a double-sided razor blade. She then shaved his eyebrows off. The new face of Risee was clean and proud. Mama said that I could keep Risee's circlet as long as I left it in my house and did not take it away to Australia. Usually, the head decorations are tossed into the calf-pen inside the house.

I saw Risee again later that night when he was freshly scrubbed and in his brand-new garments. He now looked like a real *morani* in his red blanket and new jewellery given to him by Nosotua. Three important elders had now arrived: the Olaigwanani, or speaker of Ilampala's age group, and John, the government-appointed subchief for the location, and a minor Oloiboni. We all gathered inside Nosotua's house. The men drank the honey beer. Mama was allowed a mug of the brew, but it was strictly rationed after that. Nosotua and I did not drink. The elders blessed Risee with eloquent words, wishing him cattle and bidding him to show respect for the elders all his life.

The next day was busy with preparations for the feast. In the forest close to the *enkang*, Robert and Morani Sapuk supervised the slaughter and cooking of a goat. I stayed in the house to help Nosotua and spent most of the morning peeling potatoes. The honey beer started to flow as more elders arrived. John, the subchief, was the only one wearing western clothing. Government appointments are largely political and have little to do with reflecting the real leadership of the elders. However John seemed a popular choice.

In the afternoon, when the elders had flaked out around the *enkang*, Risee escorted me to the edge of the forest and brought me a piece of meat. He cut small pieces off with his new knife and handed them to me to eat. Meat tastes sweetest like this. Because this was a bona fide ceremony, and not just a small family barbecue, I was not permitted to attend the actual meat camp. Earlier I was impervious to these subtleties, by this time I had begun to think more like a Maasai and wanted to show respect for their customs. It would now be unthinkable for me to attend a men's meat camp as I had done in 1990 for Daniel's *Olkiteng lorrbaa*.

Sadly, Risee was not able to continue with the traditional period of *morani*hood, because he was an orphan and therefore had no one to provide cattle for slaughtering and sharing with his age mates. Such contributions are mandatory. Because Risee was unable to meet these obligations, he was quietly promoted to the ranks of junior elder, though still only a teenager. When I met Risee again a year later (in 1993), the lack of traditional education was all too obvious. Without the strong influence of a father to guide him, without the chance to mature, acquire skills and prove himself a worthy *morani*, he was painfully adrift. The gentle boy I had first known had become shrill and coarse. He would often order children around and frighten them, playing with power without understanding the responsibility that came with it. When he took up with a group of wastrels and began drinking, I forbad him to enter my house.

ENKIYAMA (MARRIAGE)

The Maasai do not celebrate birthdays, so I had expected my birthday in November to be a bit of a non-event. It was. Robert knew some effort was required and tried very hard to find a suitable present for me. I had requested the thigh bells that he had worn as a young warrior. These were the bells Robert was wearing when he killed the lion. Normally, after each generation of warriors goes through their *Eunoto* ceremony, the bells are passed onto a younger warrior. Thus Robert's bells had been passed down to him through all his brothers. Because he was the youngest, he had passed them onto a *morani* from another family. I could see them being sold down the line for shillings, or swapped for a Mickey Mouse t-shirt. Robert struck a deal with the *morani* who now had them; the bells for two goats plus the young *morani* retained the right to wear them again at his *Eunoto* ceremony.

Robert also found four precious hen's eggs. People often express surprise when they learn that the Maasai do not keep chickens. It is easy to see why if you think back to their nomadic days herding cattle and goats across the floor of the Great Rift Valley. Chickens would never have kept up! Robert bought the eggs from a Kikuyu. I used them to make a golden steamed pudding. In my very basic kitchen, steamed puddings were the easiest things in the world to whip up, if you could just get hold of the eggs. Robert, uncharacteristically, then sat inside the house with me all day. He must have sensed that I was liable to go into a decline if left on my own that day!

If the spiritual soul of the Loita Maasai lies within the forest, then the spiritual soul of each separate *enkang* lies within its own cattle enclosure. Life revolves around the livestock. Even though I have less to do with them than the other women, I cannot help but be influenced by the daily rhythm of milking, watering, grazing, birth and death. Towards the end of 1992, I witnessed the birth of a calf. It was early evening and the cattle were being milked. A young black heifer stood by herself, head down, looking miserable. Memi called me over to watch.

The birth proceeded pretty much as I was accustomed to seeing on 'All Creatures Great and Small'; first the tiny hooves, followed by the face. The cow bellowed for all she was worth and the women stood watching until she appeared to be struggling with the whole procedure. Then three of them, Meiyoki, Memi and her daughter Nataiya each grabbed hold and pulled the calf out. They let it rest for only a moment. Then Meiyoki hoisted it up and carried it across the enclosure to the side of Memi's house. There she took a swig of water and spat it over the calf's mouth and nose, washing away any mucus. The cow finally wandered over to check on her calf. As night fell, the baby managed to take a drink of milk and was then moved inside the house next to the fire.

My first baby goat wasn't quite so skilful straight off. She was very weak when she was born, probably because her mother had been sick towards the end of the pregnancy with East Coast Fever. She was given an injection and recovered, but the kid may have been affected. I had been given the mother when she was just six months old by ten-year-old Momposhe, one of our schoolboys. She had grown into a big nanny goat, pregnant with a kid of her own. This nanny goat had no particular name. If the truth be told, I found it hard to distinguish her from all the other white goats with small horns. This is difficult for the Maasai to understand, as they know and can name all their animals by sight. She gave birth down by the stream one afternoon. The first I knew of it was Kokoo announcing the news.

The nanny goat was led up, or I should say pulled up, the hill with a leather strap around her neck. The newborn baby was carried by one of the children. We tied Nanny to a post by my house, and then I sat down to watch the baby goat adjust to her new world. At first she was just a little lump of white, streaked with mucus and blood. I wiped her mouth and nose clean, and then let the sun gently dry the rest. After half an hour, she was pure white and fluffy. Her hooves, which had been a translucent pink, began to turn an opaque cream colour.

When she finally awoke after nearly an hour sleeping in the sun, I saw that her eyes were pale blue. This was nothing special though, Narygunkishon assured me, as most goats are born with blue eyes, which turn brown later. I was anxious to see her take her first steps, but she was in no hurry. She mewed a bit, and her mother, who was new to all this business, eventually stopped calling for her friends and took notice of her baby, maaing soft nanny goat endearments.

After what seemed an eternity, the baby began to struggle to stand. It took ages perfecting this manoeuvre, and it wasn't until nearly three hours later that she took her first drink of milk.

The nanny goat didn't help matters, as she was skittish and each time the baby managed to get a good grip on a teat, she kicked out and moved. The whole exhausting process of struggling to her feet, balancing enough to walk and finding a teat had to be repeated over and over again.

The Maasai separate the mothers and kids at night. The adults sleep in the large *olale* and the kids in the smaller pen inside the main room of the house. This protects the young, not only from being squashed, but also from disease carrying fleas and ticks that proliferate among their elders. However, newborn goats, like calves, usually spend their first few nights tethered to a Maasai bed close to the fire. They drink from their mothers mid-morning, before the goat herd goes out to graze, and at dusk when they return. So after only a few hours with her mother, my baby goat was wrenched away and settled on a thick bed of straw in a corner of my house. I was fortunate to have the straw, which was a luxury most baby goats never know. When she recovered from her efforts at feeding and started to move around, we boxed her in with two chairs turned on their side against a corner to form a small pen. Before I went to bed, I swabbed the umbilical area with Betadine and popped a hot water bottle under the straw for extra comfort during the night. No goat in the history of the Maasai nation has enjoyed such a comfortable night. I was disappointed when she died three days later, after growing progressively weaker and weaker. Robert was amazed to see me weep when it became evident she was dying. He gave Matilda an oral dose of medicine, more to make me feel better I think. She died outside in the warm sun and the tiny white body was given to Simba to eat. Kokoo told me not to worry, for *Enkai* was great and would give me more goats and maybe a bull.

Not long after the baby goat had died, in early December Tropical Ice brought a small walking safari to the Loitas and invited me to join them during their four-day hike. Robert was employed as a guide, along with Ilampala, Murrianga and the puckish Ol Dorobo. I was delighted to accompany the group, partly because I enjoy being a 'bridge' between cultures, partly because I wanted to be near Robert, but mainly because of the food. There is not a single restaurant or lodge in Kenya (and only a very few in Australia) that can match the outstanding food prepared by the Tropical Ice cooks.

Out of a simple camp oven – a tin box placed on a bed of coals – emerged the most delicious food. Mostly the meals were comfortingly old-fashioned, such as roast turkey with golden potatoes and pumpkin, fried Nile perch fillets served with thick chips and whole beef fillets accompanied by a vegetable soufflé. Other delights included authentic Indian food, home-made pizza, chunky minestrone, traditional Kenyan dishes, fresh fruit, steamed puddings, and cakes and bread baked daily. Five days' worth of food can be packed at one time into a huge cool box, which is then filled with dry ice. This keeps the beer and soda cold too. I hadn't eaten so well since our own Maasai Culture and Wildlife Safari in July and I needed no prompting to accept the invitation.

On the third day walking in the Loitas, the group was invited to attend an *Emorata* (circumcision) ceremony being held at an *enkang* in Ongarua, near Morijo. It was to be a double ceremony for a brother and sister. I hadn't witnessed a circumcision since Loldudula 'faced the knife' in our own *enkang* over two years ago. I was not sure that I wanted to attend another female circumcision. Now that I understood more about the Maasai, I wondered if I would feel differently about the ceremony. Also I knew that the American women in our group would be in for an awful shock. I wanted to be there to help them understand what was going on and why. The night before the ceremony I explained as best I could all the different elements of *Emorata* and their significance. It is a very private and indeed a sacred occasion and we were privileged to be honoured with an invitation.

We drove to the *enkang* very early. Mist still lay across the Morijo valley and it was very cold. It felt strange to be driving to such an occasion; the vehicles looked incongruous parked outside the Maasai *enkang*. Walking across the plains would have been more appropriate. When we arrived, assorted elders, children and cattle were milling around inside the cattle enclosure. The sacred olive tree branches had been planted in the ground around a cowhide. Extra hides had been stretched between the branches like a windbreak.

Women were gathered in the doorways, talking in hushed

tones. The mother of the two initiates made a show of going about her chores, feigning disinterest, but her furrowed forehead gave her concern away. A trio of venerable elders were already positioned against a house, wrapped in their blankets, sucking away contentedly at their bottles of honey beer.

All of a sudden the boy initiate appeared at the family gate, dripping wet and snorting like a wild bull. From the very first instance, he seized control of his initiation. He was in a trance, but was more active, more aware than the other boys I had seen. The power he exuded was almost overwhelming. He strode to the little cowhide enclosure and unexpectedly threw himself backwards with fury. I had to jump out of the way to avoid colliding with him. He sat with his back against his sponsor, legs spread, eyes fierce and concentrated on the hands of the circumcisor.

The men had all crowded in to watch when one of the American men fainted. Fortunately there were a couple of Maasai handy to catch him. The first cut had not even been made. The Maasai of course thought this was very funny, but given the potent atmosphere, it is easy to understand how it affected this chap. He recovered quickly and managed to watch the rest of the operation. The boy did not so much as blink, and was dragged away into a relative's house to await promises of livestock from his relatives.

Next it was his sister's turn and I decided to retreat to the sidelines. I noticed all the same preparation as before: the women clearing a hole in the thatch roof of her mother's house; the bigger circumcised girls standing around giggling; the small children being shooed away but inevitably attracted to the doorway like the flies there before them. Elsewhere in the *enkang* warriors collected blood from the neck of a young bull. The men milled around, disinterested now that the male operation was over. Two of the American women had accepted an invitation from the girl's mother to watch from inside the hut. A couple of others watched from the doorway, where they could escape if they had to. However, the two women inside would have to stay until the bitter end, as it would be impossible to get past the girl and attendant women once the cutting had started.

My stomach churned and I wondered why was I there. It wasn't long until the screaming started. Even more upsetting was the cruel laughter of the older circumcised girls standing around the doorway. They seemed to find the screams of the new initiate very funny. Perhaps this was done on purpose to anger the girl and so make her forget a little of her pain. Perhaps not.

When it was all over, the Americans and the Maasai guides regrouped at the vehicles outside. The women were all pale and shaken, but had remained polite and respectful throughout. One woman inside the house had started to cry, but her friend sharply told her to stop. She pointed out that tears were inappropriate and that she had no right to impose her own emotions on what was, for the Maasai, an important and celebratory event. They talked about what they had seen, and what they noticed most of all was the vast difference between the ceremony for the boy and the girl.

There was a sense of dignity, respect and control around the boy. The ceremony was almost beautiful to behold. It was empowering and inspiring. When it came to circumcising the girl though, the women were most of all disorganised. There was no sense of ritual, just the hacking of flesh. One of the American women who had watched from inside the house was a final year medical student — she had noted everything that happened in clinical detail.

I had secretly hoped that the Loita Maasai might have practised only clitoridectomy. I now knew, from what the American student told me, that they cut away not only the clitoris, but also the labia majora and minora. On the scale of genital mutilation performed on women throughout the world, you might say that this is worse than a 'mere' clitoridectomy, but nowhere near as bad as infibulation, where the genitals are sewn up except for a tiny opening for urine and menstrual blood. This form is not practised among the Maasai, but it is still used today in northern Kenya, parts of Somalia, the Sudan and some parts of West Africa.

When it came to cutting, the women holding this particular girl were squeamish, and would look away and loosen their grip on her just when they needed to hold her the most. The girl would struggle and move, then they would have to stop cutting, reposition her, hold her down and start cutting again. On and on this process was repeated. In the end, the circumcisor had many cuts on her hands, and it was impossible to see through all the blood. Since this opera-tion had been performed on hundreds of thousands of Maasai women for centuries, the Americans couldn't figure out why the women had not become more organised. Why hadn't they worked out a better system, for example, slicing against a piece of wood, which would be more precise and hopefully quicker.

It was a fair question, but one that came from women empowered to control their own destinies and from women whose culture allowed the exchange of intimate information. The first prerequisite for any sort of change is for people to sit down together and talk. They must share their dissatisfaction. Maasai women cannot do this. Some of them secretly admit to me that they do not like female circumcision, but what can we do they ask, when the elders insist upon it. 'If I don't circumcise my daughter, then no man will marry her,' they say.

Times do change, however slowly, even in Maasailand. I have been told by school-educated Maasai that they are now practising a less radical circumcision upon their daughters and sometimes the operation is carried out in a hospital or clinic. There are even a handful of urban, Christian Maasai who do not circumcise their girls at all. I make no judgment on whether this is better or not. I am in no position to sit in judgment on the Maasai. This issue belongs to Maasai women specifically, and Kenyan women in general. Outsiders should not judge or interfere in any way. As a final observation, I should say that Maasai women are not victims. They live full and competent lives, raise many healthy children, and are far less preoccupied with their circumcised state than we are.

A month or so earlier, at the end of October, Robert had been due for an X-ray, so we were collected in a mini-van by the company who was liable for the accident and taken to Nairobi. I also had to check in with Janet Eastman about the progress of the proposed second story for '60 Minutes'. Of course by this time, the first story had been shown in Australia and I had had some feedback from my family and friends, none of which was favourable. Most telling were the comments from my brother, who had been there. He thought the story focused on the sexual morals of the Maasai and ignored the more important aspects of their culture.

The original plan with Janet had been for Robert to return to Australia with me in December. I was looking forward to having an Aussie Christmas with him. It was, after all, one of the few big ceremonies left in my culture. However, when I contacted Janet by fax it seemed that '60 Minutes' had changed the plan. Their crews went on their annual six weeks holiday over Christmas and would not be available for any filming until February. '60 Minutes' refused to hire a casual crew to film before Christmas. They wanted Robert to come over in February. Couldn't he come over at Christmas anyway, and then stay for filming in February, I asked. The reply was no, they wanted to capture his first impressions of Australia and did not want him to become acclimatised to the modern world. I pointed out that my husband rarely registered surprise and animation. In fact, when presented with an unfamiliar situation, the Maasai can be quite inscrutable. They hold their cards very close and don't like to give away their true feelings. However Janet felt that if she told '60 Minutes' that, then they might be inclined to call the whole thing off. I mean, why do a story about someone who is not going to express their feelings on camera? Why indeed! However, '60 Minutes' had offered to pay another $5000 for the follow-up story and I really needed the money.

The proposed change of Robert's arrival in Australia from December to January spoilt all our plans, including my own work arrangements. Deep in the pit of my stomach, I felt that we should not proceed with this second story. There was no new development in our relationship; we had nothing more to say. After the colour and spectacle of our wedding, what could we possibly do as a follow up? As I saw it, the only angle they had was the 'dumb African' all agog in the 'modern world', which sucked.

From Nairobi I faxed Janet in Amsterdam and suggested that, life being too short, we should call the whole thing off. I was willing to forgo the money and was prepared to borrow more for Robert to fly to Australia, where he could enjoy a straightforward holiday. Two things prevented me from following through this course of action. One was a very diplomatic fax from Janet, pointing out that she had invested her own time and money in the documentary project and that if we opted out now it would leave her holding the can. True enough. The second one was Robert who wanted to meet my family in Australia but was not happy at the prospect of me paying for it. He also felt that it was 'bad to change our talking now'. We did have an agreement with Janet and it would be dishonest to back out.

In true Maasai fashion, Robert felt that this decision (to cancel the second story) was too serious for us to handle by ourselves. He wanted us to consult an elder. As we were in Nairobi we turned to Iain Allan. Iain counselled us to accept the change of plans gracefully, get a free flight for Robert and as much free publicity as possible for our Maasai Culture Wildlife Tours. Robert agreed with him, so I was outnumbered, and our plans for Robert's first trip outside Kenya swung into full force.

The preparations included applying for a passport, which is not an automatic right in Kenya as it is in Australia. But before we could do this, Robert needed a birth certificate. The Maasai don't record birthdays, let alone bother with minor administrative details such as birth certificates. Very few Maasai women give birth in hospital. There is no system for recording births in the Loitas, except for memories of the old women, which have served very well until now. As even fewer Maasai ever require a passport, it doesn't really matter. After trailing around various government offices and standing in innumerable queues, we were given two forms that needed to be completed in duplicate, signed by a government chief and co-signed by the district commissioner.

This is not as simple as it sounds. The signed forms were eventually taken to a small demountable office in the grounds of Narok Hospital, where we paid a fee and then waited for half an hour for the secretary to return from tea to type out Robert's birth certificate. Then there was the passport application to be submitted, an Australian visa to be obtained and plans explained to Robert's family, none of whom had any idea of what it meant to travel across the Indian Ocean for fourteen hours by plane. Mama was quietly resigned to never seeing her son again.

I flew out of Kenya by myself in the third week of December. Robert, Ndoondo and I spent the week before this together in Nairobi and the weekend at Lake Naivasha. This was a big adventure for Ndoondo who had never travelled further than two kilometres beyond her home. We also took the opportunity to visit the airport so things would be a little more familiar to Robert on the day of his flight which was booked for the end of January. The security guards were very kind and explained the rather convoluted check-in procedure. Then we went up to the observation deck and watched the planes take off and land for a while. This was Robert's first close-up look at an aeroplane. I asked him what he thought of it all. 'I think it's crazy,' was his reply.

During this time, Robert also received the all clear from his surgeon that his arm was healing well. There had been a small chance that if the ends of the bone did not knit together a bone graft operation might be needed. We were all relieved to learn that it was not necessary.

On the Thursday Robert and Ndoondo returned to Loita and I went by taxi to the airport later that morning.

CHAPTER TWELVE

INTRODUCTIONS

January and February 1993

Melakua anginchu

Home is not far when you are
alive

MAASAI PROVERB

I SPENT A PEACEFUL CHRISTMAS WITH MY FAMILY ON THE NEW SOUTH Wales Central Coast. Though it was disappointing not to have Robert there to spend Christmas with me, I made the best of it by recharging my own batteries so that I would be ready to look after him when he finally arrived.

Robert's trip to Australia was an enormous event in his life and, as I was not there to help him, we called on a number of people. After the New Year I heard from Anne Waudo, hired by '60 Minutes' to look after Robert and the arrangements in Nairobi, that Robert's passport had come through. She arranged his inoculations and helped him negotiate his way through the minefield of check-in procedures. I spoke to Robert by phone in Nairobi; he seemed happy and excited with everything. He had to spend a day and night in Harare, where he was met by staff from tour operators, Abercrombie and Kent. Harare airport is very confusing for anybody. I knew that coming out and going back through customs would be a baptism of fire for Robert. I called him twice in Harare and he was pretty impressed with flying. Nairobi to Harare is only a short flight though. I wondered how impressed he would be with the long haul to Australia. We also talked on the phone about clothing. '60 Minutes' would be filming his arrival at Sydney airport and wanted him to go through customs in his traditional Maasai clothes. Robert would of course be wearing western clothes on the plane, and had been since leaving the Loita Hills. I told Robert that it was his decision, but that if he decided to change into Maasai gear, he could do it inside the terminal building.

The Qantas flight from Harare arrives every Friday night. On this Friday night at the end of January Mark came out to the airport with me. The thrill of seeing Robert again was definitely tinged with the dislike of being filmed. As it turned out, '60 Minutes' sent along a freelance crew. Why couldn't they just have agreed to do that in December? Finally Mark spotted Robert.

'He's wearing Maasai clothes,' he said. Under the intrusive glare of the camera, I shook Robert's hand. 'Supa,' we greeted each other. A thousand people stared at us. Robert looked tired and uncomfortable. I could see he wasn't happy about the change of clothes. Later he told me that he had been escorted to a room inside the terminal and felt pressured into changing. To make matters worse, there were some Kenyans meeting the plane, who came up to greet Robert and me. One of them exclaimed in Swahili about Robert's Maasai clothes, and accused him of letting all of Kenya down by arriving in his traditional clothes. It was not what he needed to hear. Filming over, we made our getaway. '60 Minutes' put us up in an apartment at Milsons Point. The city lights across the harbour were dazzling. A big city, Robert kept saying. It was good to have my *morani* home.

The next day, Saturday, was to be spent filming. The '60 Minutes' team were keen to capture Robert's first impressions of the big city. As I had told Janet many times, the Maasai don't like to show surprise and I didn't expect too many oohs and aahs after the long journey. Robert was exhausted and disorientated after fifteen hours of flying. The first sequence to be shot was at Just Jeans in the Queen Victoria Building. This is where the 'African Warrior' could assume the appearance of the 'white man'. At least Robert got some good clothes out of it; 501s, a chambray shirt, socks and shorts. He looked cool, but then again he always looks cool whatever he wears.

The sequences kept coming: Pitt Street Mall, street theatre, the monorail, Darling Harbour, a water taxi took us back and forth past the Sydney Opera House. (Robert: 'What's opera?' Me: 'Well, it's a long story.') We headed back to Milsons Point where Robert was interviewed about his first impressions and then we were released.

That night we had dinner with my Aunt Denise and her family. Robert was amazed at the harbour and very impressed with the roads, traffic lights and new cars. While I talked with Denise, my cousin Charlie took Robert into the TV room where he saw the first '60 Minutes' story. They must have watched it at least four times. Robert's only comment that night was that he wished he could see it without the reporter talking all the time.

The next day we were filming at my mother's on the Central Coast. It was awful that Mum, who is as shy as Robert, had to meet her son-in-law for the first time under the camera. The day was stilted and horrible. I just wanted it to end so we could relax and Robert could start to enjoy his visit here. More sequences: Robert meeting Mum, another lunch sequence, Robert down at the beach, perv shots of girls in bikinis, Robert and Mark throwing spears on the beach. While Janet was busy elsewhere, Mark made the camera-man, Paul, promise that he would not film them while he took Robert waist deep into the ocean. Paul agreed. True to his word Paul left them alone while Robert enjoyed his first dip in the sea. He couldn't swim of course, so Mark held his hand and they jumped small breakers just beyond the shore. It was the one real moment of the day. We returned to the house, were interviewed one by one upstairs, while the rest of us waited downstairs trying to keep my dog from barking. While Mum was being interviewed upstairs, my Uncle Tim arrived.

'This feels like a funeral,' he said, looking at our faces.

'Yeah,' was all Mark and I could say. Then it was over. '60 Minutes' blew out of our lives, leaving us in peace for two weeks. Then we would be required in Alice Springs.

We had a lovely fortnight at the beach. We did little more than sleep in, go for drives and watch videos while Mum cooked wonderful meals for us and generally fussed over Robert. He met the relatives and saw all my baby pictures. He started swimming lessons and learning the Australian road rules. We took Raa for walks. Mum was impressed that the dog accepted Robert immediately. This was probably because Robert is the first person to have ever treated him as a dog. We went shopping at Grace Bros where Robert became thoroughly depressed at all the consumer goods he wanted. We stopped going into shops after that. Neither of us had any money.

This was a very important time for both of us. This was Robert seeing my culture. It was his turn to be surrounded by people who spoke a foreign language. It was his turn to be without his support system and his cronies. He could begin to see why I am like I am. Robert told me that he had expected Australia to be like Nairobi, only bigger. The affluence, the sense of order, and the beauty of rural and urban Australia surprised and delighted him. He gained a new appreciation of just how tough I was to live in a mud hut. 'You're tough,' he would often say.

Two weeks later we left our idyllic existence and prepared to join the '60 Minutes' crew in Sydney before flying to Alice Springs. We drove from Alice Springs four hours north-west to Watarrka National Park (formerly Kings Canyon). This was more than just a scenic location to add to the story. Robert and I were particularly interested to visit this area because the traditional Aboriginal owners, the Loritdja people, were trying to establish cultural tourism activities on their land. Their company, Kurkarah Tours, had been conducting walking tours of the canyon for over a year.

A newly built lodge was responsible for bringing more tourists into this area. Aboriginal money was invested in the lodge. There was also a cultural site where the Aboriginal men and women taught tourists about their bush tucker, traditional housing, hunting and social laws. I hoped that in this story '60 Minutes' would include information about our own Maasai Culture & Wildlife Safari. Discussing cultural tourism with the Loritdja people of Watarrka would be a good way to bring our work into the story. We all agreed it would broaden it beyond the personal relationship aspect.

We were warmly welcomed at the Frontier Lodge where we stayed for the next four days. Apart from a glaring Mobil sign, the lodge had been artfully blended into the arid landscape. Low brick buildings merged in with the red rocks and soft green grey foliage where small wallabies lived. Despite the beautiful surroundings, the atmosphere was gloomy. Robert had finally admitted how upset and confused the first '60 Minutes' story of our wedding had made him feel. In particular Robert was deeply offended by the stuff about the spear in front of the house. He felt '60 Minutes' had betrayed his trust. I felt the same way. Janet promised Robert that this second story would redress any mistakes from the first story, especially the reference to the 'spear in the ground'.

The highlight of our stay at Watarrka was meeting the traditional owners. Over cups of instant coffee and some excellent homemade scones, members of the community explained what they were hoping to achieve with cultural tourism. Their most ambitious, and exciting, idea was to develop a three-day walking trip around the canyon. The area was beautiful beyond words and rich in Aboriginal sacred sites. The current two-hour walk had whet our appetite for more. We agreed that a three-day walking safari would be superb. The government, in its wisdom, had only funded the group for one year, so their immediate challenge was to secure funding for three years. We wished them luck and promised to return for the three-day walk. Everyone was very interested in Maasai culture, so that evening Robert returned from Frontier Lodge with a video of a Maasai ceremony (not our wedding) and talked about his culture.

We met Old Ben, Aunty Nora, Coral and other members of their extended family who gave much of their time and energy to the filming of the '60 Minutes' story. No doubt, just like me, they hoped to have their trips promoted. We filmed a number of sequences with them. I was initially wary of this looking patronising, but the down-to-earth nature and quiet dignity of the Loritdja soon made me feel comfortable. I forgot about the camera filming us and concentrated on what the women were teaching me about bush tucker and other women's business. Over on the other side of the cultural site, the men's side, Robert was creating quite a stir with the spears and woomera. Hundreds of people must have had a go at throwing one of the long, thin Loritdja spears. I'm sure nobody handled them as well as Robert, who earned nods of approval and then cheers at his long, clean throws.

On our last day, we stopped by the community to say goodbye. They had previously given Robert a tin of red ochre and some handmade jewellery. Robert had brought some Maasai beadwork to give them. Now they presented Robert and me with a very special wedding present on behalf of everyone, a large and intricate painting depicting the Witchetty-grub, Makwa Dreaming. Linda, a member of the community, had painted it. It wasn't just that her work was superb, or that the gift was so unexpected. I was overwhelmed by the sheer loving generosity of these people and felt tears sting my eyes. Once again I felt humbled to be accepted by a group of people who knew nothing about me, but this time it was in Australia instead of Kenya.

The next morning we left very early for the five-hour drive back to Alice Springs. Today was a wonderful day, because the ordeal of filming was over. I felt the black cloud lifting and with a light heart waved goodbye to the crew. Robert and I were staying in Alice Springs for a few extra days to spend time with some dear friends.

After returning to Sydney, the next two weeks were spent with other friends and family. I took Robert to one of my favourite childhood places, Taronga Park Zoo. A touring white tiger was in residence, but the animal that really caught Robert's eye was the solitary cow in Friendship Farm. We caught the train down the New South Wales south coast past Ulladulla. This lush dairy country was practically Robert's favourite spot in Australia. We kept up a running joke about how he would have to immigrate and we would set up a dairy farm on the south coast. Next we flew to Melbourne, where Robert met some more of my friends and got a brief taste of how I usually live. We journeyed down the Mornington Peninsula to Fish Creek, where my friends arranged for Robert to go to a modern dairy farm, and the next day we attended the Stony Creek races. He really saw life in Australia!

Five weeks in Australia was enough this first time for Robert. The '60 Minutes' story that was seen two months later made out that the visit had been unsuccessful, but this was untrue. Robert had a great time and we'd been very happy (apart from the time spent filming of course). Mum and Robert had felt comfortable with each other. Meeting Mum was the main reason that Robert had wanted to come to Australia. In Maasai culture, the relationship between a son and mother-in-law is a very important one.

I am usually the one getting on planes and flying off to another life. So it came as an unexpected shock how miserable I felt when Robert flew out at the end of February. Now fully versed in the art of international air travel, my *morani* was making the long journey home by himself. I felt utterly lost and depressed without him for the first few days. So to fill the void left by Robert, I sat down and started writing.

When I am in Australia, people ask me all the time if I miss Robert. It must be hard, they nod in sympathy. I missed him dreadfully when he first left Australia, but as a general rule I don't agonise over it. In Kenya, where husbands and wives spend a lot of time apart, it is taken for granted that we cannot be together all the time. I miss Ndoondo a whole heap and I would like to be near her all the time, but I don't always miss Robert. At the end of a bad day when I'm tired and feeling low, I feel it would be nice to see him and talk. However, most of the time I am fine on my own.

If I concentrate, sometimes I can connect with him mentally. If I have a particularly clear dream about Robert, then I know he has been thinking about me. I like to imagine what he might be doing. I hope he has eaten well, has a good place to sleep and not too many family problems to worry about. I hope rain has fallen and his cattle have plenty of grass. I know Robert can look after himself, and that though he chooses to be with me, he has his own stuff to do and can do it better without me around all of the time. I think I can say that, for both of us, our relationship has provided a firm base from which we have been able to grow as individuals, as well as a team.

For myself, I love being in Australia and being competent and articulate in my own culture. I enjoy the break from my primary relationship. And I like being celibate for part of each year and putting that energy into my own creativity and spirituality. The more I grow and learn in Kenya, the more comfortable I am in the West. I guess this has a lot to do with confidence and growing up.

Love doesn't stop at the coast, so across the expanse of the Indian Ocean I am still nourished and supported by Robert's love for me. I don't have to see him, or even talk to him on the phone, in order to feel it. I have things to discover and accomplish on my own, the same as Robert has. But we know we also have a journey to make together.

Some time apart for both of us is a key ingredient to the success of our relationship. In a perfect world, without financial constraints, I would choose to spend most of my time in Maasailand with my Kenyan family and some time each year in Australia. However, for the time being it is split about six months in both.

If it seems like cheating to have the best of both worlds and be happy in each of them, then call me a cheat. To me the lessons learnt in my two cultures and countries complement each other, help make sense of the world as a whole and fuse to make me complete. *Aserian.*

EPILOGUE

Some readers will be aware that Robert came to Australia with his cousin, whose name I have not mentioned in Chapter 12. This cousin was also offended by the '60 Minutes' story, but he chose to see Robert and I as perpetrators of the inaccuracies, rather than victims. The cousin took back a video copy to the Loita Hills, organised a generator and travelled around showing it to the community, with the intention of hurting Robert and me. There are in fact three or four video machines in Loita that run on generators or solar power. Copies of the video were made and are often shown, so I can expect to be haunted by it for a long time. His actions have caused a split in the family. For this reason I have honoured Robert's request to omit any mention of him in the final chapter. An episode which in Australia would seem petty has had great impact within the closeknit Maasai community.

The best news in Maasailand is always the birth of babies. In our *enkang* Robert's sister-in-law, Meiyoki, gave birth to a baby boy early in 1993 and around 9 pm on Sunday, 26 September 1993, Nolmemeri gave birth to a son, her ninth child. At the time of writing (December 1993) no significant rain has fallen for over two years in the Loita Hills. The drought is affecting both cattle and people, who are dependent upon their milk. Many elderly people suffer from constant hunger, and livestock have started to die now. Illampala still has grass and water at Empurpitia, so Robert has taken all our cattle there. He plans to split his time between overseeing the cattle and organising our new *enkang*, in between guiding the odd safari. We plan to build a new *enkang* high on a hill overlooking Narotian.

Our goats remain at Morijo under the care of Mama. Memi's daughter Toonga has left for her new husband's *enkang* near the Maasai Mara. Robert's sister Nasango also has finally married a young man and now lives in Olmesutye. She has given birth to her third child, a boy.

The three big schoolchildren, Momposhe, Leseamon and Sitaiyo, have all been enrolled in better schools outside of the Loita Hills. Leseamon and Sitaiyo live with their mother's relatives and Momposhe is a boarder at Olololunga Primary School. However, taking children out of Loita is an unsatisfactory solution. It remains the recourse of wealthy families only and removes the child from his or her community at a crucial age. The Loita community continues to demand better schools. One of the better things to come out of '60 Minutes' was a donation of extra money which we used to send Momposhe to school this year. Robert spent the balance on food for members of our family. It would be impossible for Memi to find money to educate Momposhe and he badly wants a formal education, so I have taken on that responsibility. Now he is in a better primary school, it is my wish to find a good high school to take him in two years' time.

In 1993 my own finances have been stretched to the limit as I have tried to help our family during the drought. To have relatively a lot when so many people I care for have little is a dilemma I constantly wrestle with.

The Catholic missionaries have begun to build a health centre at Entasekera Centre. Morani Sapuk was helping to build it, by shifting heavy blocks of stone for one shilling per block. It will have a resident doctor, a maternity ward and operating theatre, and will be of enormous benefit to the community. We all eagerly await its completion sometime in 1994.

While I am in Australia, and Robert is on the move with our cattle, Morani Sapuk is staying in our house and helping keep an eye on Ndoondo. I have been able to send extra food and UHT milk through Tropical Ice, for Morani Sapuk to share with her. This food became essential after he injured his legs when chased by a buffalo one night while he was out searching for missing cattle. The buffalo didn't catch him, but he cut his legs running through the bush, and the cuts became infected. This has laid him low for a while. Of course Ndoondo has moved back next door with Narygunkishon and her siblings. She enjoyed her second year in nursery class at Entasekera Primary and will start primary school proper in 1994. When not at school, Ndoondo is busy helping watch calves and goats and chasing monkeys from Narygunkishon's garden. She will be seven years old next May.

As for me, after these years of going back and forth between Kenya and Australia, I do know that I must find some way to settle more permanently in Kenya. I need to help Momposhe and soon

Ndoondo with their education, and I want to spend more time with them and Robert. I'm not sure what will turn up next, but whatever it is, I'm sure it will be wonderful.

GLOSSARY

Adumu Spectacular leaping dance performed by *moran*.

Alamoratani Circumciser.

Apa Long ago.

Aserian I am at peace.

Askari (Swahili) Guard or night watchman.

Boma (Swahili) Literally a fort, but now a thornbush cattle enclosure.

Boo The area just outside the house inside an *enkang*.

Calabash (English) Gourd used for collecting milk and blood.

Duka (Swahili) Shop.

Emorata Circumcision ceremony.

Ene Daughter of.

Enhorit Friend.

Enkai God.

Enkaiyoni Little boy (The feminine prefix 'enk' and 'ink' are used to denote items associated with women, and anything which is small. The masculine is 'ol' and 'il'. For example, a mountain is *ol-doinyo*, while a hill is *en-doinyo*).

Enkang Maasai family settlement.

Enkarna Name.

Enkarna enkerai Naming ceremony.

Enkashumpai White woman.

Enkidong (singular), **Inkidongi** (plural) Special ox horn used by the Iloibonok to keep their divining stones in. Only black or white horns are used. The ox is slaughtered at a special *olpul*, where the horn is lightly carved, and wet skin from the chest used to fashion a handle and a lid.

Entende Elaborate beaded wedding necklace.

Entito Girl.

Esita Thorn fence.

Eunoto Literally planting or establishing. Rite of passage ceremony to mark the upgrading of junior warriors to the ranks of senior warriors.

Githeri Beans and maize meal cooked together.

Ilaiser One of the five original Maasai clans, said to be descended from Aiser, one of the five sons of *Naiteru-kop*.

Ilasho Calves.

Ilkisaiyia The right hand age group of the *Ilkitoip* generation, currently junior elders. The name alludes to 'those who wish to be alone in the forest'.

Ilkishili The name of Robert's age group, currently the right hand senior *moran*. The name alludes to 'those who go to see new things', possibly reflecting the elders' confusion over a generation who no longer follow the traditional ways.

Ilkitoip The generation that are currently junior elders.

Ilmarjeshi The current left hand warrior age group.

Ilmauya The left hand age group of the Iseuri generation, currently at the height of their political power. Daniel's age group.

Ilmolelian One of the five original Maasai clans, said to be descended from Lelian, the firstborn son of *Naiteru-kop*.

Iloshon See **Olosho**.

Ilrandai The left hand age group of the *Ilkitoip* generation, currently junior elders. The name implies 'those who are fully satisfied'. Ilampala's age group.

Ilterito Robert's father's generation, who were warriors between 1926 and 1948. The name means 'those who are rich'.

Impala Books.

Inaishi Honey beer.

Kanga (Swahili) Brightly patterned cloth worn by women throughout Kenya.

Kidongoi According to oral traditions, he was the first heaven sent Oloiboni of the Maasai. Sometimes known as Lemuya Kidongoi or ole Mweyia. Not all Maasai elders or western scholars are agreed that Kidongoi was the first.

Kule Milk.

Kyondo (Kikamba) Woven bag made from sisal, wool or even plastic bags!

Laibon/s Anglicised version of Oloiboni and Iloibonok.

Laiyoni Uncircumcised boy.

Langata Nairobi estate, from the Maasai word *elangata*: a river crossing.

Mandazi Sweet fried dough.

Manyatta Special temporary ceremonial settlement used for a number of important cultural and spiritual occasions, including the fertility ceremony for women. The word is most often associated with the social and training base used by *moran*. Incorrectly used to refer to all Maasai settlements collectively.

Memsahib Colonial form of address used for European women.

Moran Warriors (plural).

Morani Warrior (singular).

Motonyi Bird.

Mzungu (Swahili) European.

Nairobi Capital of Kenya. From the Maasai *engare nairobi*: the water which is cold.

Naiteru-kop Literally the beginner of the earth, the Creator.

Ndorobo Anglicised version of the Maasai word *torobo*, used to describe the Okiek people, the original hunter gatherers of East Africa. The word was originally intended as derogatory, but seems less so nowadays.

Ngong Outer district of Nairobi. From the Maasai *enkongu e muny*: the eye of the rhino, referring to a small eye-shaped pool or well. Still a Maasai stronghold today, though much land has been lost to agricultural tribes and developers.

Ngoto Mother of.

Nkidongi An elite dynasty or subclan within the Ilaiser clan. All Iloibonok are from this family. The Nkidongi live in isolation and quite differently from secular Maasai; to give just two examples, they live together, with fathers, sons and brothers often in the same *enkang*, whereas secular Maasai prefer to live away from their immediate relatives. The power to prophesy and interpret the will of *Enkai* is passed on through the male line, and blood purity is of the utmost importance. If the much reported practice of polyandry exists among other sections of the Maasai (and I have no direct evidence to suggest that it does), then it is certainly unknown among the Nkidongi. The best scholarly work about the Nkidongi is by John L. Berntsen, whose numerous sources included Robert's father.

Berntsen has identified four Nkidongi communities: two groups who are the descendants of Olonana (one around Ngong and another settlement at Meto on the Kenya-Tanzania border) and the descendants of Nelian, a brother to Mbatiany, who have settled below the Ngong Hills near Ol Ariak. To quote from Berntsen, 'The largest and most important community of Inkidongi prophets in the twentieth century has been that of the Senteu ole Mbatian at Kisokon in the Loita Hills. Today the *emurua ooNkidongi* (living area of the Inkidongi) extends from Morijo Loita to Entasekera, and from the main road to the Rift Valley (Nguruman) escarpment. Within these rough borders most of the independent cattle owners are Inkidongi, and very few of the Senteu family live outside of it. In addition, several Inkidongi still live in the Sikirari region around Mt Meru, but perhaps due to pressure from central government, the important prophets have moved to more remote areas inaccessible to government officials.'

Olaibartani Recently circumcised youth who wears the black robes of the initiate, and may not wash or shave his hair.

Olaigwanani Spokesperson, age group official.

Olale Calf-pen inside the home.

Olashumpai (singular), **Ilushampa** (plural) White man/men.

Olbarnoti Literally 'the shaved one'. The name for junior warriors who have emerged from their time of healing *(Olaibartani)*, but have not yet grown their hair long.

Olchani Medicine; literally tree.

Ole Son of.

Olgilata (singular), **Ilgilat** (plural) Clan/s. There were originally five clans of pastoral Maasai: Ilmolelian, Ilmakesen, Iltaarrosero, Ilaiser and Ilukumai. Traditionally, the Maasai marry outside of their own clan, though within the larger clans this is breaking down to the extent that it is now restricted only to the subclan level. A fine of one calf is paid in this case to wipe away the wrongdoing.

Olkiteng lorrbaa Literally 'ox of the injuries'. A purification ceremony performed individually by senior elders. The ritual slaughter of an ox wipes away all past transgressions, and returns the elder to a 'pure' state. This ceremony must be completed before a man can arrange for the circumcision of any of his children. A variation is the *Olkine lorrbenig* ceremony, where a goat is slaughtered instead of an ox. A man must slaughter the same animal as his father did before him.

Olkurkurto   Calabash made from a dried gourd.

Olngesherr   Ceremony to join the right and left hand warrior age groups together. They are given a generational name, and officially become junior elders.

Oloiboni (singular), **Iloibonok** (plural)   Ritual expert, prophet, healer, diviner, and spiritual leader of the pastoral Maasai nation.

Olorien   Olive tree.

Olosho (singular), **Iloshon** (plural)   This word has been variously translated as meaning tribe, subtribe, tribal section and nation. Today there are at least fifteen geographically defined, autonomous, politically independent *iloshon* of pastoral Maasai in Kenya and Tanzania: Uasinkishu, Moitanik, Siria, Purko, Damat, Keekonyokie, Loitai, Loodokilani, Kaputiei, Dalalakutuk, Matapato, Loitokitoki, Salei, Serenget and Kisonko. There are more if you include the pastoral Samburu, and Maa-speaking groups such as the Baraguya, Ilarusa and Ilkurman who practise mixed farming. It is useful to remember that while your clan *(olgilat)* defines where you came from, and who you might marry, it is your section *(olosho)* that defines where you live, where you graze your stock, how you dress, speak, etc. Maasai men are circumcised, not into their *olgilat*, but into their *olosho*.

Olpayian   Elder, husband.

Olpiron   Literally firestick. The *olpiron* elders are the men who 'kindle the fire' for a new age group of warriors. A man's *olpiron* elders are usually two generations ahead of his own. Such elders are teachers and guardians for the younger age group, and traditionally accorded great respect.

Olporror   A complete generation, i.e. two age groups that are joined together make a generation.

Olpul   Temporary camp in the forest where men gather to eat meat and commune with *Enkai* and the forest, their spiritual home.

GLOSSARY

Oltirpe Beaded round collar worn by Maasai women.

Orinka Wooden club carried by men. Without an *orinka* and a walking stick, a Maasai man does not feel properly dressed. Used for personal protection against wild animals and as a herding tool.

Paashe When a friend or relative gives you a calf *(olashe)*, or vice versa, from that time on you call each other *Paashe* in recognition of that gift. Other special names for these 'stock relationships' include *pakiteng* (the bullock), *pakishu* (the cow), *pakwuo* (the goat), and *pantawou* (the heifer).

Papa Father.

Papatee Little Father. The pet name that Mesianto and the other children use for Robert.

Sandukus Tin boxes for storing and carrying things.

Shamba (Swahili) Plot or garden of crops.

Shuka (Swahili) Cotton cloth worn as a cloak or shawl, or across the body and tied at the shoulders. The Maasai equivalent is *karasha*.

Siangiki Young woman, bride.

Sidai Fine, beautiful, nice.

Soiyaan Greyish colour for cattle (also *suyaan*).

Suguru Sausage fruit tree.

Supa One of many Maasai greetings.

Syce A groom or mounted attendant, from the Hindustani word *sais*.

Toto, *mtoto* (Swahili) Child.

Ugali Maize meal cooked with hot water.

Wazungu (Swahili) Europeans (plural).

Yeiyio Mother.

ACKNOWLEDGMENTS

I MANAGE TO WALK IN TWO WORLDS BECAUSE A LOT OF PEOPLE ENCOURAGE and support me. Financially, it has always been a difficult balancing act and I would like to thank the following friends and colleagues for making it all possible. Carolyn Logan, Andrew Penney, Nanette Fox, Nadine Coleman, Helen Simondson, Lisa Logan and my aunt, Denise Tame, for sharing their homes (and a whole lot more) with me. Elena Martinez, David Foster, Greg Hocking, Tim Woods, Glenn Elston, Zane Trow, Linda Sproul, Miranda Brown, Colin Lane, Scott Casley, Frank Wood, the Melody Lords, Mark and Cath Little, Liz Baillie, Mary, Nick and Con for keeping me gainfully employed in Australia.

Lorraine Islaub, Caroline Smith and the team at Apple Mac in Australia for providing the means to write this book. Richard Potter at Elante and Simon Tan at Showa Sola for the solar panel that powered the Mac. In Nairobi, Robert Anyango at Mayfield International, who provided advice, assistance with printing and emergency back up for the Apple Mac. Ken Groves and Qantas Airways for generously providing freight for bags of school clothes for Maasai children.

I must also thank Linda Tellington-Jones, who got me to Kenya in the first place, and taught me how to be fearless; my friends Sorrel Wilby and Chris Ciantar for their inspiration and the beautiful photographs they have kindly let me use in this book; and Selwa Anthony for guiding me.

To the three artists who have given their time and energy to various projects of mine over the years: Rod Gilbert, Andrew Hoyne and Ian Stokol. Wiggy Brennan for all my beautiful clothes, Jim Cathcart for spinning plates back in the office, my buddy from way back Bronwyn Morgan, and Moonyeen Atkinson for being a piece of Africa in Australia.

My lifelines in Kenya; I could not survive without Iain Allan from Tropical Ice. I am indebted to Iain and his wife Lou, Joyce and Lucy in the office, and the best drivers and safari crew in Kenya; the

ACKNOWLEDGMENTS

whitest African in Africa, Clive Ward; and Mitch Reardon for brotherly advice. Susan and Martin Murage and their families; the Jogoo, Richard Nzomo; all the staff at the Fairview Hotel and Heron Court in Nairobi, and the Spear Hotel in Narok. *Asante sana* to everyone for making me feel 'at home'.

Thanks to my Mum Marie Oddie and bro Mark Oddie, for putting up with me, among other things.

To my Maasai friends and family, thank you for sharing your world and wisdom with this *mzungu toto*.

And lastly, I would not have been able to follow this dream if others had not been there to look after another one – my horse Siska. Thanks to Jaqui Baker and Robyn Pettifer and family, and everyone at Lysterfield Equestrian Centre who has groomed, ridden, or stopped to pat Siska, thank you with all my heart.

CONTACT LIST

Australia

Maasai Culture & Wildlife Safari and Trust
PO Box 224
Kincumber NSW 2251
or through specialist African and adventure travel agents

Kurkarah Tours
Watarrka National Park
Private Mail Bag 136
Alice Springs NT 0870
Tel (089) 567 865
or through travel agents

Kenya

Tropical Ice Safaris
(top quality walking and mountain safaris)
Iain Allan
PO Box 57341
Nairobi Kenya
Tel 254 2 740 811
Fax 254 2 740 826
or through the Africa Travel Centres in Sydney or Melbourne

Safaris Unlimited
(horseriding safaris)
Tony Church
PO Box 24181
Nairobi Kenya
Tel 254 2 891 168
Fax 254 2 891 113